Message

We are inviting you to a zagat.com subscription at the price of only $9.95 (a membership charge).

The benefits of membership include:

- **Ratings and Reviews:** Our renowned restaurant ratings and reviews for over 70 major cities worldwide.

- **New Restaurants:** A look at important restaurants as they open throughout the year.

- **ZagatWire:** Our monthly e-mail newsletter covering the latest restaurant openings, closings, chef changes, special offers, events, promotions and lots more.

- **Advanced Search:** With 50+ search criteria, you can find the perfect place for any occasion.

- **Discounts:** Up to 25% off at our online Shop.

We also encourage you to visit zagat.com to vote or make reservations at your favorite restaurants.*

Given all these benefits, we believe that your zagat.com membership is sure to pay for itself many times over – each time you have a good meal or avoid a bad one.

To redeem these benefits, go to zagat.com and enter promotional code WASH2004 when you subscribe.

Please join us.

Nina and Tim
Nina and Tim Zagat

*Voting at zagat.com requires independent registration but otherwise continues to be free of charge.

Offer expires 3/31/04. Cannot be combined with any other offer.

Message about zagat.com

We are inviting you to become a Charter Member of our zagat.com subscription service for a special introductory price of only US$19.95, a 33% discount off the normal membership annual

The benefits of membership include:

- Ratings and reviews of the renowned restaurants in these top American cities.

- Advice on where to go for all the city's attractions, the cuisine, nightlife, the food.

- Information on booking a table, reservations, wine list, services, as well as opening hours, closing times, and more.

- Updated Search, with full-text search, so that you can find the right place for any occasion.

- Frequent updates of the restaurant line-up.

- We also include archives, with tastefood in your area. Everything is available in real time.

- Plus all these benefits we also offer free, with your membership, the choice of a hard-copy zagat guide, plus if you have a magazine or newspaper of choice.

We look forward to welcome you as a new member of zagat.com and thank you.

[signature]

Nina Zagat
Tim Zagat

We hope you enjoy our new zagat.com and we look forward to receiving your feedback.

ZAGATSURVEY.

2004

WASHINGTON, DC BALTIMORE RESTAURANTS

**Local Editors and Coordinators:
Olga Boikess and Marty Katz**

Editor: Liz Daleske with Sinting Lai

Published and distributed by
ZAGAT SURVEY, LLC
4 Columbus Circle
New York, New York 10019
Tel: 212 977 6000
E-mail: washbalt@zagat.com
Web site: www.zagat.com

Acknowledgments

We thank Charles Adler, Chuck Alexander, Bernice August, Alicia Ault, Richard K. Bank, Gloria Berthold, Greg Bland, Mary Ann Brownlow, Tom Bryant, Karen Cathey, Lisa Cherkasky, Jean and Gary Cohen, Kerry Craven, Tony Curtis, Fred Deutsch, Lori Edwards, Elaine Eff, Lorraine and Megan Fitzsimmons, Gail Forman, Mary Frank, Eliza Gonzalez, Alexandra Greeley, Linda Gregory, Judy Harris, Kelly Hereth, Bonnie Hockstein, Colin Hood, Hoppy Hopkins, Michele E. Jacobs, Barbara Johnson, Michael Karlin, Danny Katz, Bill Kopit, Dennis Kurgansky, Judy Levenson, Sue Ellen Malone, Jim Marley, Angie Miller, Lynda Mulhauser, Jack Nargil, Jo-Ann Neuhaus, Kendi O'Neill, Nancy Pollard, Megan Ryan, Alan Schlaifer, Susan K. Shuman, Robert Singleton, Sol Snyder, Ken Tomashiro and Juliet Zucker for their support. Our special thanks go to Sawanee and Pete Nivasabutr and Pamela Horvath for their assistance.

This guide would not have been possible without the hard work of our staff, especially Reni Chin, Schuyler Frazier, Shelley Gallagher, Katherine Harris, Natalie Lebert, Mike Liao, Dave Makulec, Jennifer Napuli, Emily Parsons, Rob Poole, Robert Seixas and Sharon Yates.

The reviews published in this guide are based on public opinion surveys, with numerical ratings reflecting the average scores given by all survey participants who voted on each establishment and text based on direct quotes from, or fair paraphrasings of, participants' comments. Phone numbers, addresses and other factual information were correct to the best of our knowledge when published in this guide; any subsequent changes may not be reflected.

© 2003 Zagat Survey, LLC
ISBN 1-57006-533-0
Printed in the United States of America

Contents

	DC	BA
About This Survey	5	
What's New	6	
Key to Ratings & Symbols	7	

TOP RATINGS
	DC	BA
• Most Popular Places	9	157
• Food; Cuisines, Features, Locations	10	158
• Decor; Outdoors, Romance, Rooms, Views	14	161
• Service	15	161
• Best Buys	16	162

RESTAURANT DIRECTORY
	DC	BA
Names, Addresses, Phone Numbers, Ratings and Reviews	17	163

INDEXES
	DC	BA
Cuisines	124	206
Locations	131	210
Special Features	138	213
Additions	138	213
Breakfast	138	213
Brunch	138	213
Buffet Served	–	213
Business Dining	139	213
BYO	–	213
Catering	140	213
Chef's Table in Kitchen	140	–
Child-Friendly	140	214
Delivery/Takeout	141	214
Dessert	141	214
Dining Alone	142	–
Entertainment	142	214
Family-Style	143	–
Fireplaces	143	214
Historic Places	143	214
Hotel Dining	143	214
Late Dining	144	215
Meet for a Drink	144	215
Offbeat	145	215
Outdoor Dining	145	215
Parking	147	216
People-Watching	148	216
Power Scenes	148	216
Pre-Theater Menus	149	–
Private Rooms	149	216
Prix Fixe Menus	150	217
Quiet Conversation	150	217
Raw Bars	151	–
Reserve Ahead	–	217

	DC	BA
Romantic Places	151	217
Senior Appeal	151	218
Singles Scenes	152	218
Sleepers	–	218
Tea Service	152	218
Theme Restaurants	152	–
Transporting Experiences	152	–
Views	152	218
Visitors on Expense Account	153	218
Winning Wine Lists	153	218
Worth a Trip	154	218
Wine Chart		220

About This Survey

For 24 years, Zagat Survey has reported on the shared experiences of diners like you. This *2004 Washington, DC/Baltimore Restaurant Survey* is an update reflecting developments since our last *Survey* was published. For example, we have added 111 places not in the previous edition, as well as indicating new addresses, phone numbers, chef changes and other major developments. All told, this guide covers some 855 restaurants.

By regularly surveying large numbers of avid local restaurant-goers, we hope to have achieved a uniquely current and reliable guide. For this book, more than 4,300 people participated. Since they dined out an average of 2.6 times per week, this *Survey* is based on nearly 586,000 meals annually. We sincerely thank each of these surveyors; this book is really "theirs."

Of course, we are especially grateful to our editors, Olga Boikess, a Washington lawyer and avid restaurant-goer who has edited this *Survey* since it was first published in 1987, and Marty Katz, a Baltimore writer and photographer.

To help guide our readers to Washington, DC/Baltimore's best meals and best buys, we have prepared a number of lists. See Washington, DC's Top Ratings, including Most Popular (pages 9-15) and Best Buys (page 16); and Baltimore's Top Ratings, including Most Popular (pages 157-161) and Best Buys (page 162). In addition, we have provided 75 handy indexes and have tried to be concise. Finally, it should be noted that our editors have synopsized our surveyors' opinions, with their comments shown in quotation marks.

As companions to this *Survey*, we publish other guides to restaurants worldwide, as well as nightlife, hotels, resorts and spas, golf courses, shopping, movies, theater and, soon to be released, music. Most of these are also available on mobile devices and at **zagat.com**, where you can vote and shop as well.

To join any of our upcoming *Surveys*, just register at **zagat.com**. Each participant will receive a free copy of the resulting guide when it is published.

Your comments and even criticisms of this guide are also solicited. There is always room for improvement with your help. You can contact us at washbalt@zagat.com or by mail at Zagat Survey, 4 Columbus Circle, New York, NY 10019. We look forward to hearing from you.

New York, NY
August 5, 2003

Nina and Tim Zagat

What's New

Bearish economic forecasts aside, the Washington, DC/Baltimore area's dining indicators are favorable for local, value-driven, innovative – and just plain good – eating.

Talented Toques, New Territory: Since last year's *Survey*, sophisticated new settings for local chefs are drawing crowds in the DC area, most notably Zaytinya, the Mediterranean venue of Jose Andres, and the design-award winning New American Poste, helmed by Joseph Comfort, both in the Penn Quarter, as well as Restaurant 2941, Jonathan Krinn's recently debuted American, in Falls Church. At the same time, the area's demographics have attracted the likes of Charlie Palmer, whose eponymous steakhouse in Capitol Hill is already a power scene. And there's more to come from Andres, as well as from the DC Coast/TenPenh pros: Each plans to open an establishment inspired by Mexican and Latin American culture and cuisine, in the Penn Quarter and Rosslyn, respectively.

Sexy Sipping/Supping: Mixing chic decor, exotic cocktails and interesting small plates, restaurant/lounges are answering the need for casual, affordable social or solo stops. Helix Lounge, The International and the New American 15 ria, near Logan and Scott Circles in DC, as well as Cleveland Park's Indique, are offering creative, budget-wise dining. Coming soon in this genre are Cafe Milano's Dupont Circle enoteca, Sette, and Ginger Cove, a Penn Quarter Caribbean cafe from Sharon and Jimmy Banks (ex Hibiscus).

Style and Ease in the Suburbs: In the outlying areas, savvy restaurateurs are offering value-driven eating in visit-worthy surroundings, like Harry's Tap Room in Clarendon (an offshoot of Sam & Harry's) and Tower Oaks Lodge in Rockville, a must-see from the Clyde's Restaurant Group. While on the quick and casual side, Five Guys is franchising its winning formula in DC and nearby Maryland.

Mellow Maryland: Around Baltimore, stress-weary diners are being soothed by new local spots whose proprietor is on the premises. Some are siblings of successful establishments, like b, a new member of the Helmand and Tapas Teatro family, while Abacrombie, 4 West and Tiburzi's are also family-staffed, homegrown entries. In Annapolis, the non-touristy Italian La Mona Lisa, the comfort-fooder Paul's Homewood Cafe and the Colonial pub Reynolds Tavern are packing them in. In Maryland, warm and inviting works.

For Comparison's Sake: Dining in DC and Baltimore costs an average of $31.86 and $30.08, respectively. This is slightly above the national average of $28.87.

Washington, DC
Baltimore, MD
August 5, 2003

Olga Boikess
Marty Katz

Key to Ratings/Symbols

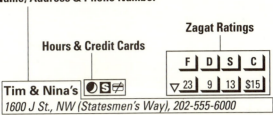

Name, Address & Phone Number

Hours & Credit Cards

Zagat Ratings

F	D	S	C
▽ 23	9	13	$15

Tim & Nina's ◐ 🅂 ⌀

1600 J St., NW (Statesmen's Way), 202-555-6000

▣ This "meat-and-greet mecca" (dubbed Prime Stakes) boasts the ultimate "see-or-be-seen dining" experience, featuring reversible one-way glass booths ("look out or let others look in") and "hot lines to the White House and The Hill"; you can "pick your own salad" from the hydroponic planters, but it's the "cameo appearances" by investors, including all living past presidents and the *West Wing* cast, that are the real "star attraction here."

Review, with surveyors' comments in quotes

Restaurants with the highest overall ratings and greatest popularity and importance are printed in CAPITAL LETTERS.

Before reviews a symbol indicates whether responses were uniform ■ or mixed ▣.

Hours: ◐ serves after 11 PM
🅂 open on Sunday

Credit Cards: ⌀ no credit cards accepted

Ratings: Food, Decor and Service are rated on a scale of **0** to **30**. The Cost (C) column reflects our surveyors' estimate of the price of dinner including one drink and tip.

F	Food	D	Decor	S	Service	C	Cost
23		9		13		$15	

0–9 poor to fair
10–15 fair to good
16–19 good to very good

20–25 very good to excellent
26–30 extraordinary to perfection
▽ low response/less reliable

For places listed without ratings or a numerical cost estimate, such as an important newcomer or a popular write-in, the price range is indicated by the following symbols.

I $15 and below
M $16 to $30
E $31 to $50
VE $51 or more

vote at zagat.com

Washington, DC's Most Popular

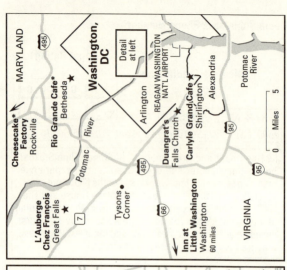

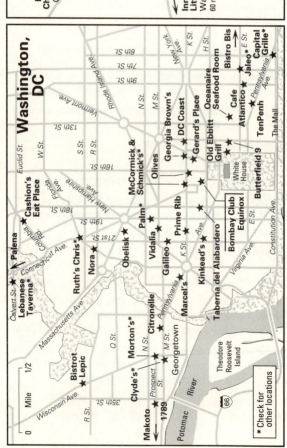

Washington, DC's Top Ratings

Excluding places with low voting. An asterisked restaurant is tied with the one directly above it.

40 Most Popular

1. Kinkead's
2. L'Auberge Chez François
3. Inn at Little Washington
4. Citronelle
5. Galileo
6. Jaleo
7. DC Coast
8. Carlyle Grand Cafe
9. TenPenh
10. Vidalia
11. Obelisk
12. 1789
13. Nora
14. Cashion's Eat Place
15. Ruth's Chris
16. Gerard's Place
17. Prime Rib
18. Cheesecake Factory
19. Clyde's
20. Equinox
21. Marcel's
22. McCormick & Schmick's
23. Cafe Atlantico
24. Lebanese Taverna
25. Palm*
26. Bistrot Lepic
27. Oceanaire Seafood Rm.
28. Morton's
29. Capital Grille
30. Butterfield 9
31. Old Ebbitt Grill
32. Georgia Brown's
33. Bistro Bis
34. Makoto
35. Taberna del Alabardero
36. Palena
37. Bombay Club
38. Duangrat's
39. Olives*
40. Rio Grande Cafe*

It's obvious that many of the restaurants on the above list are among the Washington, DC area's most expensive, but if popularity were calibrated to price, we suspect that a number of other restaurants would join the above ranks. Given the fact that both our surveyors and readers love to discover dining bargains, we have added a list of 80 Best Buys on page 16. These are restaurants that give real quality at extremely reasonable prices.

Top Food

Top 40 Food

- **29** Inn at Little Washington
- **28** L'Auberge Chez François
- **27** Makoto
  Kinkead's
  Maestro
  Gerard's Place
  Citronelle
  Prime Rib
  Obelisk
- **26** Marcel's
  Galileo
  Melrose
  Vidalia
  Four & Twenty Blackbirds
  1789
  Tosca
- **25** Taberna del Alabardero
  Nora
  L'Auberge Provençale
  Bistrot Lepic

  Seasons
  Duangrat's
  Colvin Run Tavern
  La Bergerie
  Palena
  Persimmon
  DC Coast
  TenPenh
  Ashby Inn
  Equinox
  i Ricchi
  Hollywood East Cafe
  Cashion's Eat Place
  Jerry's Seafood
  Le Relais
  Pizzeria Paradiso
  Peking Gourmet Inn
  Tachibana
  Heritage India
  Rabieng

By Cuisine

American (New)
- **27** Kinkead's
- **26** Melrose
  Vidalia
- **25** Nora
  Seasons

Chinese
- **25** Hollywood East Cafe
  Peking Gourmet Inn
- **23** Mr. K's
  Full Kee
- **22** New Fortune

French
- **28** L'Auberge Chez François
- **25** La Bergerie
- **24** La Chaumiere
- **23** La Miche
  Le Gaulois

French (Bistro)
- **25** Bistrot Lepic
- **24** Bistro Bis
- **23** Montmartre
- **21** Lavandou
  Petits Plats

French (New)
- **27** Gerard's Place
  Citronelle
- **26** Marcel's
- **25** Le Relais
- **24** Willard Room

Hamburgers
- **24** Five Guys
  Carlyle Grand Cafe
- **23** Addie's
- **22** Occidental
- **18** Clyde's

Indian
- **25** Heritage India
  Bombay Club
- **24** Connaught Place
  Haandi
- **23** Bombay Bistro

Italian
- **27** Maestro
  Obelisk
- **26** Galileo
  Tosca
- **25** i Ricchi

Top Food

Japanese
- 27 Makoto
- 25 Tachibana
  Sushi-Ko
- 24 Sushi Taro
  Kaz Sushi Bistro

Latin/South American
- 23 Cafe Atlantico
- 21 Lauriol Plaza
- 20 Grill from Ipanema
- 19 Green Field
  Andale

Louisiana
- 23 RT's
- 22 Black's Bar
- 20 Louisiana Express
- 19 219
  Warehouse B&G

Mediterranean
- 23 Mediterranee
  Olives
  Le Tarbouche
- 22 Kazan
  Neyla

Mexican/Tex-Mex
- 21 Rio Grande Cafe
  Lauriol Plaza
- 19 Guajillo
  Mi Rancho
  Cactus Cantina

Middle Eastern
- 23 Lebanese Taverna
  Le Tarbouche
- 22 Bacchus
- 21 Faryab
- 20 Skewers/Cafe Luna

Pan-Asian
- 25 TenPenh
- 24 Yanÿu
  Asia Nora
- 21 Cafe Asia
- 20 Spices

Pizza
- 25 Pizzeria Paradiso
- 24 Pasta Plus
- 23 Dolce Vita
- 22 2 Amys
- 20 Faccia Luna

Seafood
- 27 Kinkead's
- 25 DC Coast
  Jerry's Seafood
- 24 Pesce
- 23 Blue Point Grill

Southern
- 26 Vidalia
- 23 Majestic Cafe
- 22 Georgia Brown's
- 20 Florida Ave. Grill
  B. Smith's

Spanish
- 25 Taberna del Alabardero
- 23 Jaleo
- 21 Mar de Plata
  Lauriol Plaza
- 20 Andalucia

Steakhouses
- 27 Prime Rib
- 24 Ruth's Chris
  Sam & Harry's
  Morton's
  Palm

Thai
- 25 Duangrat's
  Rabieng
- 23 T.H.A.I.
  Sweet Basil
- 22 Neisha Thai

Vietnamese
- 24 Huong Que
  Taste of Saigon
- 22 Pho 75
  Nam Viet
  Saigonnais

vote at zagat.com

Top Food

By Special Feature

Breakfast†
- **23** Bread Line
- **22** La Colline
- **20** Old Ebbitt Grill
  - Louisiana Express
  - Ben's Chili Bowl

Brunch
- **27** Maestro
- **26** Melrose
  - Four & Twenty Blackbirds
- **25** Seasons
  - Cashion's Eat Place

Chef's Table
- **27** Citronelle
- **26** Marcel's
  - Galileo
  - Tosca
- **20** Matisse

Dining Alone
- **27** Kinkead's
- **25** DC Coast
- **24** Kaz Sushi Bistro
- **23** Johnny's Half Shell
- **21** Grapeseed

Family Dining
- **23** Lebanese Taverna
- **22** Matuba
  - 2 Amys
- **21** Tara Thai
  - Rio Grande Cafe

Hotel Dining
- **27** Maestro
  - Ritz Tysons Corner
  - Citronelle
  - Latham Hotel
- **26** Melrose
  - Park Hyatt Washington
- **25** Seasons
  - Four Seasons
- **24** Bistro Bis
  - Hotel George

Meet for a Drink
- **24** Bistro Bis
- **23** 701
  - Jaleo
- **22** Bardeo Wine Bar
- **21** Red Sage

Newcomers
- Charlie Palmer Steak
- 15 ria
- Poste
- Restaurant 2941
- Zaytinya

Power Scenes
- **27** Maestro
- **24** Bistro Bis
- **23** Capital Grille
- **22** Caucus Room
- **16** Monocle

Private Rooms
- **27** Maestro
  - Citronelle
- **26** Galileo
- **25** Seasons
- **21** Red Sage

Worth a Trip
- **29** Inn at Little Washington
  - Washington, VA
- **26** Four & Twenty Blackbirds
  - Flint Hill, VA
- **25** L'Auberge Provençale
  - Boyce, VA
  - Ashby Inn
  - Paris, VA
- **21** Rail Stop
  - The Plains, VA

---

† Other than hotels

Top Food

By Location

Adams Morgan/Dupont Circle East
- 25 Cashion's Eat Place
- 24 Sushi Taro
  - Pasta Mia
- 22 Saigonnais
  - Meskerem

Bethesda
- 25 Persimmon
- 24 Ruth's Chris
  - Haandi
- 23 Jaleo
  - Cafe Bethesda

Capitol Hill
- 24 Bistro Bis
- 23 Montmartre
- 22 La Colline
- 21 Barolo
  - La Brasserie

Downtown
- 27 Gerard's Place
- 26 Tosca
- 25 DC Coast
  - TenPenh
- 24 Willard Room

Dupont Circle
- 27 Obelisk
- 25 Nora
  - Pizzeria Paradiso
- 24 Pesce
- 23 Johnny's Half Shell

Georgetown/Glover Park
- 27 Citronelle
- 26 1789
- 25 Bistrot Lepic
  - Seasons
  - Heritage India

Golden Triangle
- 26 Galileo
  - Vidalia
- 25 Taberna del Alabardero
  - Equinox
  - i Ricchi

Old Town, Alexandria
- 25 La Bergerie
- 24 Five Guys
- 23 Blue Point Grill
  - Le Gaulois
  - Majestic Cafe

Penn Quarter/MCI Center/Chinatown
- 23 Capitol Grille
  - Cafe Atlantico
  - 701
  - Jaleo
  - Full Kee

Tysons Corner
- 27 Maestro
- 25 Colvin Run Tavern
- 24 Sam & Harry's
  - Morton's
  - Palm

West End
- 26 Marcel's
  - Melrose
- 24 Asia Nora
- 22 Meiwah
- 20 Ritz, Grill (Wash. DC)

Woodley Park/Cleveland Park
- 25 Palena
- 24 New Heights
  - Yanÿu
- 23 Lebanese Taverna
- 22 Nam Viet

vote at zagat.com

Top 40 Decor

- **28** Inn at Little Washington
  Maestro
- **27** L'Auberge Chez François
  Willard Room
- **26** Seasons
  Lightfoot
  Taberna del Alabardero
  Citronelle
  Bombay Club
  Prime Rib
  L'Auberge Provençale
- **25** 1789
  Colvin Run Tavern
  Teatro Goldoni
  TenPenh
  Marcel's
  Ashby Inn
  Ritz, Grill (Pent. City)
  Ritz, Grill (Wash. DC)
- **24** Le Tarbouche
  Melrose
  Bistro Bis
  Morrison-Clark Inn
  Old Angler's Inn
  La Ferme
  Sequoia
  DC Coast
  Butterfield 9
  Neyla
  Caucus Room
  Kinkead's
  Tosca
  Yanÿu
  Makoto
- **23** Two Quail
  Palena
  Tabard Inn
  Nora
  Oceanaire Seafood Rm.
  Asia Nora

Outdoors

Cafe Milano
Gerard's Place
L'Auberge Chez François
Lauriol Plaza
Old Angler's Inn
Perry's
Sea Catch
Sequoia
701
Zaytinya

Romance

Asia Nora
La Bergerie
Le Tarbouche
Nora
Palena
Tabard Inn
Two Quail
Yanÿu

Rooms

Citronelle
DC Coast
Galileo
Lafayette
Maestro
Melrose
Red Sage
Taberna del Alabardero
TenPenh
Tower Oaks Lodge
Willard Room
Zaytinya

Views

Charlie Palmer Steak
New Heights
Perry's
Restaurant 2941
Rico y Rico
Ruth's Chris
Sequoia
701

Top 40 Service

- **29** Inn at Little Washington
- **28** Maestro
  L'Auberge Chez François
- **26** Obelisk
  Prime Rib
  Seasons
- **25** Citronelle
  Makoto
  Kinkead's
  L'Auberge Provençale
  Melrose
  Bombay Club
  Taberna del Alabardero
  Willard Room
  1789
  Marcel's
- **24** Gerard's Place
  Colvin Run Tavern
  Ashby Inn
  Ritz, Grill (Pent. City)

  La Bergerie
  Vidalia
  Sam & Harry's
  Galileo
  Mr. K's
  Nora
- **23** Ruth's Chris
  Connaught Place
  Four & Twenty Blackbirds*
  Morrison-Clark Inn
  Palm
  i Ricchi
  701
  Morton's
  La Chaumiere
  Caucus Room
  Capital Grille
  Oval Room
  TenPenh
  Tosca

Best Buys

Top 40 Bangs for the Buck

1. Five Guys
2. Ben's Chili Bowl
3. California Tortilla
4. Firehook Bakery
5. Burro
6. El Pollo Rico
7. Bob & Edith's Diner
8. Burrito Brothers
9. Bread Line
10. Florida Ave. Grill
11. A&J
12. Pho 75
13. Crisp & Juicy
14. C.F. Folks
15. Tryst
16. Hard Times Cafe
17. Moby Dick
18. Teaism
19. Diner
20. Visions
21. Hope Key
22. Rocklands
23. Udupi Palace
24. Generous George's
25. Vegetable Garden
26. Delhi Dhaba
27. Parkway Deli
28. Haad Thai
29. Dean & DeLuca
30. Faccia Luna
31. Chi-Cha Lounge
32. Hollywood East Cafe
33. Havana Breeze
34. Pizzeria Paradiso
35. La Madeleine
36. T.H.A.I.
37. Oodles Noodles
38. Benjarong
39. Joe's Noodle House
40. Connaught Place

Other Good Values

Afghan
Amma Vegetarian
Ben's Whole Hog
Bombay Club
Cactus Cantina
Cafe Asia
Cafe Divan
Café Olé
Caribbean Feast
Carlyle Grand Cafe
Ching Ching Cha
Colorado Kitchen
Cubano's
Dukem
Eat First
Franklins
Full Key
Huong Que
Islander Caribbean
Johnny's Half Shell
Kuna
Kuzine
Lauriol Plaza
Lebanese Taverna
Little Saigon
Mark's Kitchen
Meze
Myanmar
Nam's of Bethesda
Negril
Noodles & Co.
Pasta Mia
Ray's The Steaks
Skewers/Cafe Luna
Taqueria Poblano
Taste of Morroco
Temel
Thanh Thanh
Washington Cafe
Wok & Roll

Washington, DC
Restaurant Directory

Washington, DC

| F | D | S | C |

A&J 🆂 🚫   21 | 8 | 16 | $13
Woodmont Station, 1319C Rockville Pike (bet. Talbott St. & Templeton Pl.), Rockville, MD, 301-251-7878
4316B Markham St. (Little River Tpke.), Annandale, VA, 703-813-8181
◾ Discover Beijing in your own "backyard" at these "bare-bones" suburban quick stops in Rockville and Annandale, where the "buzz of Chinese speakers vouches for their dim sum", noodle soups and "street-food" dishes; adventurous types who "line up for the food, not the ambiance" or the service ("courteous", if often uninformative), are always eager to "try new things" at "unbeatable" prices; N.B. no reservations, no booze, no plastic.

Acropolis ●   ✕   – | – | – | M
1337 Connecticut Ave., NW (bet. Dupont Circle & N St.), 202-496-5480
This year-old late-night scene just below Dupont Circle features flashy decor (envision classic Greek motifs, deep blue velvet, a faux fountain) and an endless bar (measuring 65 feet, it's reputed to be the longest in DC); the menu spotlights Greek specialties, along with sushi, plus there's occasional live jazz and dancing on weekends.

Addie's 🆂   23 | 15 | 20 | $35
11120 Rockville Pike (Edson Ln.), Rockville, MD, 301-881-0081
◾ Legions laud the "creative comfort food" and "civility" that mark this "vibrant" New American set on strip mall–lined Rockville Pike; while its cheery decor complements its unique bungalow setting, some complain of "tight quarters" and wish its "homey" looks were as "sophisticated" as its cooking, though in nice weather the patio is a "particular delight"; Sunday brunch is a recent addition.

Afghan 🆂   – | – | – | M
2700 Jefferson Davis Hwy. (Raymond Ave.), Alexandria, VA, 703-548-0022
"It's not that the menu is extraordinary", it's how carefully the kitchen prepares its "authentic" "Afghan comfort foods" that sets apart this "friendly", "family-owned" standby in Alexandria; it draws customers from around the Beltway with its "amazing appetizers (the best part of the dining experience)", "really tasty" kebabs and weekday lunch buffet (an especially "good value"); the consensus: it's a "solid" bet.

Washington, DC   F | D | S | C

Agua Ardiente ◐ S   – | – | – | M
1250 24th St., NW (N St.), 202-833-8500
Maricio Fraga-Rosenfeld's (Chi-Cha Lounge and Gua-Rapo) opulent recasting of this West End space (formerly West 24) into a Nuevo Latino restaurant and lounge invites the MTV generation to sip, sup and socialize amid flickering candles, gilded walls and Hispanic religious artifacts; it's named for a popular Latin American liqueur translated as 'fire water', used in potent drinks that can be paired with chef Hector Guerra's (ex Galileo) inventive, healthy tapas-style fare and more sizable entrees.

Al Tiramisu S   22 | 18 | 21 | $39
2014 P St., NW (bet. 20th & 21st Sts.), 202-467-4466
◪ "Charming and intimate", this Dupont Circle trattoria "takes you to Italy" with its "glorious, fresh" fare, "superior" regional wines, "hideaway" feel and "warm" service; the "ebullient" chef-owner describes his nightly specials in an irresistible way, but cynics warn "watch out for the [off-menu] prices" because his "magic with truffle oil and pasta" sometimes comes with an "ouch factor."

Amada Amante S   – | – | – | E
9755 Traville Gateway Dr. (Shady Grove Rd.), Rockville, MD, 301-217-5900
Kobe beef and foie gras are among the luxury ingredients in ambitious dishes that lure Potomac and Rockville high-rollers to this glossy Mediterranean where gleaming wood floors, richly appointed dining rooms and floor-to-ceiling wine racks all signal to Montgomery County patrons that this is a deluxe dining option.

Amma Vegetarian Kitchen S   ▽ 20 | 10 | 17 | $13
3291 M St., NW (bet. Potomac & 33rd Sts.), 202-625-6625
344A Maple Ave. E. (bet. Beulah Rd. & Park St.), Vienna, VA, 703-938-5328
◪ Herbivores "have to have the dosas and the coconut chutney" at this "dependable" Southern Indian kitchen in Georgetown (where the upstairs table dining is spare but "sunny") and its "simply" appointed, self-serve Vienna sibling; despite a few gripes about the "boring" menu (basically, "variations on a few basic dishes"), they provide a "fast, cheap" "veggie option."

Andale   19 | 20 | 19 | $33
401 Seventh St., NW (D St.), 202-783-3133
◪ "Alison Swope's love affair with contemporary Mexico" is clearly evident at her "lively" Penn Quarter bistro that's staffed by "attentive" people who "get you out in time" for an event at the nearby Shakespeare Theatre or MCI Center; a few "kinks" notwithstanding, the "upscale" menu is "promising", featuring "imaginative" "nuevo" "twists" on

Washington, DC | F | D | S | C |

the classics, all "artfully presented"; P.S. "don't miss the churros" with hot chocolate for dessert.

Andalucia S | 20 | 16 | 20 | $34 |
12300 Wilkins Ave. (Parklawn Dr.), Rockville, MD, 301-770-1880
■ This "old-world" Iberian in Rockville is known for its "way with fish", "great" paella and other "tasty", "authentic" Andalusian dishes, a "family"-friendly atmosphere and flamenco entertainment (on Thursdays).

Angelo & Maxie's Steakhouse S | 18 | 19 | 18 | $42 |
901 F St., NW (9th St.), 202-639-9330
Reston Town Ctr., 11901 Democracy Dr. (bet. Library St. & Reston Pkwy.), Reston, VA, 703-787-7766
◪ "Trying hard to skew young", this pair of "red-meat havens" near the MCI Center and in Reston features white-chocolate martinis ("a must"), bargain happy-hour deals, "blaring" pop sounds, even a cigar store on-site; the concept dinery earns points for "dark", retro ambiance and "delicious" steaks, but connoisseurs sniff that it exhibits "no real sophistication" and beef too about "uneven" service.

Anzu S | – | – | – | M |
2436 18th St., NW (Columbia Rd.), 202-387-5600
Pizza, pasta and Spanish tapas are the focus at this recent Adams Morgan entry, whose sophisticated recast of I Matti's space provides a softly lit, polished-wood-and-white backdrop for convivial sharing and leisurely sampling of its mid-priced plates; its comfortable bar and cosmopolitan mien seem destined to appeal to the area's Euro-scene seekers, and its windowside tables make for a good people-watching perch.

Arbor S | ▽ 16 | 17 | 16 | $28 |
2400 18th St., NW (Belmont Rd.), 202-667-1200
■ "Hip but accessible", this "casual, good-looking" New American's "cheerful" demeanor, updated comfort food (generally "well done") and interesting wines appeal when you're looking "for something between a diner and finer dining" in Adams Morgan; even its critics concede that it boasts one of the city's "best" people-watching patios, making it a "lovely" spot for Sunday brunch; dinner Wednesday–Saturday only.

Ardeo S | 21 | 21 | 20 | $40 |
3311 Connecticut Ave., NW (Macomb St.), 202-244-6750
◪ "Classy" and "customer-conscious", this Cleveland Park spot cossets clients in "posh yet comfortable" postmodern surroundings that showcase "tasteful" New American dishes that are "art nouveau on a plate"; celebrity-spotting ("pundits and Bushies" alike) gives it an edge, even if a few doubters drub it "overpriced and overhyped."

Argia's [S] 18 17 17 $29
124 N. Washington St. (bet. Broad St. & Park Ave.), Falls Church, VA, 703-534-1033
◪ Loyalists who maintain "high hopes" for this modern Italian bistro in Falls Church "arrive early" for "homemade" pastas and "hearty" entrees (available in both individual and sharing portions) delivered in an "attractive", mural-dominated space; detractors, however, complain about food that "doesn't always measure up" ("bland" flavors), "excessive noise" and "slow" service.

Artie's [S] 21 18 21 $27
3260 Old Lee Hwy. (south of Fairfax Circle), Fairfax, VA, 703-273-7600
■ "Deservedly popular", this Fairfax "standby" earns praise for "consistently good American food at reasonable prices", served by a "well-trained" staff in a room with a New England boathouse motif; note that it doesn't accept reservations (though you can call ahead to put your name on a list), so it can be "tough to get in on weekends", when the crowds descend for its "outstanding" "blackened prime rib special" (available Thursday–Saturday), but regulars agree it's "worth the wait."

Arucola [S] 17 14 17 $29
5534 Connecticut Ave., NW (Morrison St.), 202-244-1555
◪ Surveyors are decidedly divided about this Upper NW Italian osteria – proponents tout it as a "delightful meeting place" that offers rustic dishes like "scrumptious" roast chicken and homemade pastas (plus, kids are sure to be "happy with the pizzas" from the wood-burning oven), but opponents nix "hit-or-miss" cooking served by "arrogant" "Fabio look-alikes"; the "great summer dining" on the deck, however, gets everyone's blessing, and a second floor should ease complaints about "cramped" quarters.

Ashby Inn, The [S] 25 25 24 $50
692 Federal St. (Rte. 17), Paris, VA, 540-592-3900
■ "Love is in the air" at this "delightfully" "romantic" 1829 inn set in the tiny village of Paris in Virginia's hunt country, and it's only enhanced by the "marvelous" vista of the Blue Ridge Mountains ("look for stars"); the smitten swoon over the "first-rate" daily New American menu and weekly changing global wine list and recommend that you pair a leisurely meal with "a tour of the local wineries"; N.B. dinner Wednesday–Saturday and Sunday brunch only.

Asia Nora 24 23 23 $45
2213 M St., NW (bet. 22nd & 23rd Sts.), 202-797-4860
◪ "Elegant", "imaginative" Pan-Asian fusion cuisine "beautifully" presented by a "quietly attentive" staff in "relaxing Zen"-like environs draws an "interesting" clientele to this West End boîte for a "romantic night out" or an

"urbane" business dinner; enamored epicures celebrate an "exquisite" organic menu filled with "bites of joy", but big appetites balk at the inverse relationship between portions ("small") and tabs ("pricey").

Austin Grill [S] 16 15 16 $21

750 E St., NW (bet. 7th & 8th Sts.), 202-393-3776
2404 Wisconsin Ave., NW (bet. Calvert St. & Observatory Ln.), 202-337-8080
7278 Woodmont Ave. (Elm St.), Bethesda, MD, 301-656-1366
8430A Old Keene Mill Rd. (Rolling Rd.), Springfield, VA, 703-644-3111

South Austin Grill [S]

801 King St. (Columbus St.), Alexandria, VA, 703-684-8969

◪ Brace yourself for a cattle call at this "affordable" chain of Tex-Mex cantinas, which ropes in plenty of revelers with its "bustling" under-30 bar scene that's fueled by "high-octane" swirlies; heavy traffic notwithstanding, purists gripe about "greasy" "gringo" grub, dismissing it as an "insult to Dubya's Administration."

Bacchus 22 17 20 $29

1827 Jefferson Pl., NW (bet. 18th & 19th Sts.), 202-785-0734
7945 Norfolk Ave. (Del Rey Ave.), Bethesda, MD, 301-657-1722 [S]

◪ "A grazer's delight", this "long-running" pair of Middle Eastern meccas below Dupont Circle and in Bethesda pleases palates with a wide "variety" of "authentic" meze that taste "like grandma's (if you happen to be Lebanese)"; the waiters "love to give advice" about the "alluring" menu, so come prepared "to share" and "make a meal of the appetizers"; despite somewhat "dated" decor, it's "always a good bet" for an "enjoyable" meal; P.S. the Maryland branch features "scenic courtyard" dining.

Bailiwick Inn [S] ▽ 22 23 23 $52

4023 Chain Bridge Rd. (Seger Ave.), Fairfax, VA, 703-691-2266

◪ "For a special occasion with special people", consider this "refined" Fairfax retreat set in an 1800s Federal-style inn (on the National List of Historic Places), whose "erudite hosts" and "attentive" servers present five-course dinners that start with "drinks and hors d'oeuvres in the parlor" before moving on to the "civilized, cozy dining room"; the French-accented American fare is "well prepared", if "not terribly innovative", leading a few wallet-watchers to carp "for the price, there are more exciting options."

Bambu [S] – – – M

5101 Macarthur Blvd., NW (Dana Pl.), 202-364-3088

Broadening dining options in the Palisades, this modish Asian newcomer done up in warm cinnamon and beige colors is a suitable choice for business and family meals alike; the extensive menu encompasses Chinese (such as

Washington, DC

Peking duck), Japanese (more than 40 selections at the sushi bar, along with lunchtime bento boxes) and Thai dishes, all moderately priced.

Banana Café and Piano Bar ●S   _|_|_|M|
500 Eighth St., SE (E St.), 202-543-5906
"Arty" and "funky" yet "unpretentious", this "popular" "tropical" "jewel" on Capitol Hill is a "great" place to "try new and wonderful things"; the Latin menu features Cuban and Puerto Rican specialties that are "nothing fancy but just plain good" (especially anything with pork) and it's "reasonably priced", while the "atmospheric" "piano bar upstairs" is a "hoot"; just "plan to spend a lot of time" here, as the staff is on "slow" island time.

Bangkok Blues S   _|_|_|M|
926 W. Broad St. (West St.), Falls Church, VA, 703-534-0095
Cool jazz and hot Thai food are cooking at this Falls Church storefront where music memorabilia and videos set the scene for a broad menu that plays Siamese riffs on American favorites (like water buffalo wings with a vermouth-chile glaze and Bangkok broil with a brandy sauce), as well as offering traditional curries and such, leading fans to applaud that it's hitting all the right notes.

Bardeo Wine Bar & Cafe S   22|21|20|$29|
3309 Connecticut Ave., NW (bet. Macomb & Porter Sts.), 202-244-6550
■ "Hats off" to this "chic" "hot spot" that's helping to "turn Cleveland Park into NYC's SoHo"; "a hip singles scene and a good date place", it's where oenophiles gather for a "night's worth" of sipping "excellent wines" and nibbling "imaginative" New American tapas; it has "everything you love about Ardeo" (its next-door sibling), "only it's smaller and cheaper" (and "younger and noisier").

Barolo   21|20|19|$40|
223 Pennsylvania Ave., SE (bet. 2nd & 3rd Sts.), 202-547-5011
◪ "Talented" chef-owner Enzo Fargione's "interesting" Piedmontese dishes (always "good, sometimes great") and all-Italian wine list draw a diverse clientele of "politicians", dating duos and food-and-wine mavens to this "quaint" Capitol Hill townhouse "near the Folger Theatre"; though a few detractors detect "aloof" service, most regard it as a "charming" "treasure – if you can stand all the lobbyists."

Bar Rouge S   _|_|_|M|
Hotel Rouge, 1315 16th St., NW (bet. Massachusetts Ave. & O St.), 202-232-8000
"Would it were a restaurant, not really just a bar" sigh trend-conscious gourmands of this svelte Scott Circle

Washington, DC | F | D | S | C |

lounge concept whose low-key milieu sets the stage for sophisticated sipping and small-plate sharing; while subtle tones define the decor, the International menu is tinted crimson (as in crab and red pepper beignets with tarragon aïoli), as is the naughty house drink, currently "Hot Rox"; N.B. dinner only.

BeDuCi S | 19 | 18 | 19 | $36 |
2100 P St., NW (21st St.), 202-223-3824

◪ Partisans of this Dupont Circle Italian-Mediterranean applaud its "diverse menu" (including what some consider the "best couscous in town"), "admirable" wine selection ("masterfully" described by an "incredibly friendly" owner) and "enticing" all-weather sidewalk veranda; a vocal minority, however, is dismissive of "overpriced" food that "fails to inspire", service that can be "hit-or-miss" and a vibe that feels "touristy."

Benjarong S | 22 | 20 | 20 | $23 |
Wintergreen Plaza, 885 Rockville Pike (Edmonston Dr.), Rockville, MD, 301-424-5533

■ The ambiance is "calm" and "relaxing", but the "delicious traditional" Thai food (its "outstanding" fried mussels are "a must") at this Rockville "favorite" is a real "eye-opener", packing "lots of flavor, not just heat"; combined with "warm" service and a "tasteful" setting that belies its strip-mall surroundings, it adds up to a "good value", though the price of "popularity" is a "long wait" on weekends.

Ben's Chili Bowl ●S≠ | 20 | 11 | 16 | $9 |
1213 U St., NW (bet. 12th & 13th Sts.), 202-667-0909

■ Though the U Street corridor may be "changing", not so this "legendary" "late-night" American diner, which since 1958 has been satisfying people from all walks of life with its "sinful" half-smokes (a grilled dog split and smothered with chili and onions and served on a bun), "real-deal cheese fries" and "fabulous shakes"; it's an "extraordinary melting pot" with "interesting" people-watching, a "charged and chaotic" atmosphere and the "best juke in the 202", so "cholesterol, schlomesterol" be damned.

Ben's Whole Hog Barbecue S | – | – | – | I |
7422 Old Centreville Rd. (Yorkshire Ln.), Manassas, VA, 703-331-5980

The Sung Kim family, who lately took over this Manassas BBQ pit from its former chef-owner, Ben Morris, follows his tradition of cooking barbecue the time-honored way – slowly, over a hickory-wood fire; that's good news for the folks who "crave" the pork ribs, beef brisket and "tasty" sauces, which come heaped on plates with Southern sides; the menu hasn't changed, nor, for the most part, has the ultra-casual log-cabin setting so "funky" that "you'll always be overdressed", but sadly, the live music is gone.

Big Bowl Asian Kitchen [S] 18 | 19 | 16 | $21

2800 Clarendon Blvd. (Fillmore St.), Arlington, VA, 703-875-8925
Reston Town Ctr., 11915 Democracy Dr. (bet. Library St. & Reston Pkwy.), Reston, VA, 703-787-8852
21100 Dulles Town Ctr. (Rte. 7), Sterling, VA, 703-421-9989

◪ "Finally, some pizzazz in Reston" cheers the contingent that "mobs" this "glitzy" Asian-style dining complex for its "diverse menu", "wonderful stir-fry bar" and "fun", "kid-friendly" atmosphere (and prices); the ingredients are always "fresh" and some of the dishes are "interesting", but "don't expect authentic cooking at this Americanized chain"; outright opponents who dub it "Big Noise, Big Disappointment", though, warn "all flash and no substance"; N.B. Arlington and Dulles Town Center are unrated.

Bistro Bis [S] 24 | 24 | 22 | $45

Hotel George, 15 E St., NW (bet. N. Capitol St. & New Jersey Ave.), 202-661-2700

■ Just "steps from the Capitol", this "sophisticated" French bistro housed in the Hotel George cossets with "film noir elegance" and "polished" but "not intimidating" manners; the kitchen's "clever" takes on Gallic classics and the cellar's *très* "fine" collection of regional wines make it a "great place for celebrating an event", while the "who's who" scene around the "fabulous" zinc-topped bar earns it the sobriquet "Manhattan in DC."

Bistro Bistro [S] 15 | 17 | 16 | $28

4021 28th St. S. (bet. Quincy & Randolph Sts.), Arlington, VA, 703-379-0300

◪ "Casually upscale" with a "welcoming" atmosphere, this mural-lined "neighborhood bistro" in Shirlington satisfies supporters with a "reliable" ("competent", if "nothing special") New American–Mediterranean menu, a convivial bar and "nice" outdoor tables; doubters, however, who deem it entirely "average", point to "lackluster" fare and "spotty" service; still, it'll do "in a pinch."

Bistro D'Oc [S] – | – | – | E

518 10th St., NW (bet. E & F Sts.), 202-393-5444

Warmed by the rouge, saffron and deep blue colors of the Languedoc and Mediterranean provinces of France and prettied up with lace curtains in the windows, this engaging bistro brings the Gallic countryside to a Downtown site opposite Ford's Theatre; it's an inviting backdrop for chef Bernard Grenier's (ex La Miche) enticing cooking, which reinterprets the regional recipes of Basque, Provençal and Toulousian cuisines, with Asian grace notes.

Bistro Français ◐[S] 20 | 18 | 19 | $32

3128 M St., NW (bet. 31st St. & Wisconsin Ave.), 202-338-3830

■ "If you can't make the evening flight to Paris", this "veritable" French bistro in Georgetown will transport you

Washington, DC F | D | S | C

there with its "honest" bourgeois fare (the early-bird deal is a "brilliant" bargain) and "charming" environs, all "warm woods" and brass; it gets even "better" in the "wee hours" (open till 3 AM weeknights, 4 AM weekends), when off-work chefs and club-goers alike pile in for a "serious" meal, or just the "best" eggs Benedict around.

Bistro Lafayette   – | – | – | E
1118 King St. (bet. Fayette & Henry Sts.), Alexandria, VA, 703-548-2525
Now settled in Old Town Alexandria, owners Keo and Marie Koumtakoun replicate the formula polished at their former venture Saveur in Georgetown with boldly seasoned French bistro fare and attractive dark-wood and soft-toned surroundings; local Francophiles drawn by chef Keo's aromatic, comforting classics are beginning to dub this stretch of King Street Alexandria's Left Bank.

Bistro 123   20 | 16 | 20 | $38
246 Maple Ave. E. (bet. Glyndon & Park Sts.), Vienna, VA, 703-938-4379
■ "Don't judge a book by its cover" urge Francophiles who hail this "cozy" (despite its "strip-mall" ambiance) Vienna bistro for its "fine treatment of classic dishes", "quiet" room and "solid" service; devotees say dining is "especially enjoyable out on the patio", but the less impressed complain about food that "comes up flat" and a "stuffy" staff.

Bistrot Belgique Gourmande   ∇ 22 | 14 | 21 | $28
302 Poplar Ln. (Union St.), Occoquan, VA, 703-494-1180
■ Visit once and you'll feel like part of the "friendly", "close-knit" family that runs this "quirky" (to put it mildly) Occoquan outpost where "hearty", "authentic" Belgian bistro classics (including "incredible" *pommes frites* and for dessert, "fabulous waffles") and a "huge selection" of "wonderful", "unusual beers" ("fun to explore") make dinner well "worth the drive"; N.B. note that the hours are "irregular", so it's best to call ahead.

Bistrot du Coin S   18 | 19 | 13 | $30
1738 Connecticut Ave., NW (Florida Ave.), 202-234-6969
■ Wildly popular, this "Parisian food hall" re-creation above Dupont Circle provides a "raucous", "fun escape" to Montmartre thanks to its "smoky" zinc bar, "lively" vibe and "delicious" "tried-and-true" bistro "staples" ("great steak frites" and "remarkable mussels"); critics, though, gripe that the food, "dripping in duck fat", is delivered with Gallic "disdain" and warn too of "deafening noise."

BISTROT LEPIC & WINE BAR S   25 | 20 | 22 | $42
1736 Wisconsin Ave., NW (S St.), 202-333-0111
■ Chef-owner Bruno Fortin's "adorable little French" in Upper Georgetown turns out "top-notch" bistro dishes with

Washington, DC | F | D | S | C |

"panache" (his signature veal cheeks are the "best" in the city, and he does "wonders with fish"); the cooking is such a "treat" that his many admirers readily forgive minor flaws, namely the "tight" spacing, the "noise" and the "Franco-efficient" service; N.B. a wine bar, added post-*Survey*, offers East/West appetizers and vins de pays.

Blackie's S | 17 | 17 | 18 | $39 |
1217 22nd St., NW (bet. M & N Sts.), 202-333-1100
◪ Veterans of this vintage West End steakhouse are pleased with its "cool old DC" appeal and "inviting" surrounds, complete with French-style grillwork and "plush bar", as well as the "classics" and New American updates that emerge from the kitchen; dissenters, however, nix the merely "decent" menu, "'50s" feel and "inconsistent" service.

Black's Bar & Kitchen ◐S | 22 | 17 | 19 | $36 |
7750 Woodmont Ave. (bet. Cheltenham Dr. & Old Georgetown Rd.), Bethesda, MD, 301-652-6278
◪ A "good-looking crowd" "packs" this "easygoing" New American "hangout" in Bethesda for "absolutely delicious" seafood, notably "creative", "piquant" Gulf Coast–inspired preparations and a "great oyster selection"; the patio and rooftop deck are such "delights" that boosters can overlook the "sketchy" service, but a few dissenters feel the "noise" from the bar gets so loud "it makes eating here a chore."

Blue Iguana S | 18 | 16 | 18 | $25 |
12727 Shoppes Ln. (Fair Lakes Pkwy.), Fairfax, VA, 703-502-8108
◪ "Tucked away in a tacky" Fairfax shopping strip, this "funky oasis" with "Jimmy Buffett atmosphere", a DJ-spiked bar scene and a New American menu with a "tantalizing" twist is a "find" for local techies and shoppers; faultfinders, however, observe that the "innovative offerings often leave something to be desired", as does the service.

Blue Point Grill S | 23 | 19 | 21 | $37 |
600 Franklin St. (S. Washington St.), Alexandria, VA, 703-739-0404
◪ "Heavenly" seafood courtesy of the "Sutton Place Gourmet next door" (they share owners) is the star at this tony Alexandria "jewel" where the "beautiful" piscine specimens are "cooked just right" (it's also "the place for oysters"); though a few find it "snobby" and "overpriced", well-heeled fin fanciers who think that its "intimate" interior, "classy" bar and "relaxing" patio make it a "perfect rendezvous" retort just "point me the way to that fresh fish."

Bob & Edith's Diner S | 16 | 11 | 17 | $11 |
2310 Columbia Pike (Wayne St.), Arlington, VA, 703-920-6103 ◐
4707 Columbia Pike (Four Mile Run Dr.), Arlington, VA, 703-920-4700
■ "On weekend mornings, the line always stretches out the door" at these Arlington "dives", which satisfy the hankering

vote at zagat.com

Washington, DC

for "artery-clogging", "dirt-cheap" all-American diner eats slung by wisecracking servers who "don't take any lip"; the "small-town feel" draws everyone from "young musicians and Congressmen" to "yuppies and folks with lavender hair", so you "can't beat" the "roaring" "drama" here; N.B. 2310 Columbia Pike is open 24/7.

Bobby Van's Steakhouse — 21 | 20 | 21 | $48
809 15th St., NW (bet. H & I Sts.), 202-589-0060

"Big steaks" and dry martinis are the order of the day at this masculine "power place" Downtown, a "lobbyist's" haven that prides itself on its "porterhouse for two", "attentive" treatment (albeit "not guaranteed" for "non-star eaters") and good-weather patio; still, critical carnivores are convinced that "you can do better elsewhere for the same price."

Bombay Bistro S — 23 | 15 | 20 | $22
Bell's Corner, 98 W. Montgomery Ave. (Adams St.), Rockville, MD, 301-762-8798
3570 Chain Bridge Rd. (bet. I-66 & Lee Hwy.), Fairfax, VA, 703-359-5810

The "fabulous" lunch buffet "bargain" and "informative" service featured at this pair of "cheerful" Indian bistros in Rockville and Fairfax provide a "great" introduction to one of the ancient cuisines of the Subcontinent; the dishes on the "varied" dinner menu are just as "consistently well prepared", making it a "wonderful", "casual" option.

BOMBAY CLUB S — 25 | 26 | 25 | $40
815 Connecticut Ave., NW (bet. H & I Sts.), 202-659-3727

Only steps from the White House, this "lovely" Indian "oasis" distinguished by "refined elegance" transports visitors "back to the days of the Raj" with "gracious", "unobtrusive" pampering that makes even bureaucrats "feel like viceroys"; as "first-class" as the service is the "superb" fare, "subtly spiced" yet "bursting with flavor", making this "special-occasion" destination one of the "best dining experiences in DC."

Bombay Palace S — 22 | 20 | 21 | $33
2020 K St., NW (bet. 20th & 21st Sts.), 202-331-4200

"Generously spiced" "traditional" Northern Indian dishes marked by "complex flavors" are the focus at this K Street "standby"; with its "reliably excellent" menu, "fairly formal" surroundings and "polished" service, it's "a real deal" that's definitely "a cut above the usual."

Bombay Tandoor S — ∇ 19 | 17 | 20 | $23
8603 Westwood Center Dr. (Leesburg Pike), Tysons Corner, VA, 703-734-2202

Situated in a "boring" Tysons Corner business district with "sparse" dining options, this "commendable" Indian

Washington, DC | F | D | S | C |

"find" is a "success" thanks to its "solid cooking" (especially the "outstanding appetizers and great breads") and "warm" environs; even if "there's better" in the region, its "weekday lunch buffet" (blessed by budget-conscious dot-commers) is regarded as "one of the best in Northern Virginia."

Boulevard Woodgrill S | – | – | – | M |
2901 Wilson Blvd. (Fillmore St.), Arlington, VA, 703-875-9663
Overlooking the bustling Clarendon corridor, this casual American, centered around a wood-fired grill, serves up anything that swims, flies or grazes; grown-ups can gather at the handsome, well-stocked bar or settle into a comfortable, roomy booth, while grape nuts will appreciate the fact that the wine-loving owner sells Cabernets and Chardonnays at a fraction of what they'd cost at a Downtown restaurant.

Brasserie at the Watergate | 18 | 20 | 18 | $44 |
Watergate South, 600 New Hampshire Ave., NW (F St.), 202-337-5890
◪ Located opposite the Kennedy Center, this "attractive" French-accented American brasserie is "handy" for both pre-theater dining and "mixing with the cast" after the show; yet, while one faction calls it a "fine", "accommodating" "boon" for arts patrons, another pans it as a "disappointingly pale comparison to the original" Dominique's (its former incarnation) and cautions about "slow" service, especially irksome "when you need to get to the opera on time."

Brasserie Monte Carlo S | – | – | – | E |
7929 Norfolk Ave. (Cordell Ave.), Bethesda, MD, 301-656-9225
"One of Bethesda's nicer additions", this "petite" New French brasserie evokes the "Côte d'Azur with its colorful mural" and "lively" vibe; it's a "real find" for "simple" but "delicious" "favorites" "beautifully prepared" and delivered by a "friendly, competent" crew in "pleasant" ("charming", even) surroundings at prices that aren't out of line.

Bread Line | 23 | 11 | 14 | $12 |
1751 Pennsylvania Ave., NW (bet. 17th & 18th Sts.), 202-822-8900
◪ "Elevating fast food" to high art, Mark Furstenberg's International bakery/cafe on Pennsylvania Avenue has made many an addict out of the employees at the White House and World Bank, who can't get enough of his "fantastic" artisanal breads, "clever" sandwiches or "divine" desserts; "first-timers shouldn't be thrown off by the noise", the "spartan" decor or the "confusing lines", because this place is really an "amazingly" "well-oiled machine" and it may be the "best cheap lunch ever."

Broad Street Grill ◐ S | 14 | 13 | 16 | $22 |
132 W. Broad St. (Lee Hwy.), Falls Church, VA, 703-534-8120
◪ A "nice family place in a Falls Church neighborhood desperately in need of one", this American grill "fills a

Washington, DC F | D | S | C

void" with its "upscale pub food", while the "bustling bar" pulls in lots of sports fans, and its sidewalk cafe pleases people-watchers; new ownership may outdate the Food and Service scores.

B. Smith's S 20 | 22 | 19 | $36
Union Station, 50 Massachusetts Ave., NE (Columbus Circle), 202-289-6188

■ Both "delicious and inexplicable", the Swamp Thing (the signature dish of mixed seafood in a mustard-based sauce over greens) exemplifies the contrast between this soulful restaurant's "down-home" Southern (and Cajun-Creole) cooking and its "spectacular" "landmark" Union Station setting; while it functions as a "classy" site for a Capitol Hill business lunch, granola types gripe that it can be "hard to eat healthy" here and add that the food is as "uneven" as the service.

Buca di Beppo S 15 | 19 | 18 | $23
1825 Connecticut Ave., NW (Florida Ave.), 202-232-8466
122 Kentlands Blvd. (Great Seneca Hwy.), Gaithersburg, MD, 301-947-7346

■ "Over the top", this ultra-"kitschy", "family-style" chain is about "as Italian as Iceland", yet few seem to care because everyone's too busy stuffing themselves from the "heaping platters" of "garlicky" red-sauce crowd-pleasers while "looking at the campy masterpieces" ("love the Pope's head lazy Susan!"); egged on by the "energetic" servers, most have a "rowdy" "good time" (it's "so tacky it's fun"), but gourmands who find the whole concept "bizarre" warn that it's "all about quantity, not quality."

Burma S 21 | 9 | 16 | $18
740 Sixth St., NW (bet. G & H Sts.), 202-638-1280

■ "Worth the hunt" (it's hidden away on the second floor), this "offbeat" Burmese "alternative" in Chinatown with "very plain" "Soviet-era" decor and a "sleepy" atmosphere tantalizes curious palates with "unusual spicing" that's "quite distinct" from other Southeast Asian cuisines; with its "excellent variety of unique dishes" ("try the green tea leaf salad"), it's "a great representation of a rarely found" style of cooking and a "real bargain" to boot.

Burrito Brothers 15 | 9 | 13 | $9
1718 Connecticut Ave., NW (Florida Ave.),
202-332-2308 S
2418 18th St., NW (bet. Belmont & Columbia Rds.),
202-265-4048 S ⌑
1825 I St., NW (bet. 18th & 19th Sts.), 202-887-8266 ⌑
1815 M St., NW (bet. 18th & 19th Sts.), 202-785-3309
205 Pennsylvania Ave., SE (2nd St.), 202-543-6835
Union Station, 50 Massachusetts Ave., NE (Columbus Circle), 202-289-3652 S

Washington, DC   F | D | S | C

(continued)
Burrito Brothers
7505 Leesburg Pike (Pimmit Dr.), Falls Church, VA, 703-356-8226 S

🖼 "Cheap, fresh and fast", these Mexican franchises sustain Gen Y with "filling" burritos that are like a "three-course meal" wrapped in a soft tortilla (they're "so big" they're a "major cause of afternoon naps"); though the digs are "utilitarian" (to say the least), the eats provide a "healthier" alternative to typical "fast food", but critics feel they're getting "outclassed" by "better" (less "bland") versions from the "national chains."

Burro   16 | 10 | 13 | $9
2000 Pennsylvania Ave., NW (20th St.), 202-293-9449

🖼 "Extra spice" and a "healthy" orientation set apart this Golden Triangle Tex-Mex that's known for its "yummy burritos", "tasty" fish tacos and "rocking salsa"; "like its namesake, it's a steady" performer (aficionados insist its "quality and value" always "kick butt"), though opponents dismiss the "basic" eats ("decent" but "nothing special").

Busara S   21 | 20 | 19 | $25
2340 Wisconsin Ave., NW (Calvert St.), 202-337-2340
8142 Watson St. (International Dr.), Tysons Corner, VA, 703-356-2288

■ "Chic and trendy", with a crowd to match, these "upscale" Siamese twins "satisfy" with "zingy flavors" that'll "delight your palate"; "throngs of power-lunchers" take "clients" to the Tysons Corner branch for "something different" (such as the 'shrimp bikini' dressed in a spring roll wrapper and "spicy Bangkok-style bouillabaisse") turned out in "sexy" surroundings, while the Glover Park site's "lovely courtyard" nearly rivals the food as the "star attraction."

BUTTERFIELD 9 S   23 | 24 | 22 | $46
600 14th St., NW (bet. F & G Sts.), 202-289-8810

🖼 "All the senses are pleased" at this "swank" Downtown New American "darling" ("as cool and self-assured as *The Thin Man*" that inspired it), which "beautifully presents" "innovative" dishes and "impressive wines"; as "elegant" as the "sophisticated" setting is the "smooth" service, but some detractors feel like they've dialed the "wrong number", adding that the "erratic" menu ("sometimes wonderful, sometimes simply ok") should be better at these "upper-tier" prices.

Cactus Cantina S   19 | 17 | 17 | $21
3300 Wisconsin Ave., NW (Macomb St.), 202-686-7222

🖼 It's "a little loud and a little rowdy", but that's what makes this "festive" Cleveland Park cantina a "crowd" "favorite", not to mention the "great margaritas"; "endless chips, the freshest salsa" and "large portions" of "yummy burritos, enchiladas and other" affordable Mexican/Tex-Mex "standards" guarantee that "you won't go home hungry" or broke, but be ready for a "too-long" wait and "inexperienced" servers.

Cafe Asia [S] 21 | 18 | 17 | $21

1550 Wilson Blvd. (Pierce St.), Arlington, VA, 703-741-0870

◪ The "$1 apiece sushi may be the best happy-hour deal around" cheer boosters of this "happening" Pan-Asian cafe in Arlington, where "sharply dressed go-getters" congregate; the "diverse" Far Eastern menu "covers all the bases", and it's presented by "drop-dead" gorgeous waitresses in a "stylish", "sprawling" space that quickly gets "packed", engendering a "love-the-food, hate-the-wait" mantra.

CAFE ATLANTICO [S] 23 | 22 | 21 | $37

405 Eighth St., NW (bet. D & E Sts.), 202-393-0812

■ This "sexy", "multilevel" recently polished Penn Quarter Nuevo Latino will "spice up your evening" with "innovative" dishes such as "outstanding" guacamole ("made at the table"), "not-to-be-missed" quesadilla de huitlacoche and "dangerous" cocktails; not only is it "chaotic fun" and a "unique" "adventure", but it offers a "fabulous" weekend dim sum–style brunch; N.B. Jose Andres now oversees the kitchen and is creating art-on-a-plate for the glamorous new tapas bar (think foie gras wrapped in cotton candy).

Cafe Bethesda [S] 23 | 19 | 21 | $40

5027 Wilson Ln. (Cordell Ave.), Bethesda, MD, 301-657-3383

◪ "Treasured" for a "special night out" "off-the-beaten-path" in Bethesda, this "pretty" New American "find" is a "personalized" place in which to enjoy "creative" French-influenced cooking that remains "reliably good"; though wallet-watchers deem it "pricey", devotees appreciate its "intimate" scale and "warm", "unpretentious" ambiance.

Cafe Deluxe [S] 18 | 17 | 18 | $26

3228 Wisconsin Ave., NW (Macomb St.), 202-686-2233
4910 Elm St. (bet. Arlington Rd. & Woodmont Ave.), Bethesda, MD, 301-656-3131
1800 International Dr. (Leesburg Pike), Tysons Corner, VA, 703-761-0600

◪ "Always worthwhile", with "lots of action" going on at the "handsome" bar, this strategically located trio of bistro-style "favorites" is a "good all-purpose restaurant" with "something for everyone" on the "snazzy", "affordable" American "comfort-food" menu, including "fantastic meatloaf (nothing like mom's)"; you get "honest eats at honest prices" and the "friendly" crew is "kind to kids", but there's a drawback: "everybody likes it", so it's "perpetually" "too crowded" ("wish they took reservations") and "noisy."

Cafe Divan [S] — | — | — | M

1834 Wisconsin Ave., NW (34th St.), 202-338-1747

Cleverly designed with wraparound windows, warm cherry wood and distinctive cinnamon-and-copper-colored tiles, this eye-catching Upper Georgetown bistro provides a stylish backdrop for chef Yucel Atalay's (ex Nizam's) Ottoman cooking – meze, brick-oven pides (Turkish-style pizzas), grilled shrimp, doner kebab and pastirma (spicy sun-dried beef); it's all visually appealing, agreeably priced and available for takeout too; a liquor license is a recent addition.

Café 15 [S] — | — | — | VE

Sofitel Lafayette Square, 806 15th St., NW (bet. H & I Sts.), 202-737-8800

Contemporary French luxe is the lure at this White House precinct lobbying lair, a petite place with a seasonal menu overseen by chef Antoine Westermann that's well suited to the dignified, deco-feeling hotel dining room; Le Bar, its jewel-toned lounge with plush seating arranged for informal meetings, offers more casual dining options; be forewarned, though, that prices are as Parisian as the fare.

Cafe Japoné 🌙 [S] 18 | 15 | 16 | $26

2032 P St., NW (21st St.), 202-223-1573

◪ Stark contrasts mark this "lively" Dupont Circle boîte: in the "smoky", noirish karaoke lounge upstairs, a crowd of twentysomethings meets till "late at night" for sake, "decent" sushi and "nonstop entertainment" (including live jazz on Wednesdays), while downstairs in the all-white dining room, a more mature clientele settles in for Japanese "fusion" fare or relaxes in the new coral reef–themed lounge; purists who "give it a miss", though, say it "pales in comparison with other places" and warn "don't come looking for a quiet dining experience."

Cafe Milano 🌙 [S] 21 | 20 | 18 | $45

3251 Prospect St., NW (Wisconsin Ave.), 202-333-6183

◪ "VIP worlds collide" at this Georgetown Italian "scene" where "*Sopranos* sorts meet *Sex and the City*" wanna-bes; the "young and famous" are fawned over (and seated in the coveted downstairs room) by the "showy" staff, while mere mortals are shuttled to the "quiet" alcove upstairs, but wherever your table, you'll dine on "surprisingly good" food; even if detractors are "annoyed" by the "attitude", voyeurs "love the excitement and energy."

Café Mileto [S] 21 | 16 | 20 | $24

Cloppers Mill Village Ctr., 18056 Mateny Rd. (Great Seneca Hwy.), Germantown, MD, 301-515-9370

◪ "Large parties" of "young families" "stampede" to this "neighborhood" Southern Italian in Germantown to dig into its lunch buffet, "unusually good" pasta-night special (a "Monday tradition"), "wonderful wood-oven pizzas" and other "homey" fare; though it's stuck in a "shopping center" and the service can be "rushed", the "friendly" faces and "bargain" prices matter more to regulars.

Café Olé [S] 20 15 17 $22

4000 Wisconsin Ave., NW (Upton St.), 202-244-1330

■ Handy "before or after" a movie, this teeny Tenleytown "treasure" fills the bill with a "variety" of meze, "small plates" bursting with "great Mediterranean flavors" ("order lots" and share, easy to do when the prices are such "a wonder"); at lunchtime (self-service only), "daily customers" line up for soups, sandwiches and salads, then vie for a table out on the "thoroughly pleasant" patio (the "clincher").

Cafe Promenade [S] ▽ 20 23 20 $38

Renaissance Mayflower Hotel, 1127 Connecticut Ave., NW (bet. L & M Sts.), 202-347-2233

■ "DC's elite" can be spotted at this "ultimate power-breakfast" haunt set in the lobby of the Mayflower Hotel; it's the place to "close a deal" over lunch too while dining on "consistently" "good" Med fare in "elegant" environs "enhanced by a skylight", and it's a "Washington tradition" for an "excellent Sunday brunch" or "dainty" afternoon tea; N.B. there's a four-course seafood dinner ($39) on Fridays.

Café Salsa [S] – – – M

808 King St. (bet. Alfred & Columbus Sts.), Alexandria, VA, 703-684-4100

Pizzazz is the secret to the success of this Nuevo Latino with a spiced-up Puerto Rican, Cuban and Latin American menu and a jaunty bi-level setting in Old Town Alexandria that's an all-purpose place to grab a bite; wicked drinks at the upstairs bar enliven a scene that revs up on weekends after 10, when tables are moved aside to make room for live music and salsa dancing (lessons on Tuesdays).

Cafe Taj [S] 20 16 17 $25

1379 Beverly Rd. (Old Dominion Dr.), McLean, VA, 703-827-0444

◪ McLean's own "jewel" of India, this "cozy" fixture is "dependable" for its "especially good" lunch buffet, starring "excellent butter chicken"; service can be "perfunctory" during the day, but the dinner experience is "more refined", "attractively" presenting "well-executed" tandoori dishes and "lovely" vegetarian choices such as saag paneer in a "peaceful" atmosphere at "fair prices."

California Tortilla [S] 20 13 19 $10

4862 Cordell Ave. (bet. Norfolk & Woodmont Aves.), Bethesda, MD, 301-654-8226

Cabin John Shopping Ctr., 7727 Tuckerman Ln. (Seven Locks Rd.), Potomac, MD, 301-765-3600

■ "Witty" and "spunky", this Cal-Mex burrito team turns fast food into an "easy", "wholesome" "adventure" with

Washington, DC   F | D | S | C

its "interesting" selection of "huge", "high-quality and healthy" wraps doused with your choice of "awesome" hot sauces; the counter-people "customize" each order with a "smile", making it easy to overlook "decor shortcomings."

Cantina Marina S   – | – | – | M
600 Water St., SW (bet. Maine Ave. & 7th St.), 202-554-8396
This festive cabana cafe on the southwest waterfront (in the former Gangplank space) makes the most of sunset prospects with year-round patio seating and panoramic windows from its upstairs dining perch; its Cajun/Tex-Mex menu includes everything from boudin (spicy bayou sausage) and fish tacos to chicken-fried steak, and the margaritas are appropriately potent.

CAPITAL GRILLE S   23 | 23 | 23 | $47
601 Pennsylvania Ave., NW (6th St.), 202-737-6200
1861 International Dr. (Leesburg Pike), Tysons Corner, VA, 703-448-3900
◪ "Seeking out your Congressman?" – try the bar at this "manly" "political mecca" within sight of the Capitol, or "rub elbows with Beltway bandits" at the "elegant" Tysons Corner power hub; both "delight" conservative carnivores with "dry-aged" porterhouse steaks, a "classic" "boys' club feel" and "polished" service, but "prepare to wait" if you're not "connected" to a party "bigwig" or "celebrity."

Capri   18 | 18 | 18 | $38
Giant Shopping Ctr., 6825K Redmond Dr. (Old Dominion Dr.), McLean, VA, 703-288-4601
◪ Rechristened Capri to reflect its new seafood-strong menu and sea-blue decor, this upscale, modern Italian brings a "chic and fresh" approach to a shopping mall in McLean; at its convivial bar and well-appointed tables, you'll find tony locals meeting "old friends for good conversation", though detractors mark it down for "inconsistent" cooking.

Caribbean Feast   ∇ 22 | 10 | 15 | $12
823 Hungerford Dr. (bet. Mannakee & Washington Sts.), Rockville, MD, 301-315-2668
◪ "Don't let the nondescript exterior fool you" because inside this Rockville storefront awaits the "best jerk chicken" in town; "add some plantains, rice and beans and cornbread, listen to the reggae in the background and for just a moment you're in Jamaica"; a "cafeteria-style" "dive" it may be, but the "healthy portions" of "good, cheap eats" "make it worth it", and it's the "closest you'll get to the Caribbean" while still in Maryland.

CARLYLE S   24 | 21 | 22 | $31
4000 S. 28th St. (Quincy St.), Shirlington, VA, 703-931-0777
◪ One of Shirlington's "all-around favorites", this "lively" "pleaser" "gives the public what it wants" – an "eclectic",

vote at zagat.com

Washington, DC

"stupendous" New American menu that "accommodates any dining need", "arty", "contemporary" surroundings, "attentive" service and a "fair quality-price ratio"; its spiffy post-*Survey* redo may take care of its "acoustics problem", but impatient patrons still wish they could "make reservations" "instead of calling ahead" to put their names on a "long" waiting list.

CASHION'S EAT PLACE S | 25 | 21 | 21 | $39 |
1819 Columbia Rd., NW (bet. Biltmore St. & Mintwood Pl.), 202-797-1819

■ A "great meal is guaranteed" at this Adams Morgan New American "star" where Ann Cashion, a "dream of a chef", crafts "amazing" "seasonal" dishes that are "original without going too far"; inside, it's "romantic in a modern, edgy way", with "no pretensions", while the "neat" patio outside is a prime perch for "people-watching"; P.S. it's a "real treat" that's "not to be missed", so if it proves too "hard to get a table" try to snag a seat at the "inviting" bar.

Caucus Room | 22 | 24 | 23 | $49 |
401 Ninth St., NW (D St.), 202-393-1300

■ Just a stone's throw from Capitol Hill, this "state-of-the-art lobbyist's hangout" with an "imposing gentlemen's club" atmosphere is a "very Washingtonian" political hub; whether you opt for a "leather booth" or a "private" room, you can expect "very good" steaks ("so big it should be called the Carcass Room") and New American fare served by, "seemingly, one waiter per chair", though the powerful tabs lead pundits to quip "with these prices, [co-investors] Tom Boggs and Haley Barbour can leave their day jobs."

Centro Italian Grill S | 18 | 19 | 17 | $37 |
4838 Bethesda Ave. (bet. Arlington Rd. & Woodmont Ave.), Bethesda, MD, 301-951-1988

■ Set on a major Bethesda thoroughfare, this "sleek" and "airy" Northern Italian appeals with "flavorful" grilled fish and "modern" decor; critics (and there are more than a few), though, who cite "undistinguished" cooking and "spotty" service, dismiss it as a "triumph of style over substance", but that surely hasn't halted the traffic flow.

Cesco S | 22 | 18 | 19 | $42 |
4871 Cordell Ave. (Norfolk Ave.), Bethesda, MD, 301-654-8333

■ "Authentic" Tuscan cuisine (including the "best osso buco ever") matched by "super" regional wines brings the "pleasures" of Northern Italy to this Bethesda enclave; insiders try to go when chef-owner Francesco Ricchi is present (he spends some time at his DC venue Etrusco), because it can otherwise be "disappointing", but those who deem it "decent but way overpriced" and "overrated" "won't be back."

Washington, DC | F | D | S | C |

C.F. Folks | 23 | 10 | 18 | $15 |
1225 19th St., NW (bet. M & N Sts.), 202-293-0162
◪ Granted, this "hole-in-the-wall" International lunch counter below Dupont Circle is "dingy" and "cramped" and the service "can be pushy" (if not downright "surly"), but it has its "priorities" straight — "it's all about food" here, and it's "shockingly good"; those in-the-know advise "don't bother with the menu, just stick to the daily specials" and then "sit elbow-to-elbow with Washington bigwigs" while listening to "opera in the background."

Charlie Palmer Steak | – | – | – | VE |
101 Constitution Ave., NW (bet. 1st St. & Louisiana Ave.), 202-547-8100
Understated modern elegance pervades celebrity chef Charlie Palmer's (Aureole in NYC and Las Vegas) Capitol Hill showcase where prime beef, seafood and fowl are the centerpiece for boldly accented American dishes served in a fashionable bar and couch-filled lounge, at tables with views of the Capitol and the Mall or in private facilities, notably a rooftop terrace; the impressive 600-label wine list of exclusively American producers stored in a handheld computer is sure to be a conversation starter with the heavy-hitters who'll be coming here.

CHEESECAKE FACTORY ●S | 19 | 17 | 17 | $23 |
Chevy Chase Pavilion, 5345 Wisconsin Ave., NW (bet. Jenifer St. & Military Rd.), 202-364-0500
White Flint Mall, 11301 Rockville Pike (Nicholson Ln.), Rockville, MD, 301-770-0999
◪ "Eat dessert first" is clearly the strategy at this "horribly" "popular" chain, because given the "mammoth" size of its "solid" American dishes (from an equally "mind-boggling" menu) you risk not having precious room for its "better-than-sex" namesake cheesecakes (which, of course, is the "reason to go"); yes, the "wait" is "a killer" and the quarters a "madhouse", but few can resist its "are you tough enough to overstuff" challenge; P.S. try to "snag a table in the bar" area to avoid the reservations hassle.

Chef Geoff's ●S | – | – | – | M |
3201 New Mexico Ave., NW (Nebraska Ave.), 202-237-7800
1301 Pennsylvania Ave., NW (bet. E & F Sts.), 202-464-4461
In "tony" Foxhall Village, this "simpatico" New American bistro is known as a "welcoming", "casual" option for its "pleasing", "creative" fare paired with affordable wines by the glass and its eager-to-please manners; its Downtown junior courts professionals, tourists and nearby Warner Theatre ticket-holders within a big-windowed space with a roomy bar area and an outdoor patio, serving up a roster of creative pizzas, salads and a few more ambitious entrees with a similar "you want them to succeed" youthful charm.

Washington, DC | F | D | S | C |

Chez Marc ▽ | 23 | 19 | 21 | $40 |
7607 Centreville Rd. (bet. Leland & Rugby Rds.), Manassas, VA, 703-369-6526
☒ Marc Fusilier, who passed away shortly before we went to press, was the founding patron of this "one-of-a-kind" Classic French cafe, set in an "unlikely" Manassas location, which specializes in "authentic" dishes running the gamut from "excellent" pâté de foie gras and lobster with saffron beurre blanc to Grand Marnier soufflés; it was very much his domain, but his family, with the help of the longtime Fusilier-trained chef, plans to carry on his traditions.

Chi-Cha Lounge ●◐S | 16 | 22 | 15 | $19 |
1624 U St., NW (16th St.), 202-234-8400
☒ Twentysomethings "chill" at this "cool" New U lounge by sipping a signature Chi-Cha cocktail, smoking a hookah filled with flavored tobacco and listening to varied live music in a "sultry", "dim" "Andean village" setting; though "food isn't the main draw" here, the Latin American tapas are "perfect for sharing" while nestled into one of the "mismatched" velvet couches; P.S. you may want to "bring a flashlight" and perhaps an "iron lung."

China Star S | – | – | – | I |
Montgomery Village Shopping Ctr., 18204 Contour Rd. (Lost Knife Rd.), Gaithersburg, MD, 301-947-0104
Interesting dishes from the Shanxi province in northern China set apart this Gaithersburg fixture – many kinds of dumplings, little savory buns (try the soup-filled ones) and hand-pulled noodles, as well as multiregional entrees like crispy beef; the prices are inexpensive at any time, but the lunchtime buffet is a true bargain.

Ching Ching Cha S ▽ | 20 | 25 | 22 | $18 |
1063 Wisconsin Ave., NW (bet. K & M Sts.), 202-333-8288
■ "Welcoming sunlight" pours though the atrium of this "beautiful", "civilized" teahouse set "among the fray of Georgetown", making it a "peaceful oasis" in which to enjoy a "wonderful", formal Asian tea; the "amiable" staff is "knowledgeable about the large variety of brews available" and serious about authenticity ("don't even think of asking for sugar"), and the menu offers "tasty" "snacks" and "light and satisfying" bento boxes, but best of all is the "total relaxation for your mind."

Chopsticks | – | – | – | M |
1073 Wisconsin Ave., NW (Blues Aly), 202-338-6161
Japanese street food and serious sushi in a bento box–size setting is the story at this Georgetown sleeper prized by hip locals and sliced-fish cognoscenti; sure, its menu lists familiar noodle bowls, grills, tempura and deep-fry dishes, and its sushi specials are similar to those at other high-caliber spots, but what distinguishes it are pristine

subscribe to zagat.com

Washington, DC F D S C

ingredients, talented cooks, notably Masao Suzuki (ex Makoto), and the 'could-be-in-Tokyo' feel.

Cho's Garden S — | — | — | M
9940 Lee Hwy. (Rabel Run St.), Fairfax, VA, 703-359-9801
This smart-looking, family-oriented Fairfax Korean offers an easy introduction to a hearty, healthy, pungent cuisine featuring BBQ, stir-fries and bibimbop (a dish of rice, meat and vegetables topped with egg); its staff is eager to help with tabletop grilling and describing unfamiliar dishes, and prices are budget-friendly too, with a weekday luncheon buffet ($8.95) and happy-hour specials making it even cheaper to try something new.

Chutzpah S   18 | 10 | 14 | $16
12214 Fairfax Towne Ctr. (Monument Dr.), Fairfax, VA, 703-385-8883
■ Mavens award this busy Fairfax deli's "overstuffed" pastrami and corned beef sandwiches, "very decent chopped liver", "excellent half-sour pickles" and other "fresh quality" items the highest accolade – "just like NYC" – even though the joint is too "sterile"-looking and the help "more incompetent than rude"; sticklers, however, retort it "takes chutzpah" indeed to pass this "sandwich shop" off as a "real deli" ("who are they trying to kid?").

Circle Bistro S — | — | — | E
One Washington Circle Hotel, 1 Washington Circle, NW (New Hampshire Ave.), 202-293-5390
Recently redesigned by Adamstein & Demetriou into a sophisticated, streamlined space, this pumpkin-toned West End hotel refuge is convenient for a pre– or post–Kennedy Center supper; as stylish as the decor is Swiss-born chef George Vetsch's (ex Oval Room) distinctive, frequently changing New American–Mediterranean menu; grazers can opt for fondue or fritto misto at the sleek bar, while night owls can have a nightcap in the piano lounge.

Cities 20 | 22 | 17 | $39
2424 18th St., NW (bet. Belmont & Columbia Rds.), 202-328-7194
■ "It's all about atmosphere and attitude" at this eclectic Adams Morgan fashion plate where every year a different locale is featured (currently it's Mexico), with the theme carried out in the "high-style" designer backdrop and menu; the "*très* cosmopolitan" bar scene is its chief attraction, but those who settle in for a "leisurely" meal praise the kitchen's "originality and flair", adding that the "people-watching makes up for the spotty service."

CITRONELLE S   27 | 26 | 25 | $66
(aka Michel Richard's Citronelle)
Latham Hotel, 3000 M St., NW (30th St.), 202-625-2150
■ Revel in a "gastronomic tour de force" at this "national destination" in Georgetown, the "unforgettable" brainchild

vote at zagat.com

of "jovial" chef-owner Michel Richard; from the show kitchen emerge "intricate", "inventive" New French dishes, "accompanied by "superb" wines and "expertly served" in an "attractive" California-"chic" interior with a color-shifting mood wall; "from start to finish", "it doesn't get much better than this", but for an even more "extraordinary" evening, book the private chef's table; N.B. its bar/lounge offers more affordable luxe.

City Lights of China ◐ [S] 21 | 12 | 17 | $21

1731 Connecticut Ave., NW (bet. R & S Sts.), 202-265-6688

◪ Dupont Circle's shining source for a "Chinese-food fix", this "hole-in-the-wall" has cultivated a loyal following with its broad menu of "reliably" "above-average" "standards"; given its "cheesy" basement digs and the staff's "brusque" behavior, many prefer to take out (the "fast delivery" makes it a speed-dialer's dream).

CLYDE'S ◐ [S] 18 | 20 | 19 | $27

Georgetown Park Mall, 3236 M St., NW (Wisconsin Ave.), 202-333-9180

70 Wisconsin Circle (Western Ave.), Chevy Chase, MD, 301-951-9600

1700 N. Beauregard St. (Seminary Rd.), Alexandria, VA, 703-820-8300

Reston Town Ctr., 11905 Market St. (Reston Pkwy.), Reston, VA, 703-787-6601

8332 Leesburg Pike (Chain Bridge), Tysons Corner, VA, 703-734-1901

■ "Dependable and affordable", these "Washington institutions" are "inviting" places for "all-purpose" dining, drawing in everyone from age "3 to 83"; appointed with lots of "glass and brass" to give them "class", they feature "middle-of-the-road" American saloon eats enlivened by "good-deal" seasonal specials; considering that they're franchises, customers are glad to report "few failings."

Coeur de Lion [S] ▽ 23 | 24 | 24 | $50

Henley Park Hotel, 926 Massachusetts Ave., NW (10th St.), 202-414-0500

■ One of Downtown's "most charming brunch" sites, this "romantic" rendezvous features a series of dining rooms made "cozy" by old brick, stained-glass details and a fireplace; exuding "quiet class", it's a pleasant place for "fine" New American fare that may be "better than you'd expect" from a hotel.

Colorado Kitchen [S] ▽ 24 | 20 | 20 | $20

5515 Colorado Ave., NW (Kennedy St.), 202-545-8280

◪ Hats off to Gillian Clark for bringing her "super" American cooking, both "homey" and "inventive", to an iffy Northwest "neighborhood that needs good restaurants" like her "cute" bistro; fans appreciate the small- and large-plate options

Washington, DC F | D | S | C

on the menu and find the atmosphere "so relaxing and lighthearted" that minor service slips are easily forgiven; besides, the "staff warms up with regulars", and once you sample her "homemade doughnuts", you'll be one too.

COLVIN RUN TAVERN S   25 | 25 | 24 | $56
Fairfax Sq., 8045 Leesburg Pike (Gallows Rd.), Tysons Corner, VA, 703-356-9500

▰ An "upbeat" haven of "city sophistication among the glut of Tysons Corner steakhouses", this "exciting" venue courtesy of Bob Kinkead looks nothing like a tavern; it's a "warm", "comfortable" "class act" with an "outstanding" New American menu that specializes in "exceptional" roasted meats "carved at the table" by "polished" servers; though a few faultfinders quibble that it "needs to smooth out some edges", groupies already consider it "easily one of the best in Northern Virginia"; closed on Sundays in summer.

Connaught Place S   24 | 19 | 23 | $24
10425 North St. (bet. Chain Bridge Rd. & University Dr.), Fairfax, VA, 703-352-5959

■ Rivaling the "big name" Indian establishments in DC, this Fairfax "gem" has "outstanding everything" – "authentic", "perfectly seasoned" dishes, a "calm" atmosphere ("never a rushed feeling") and "attentive" service; it's also "one of the best values around", offering a "bargain" lunch buffet as well as a "wonderful" pre-theater menu; whether you come "in jeans or dress up for a night out", the "gracious" staff will "make you feel grand"; N.B. there's live sitar music on weekends.

Coppi's S   19 | 17 | 17 | $24
1414 U St., NW (bet. 14th & 15th Sts.), 202-319-7773

▰ "Bicycling fanatics" brake for the "eclectic" pizzas topped with "unusual combinations" at this "funky", "cycle-themed" U Street Italian; its wood-burning oven also turns out some "unique" dishes from Liguria, favored by cognoscenti, while regulars "crowd" in for the "good" "designer" pies and "divine" Nutella dessert calzones, though dissenters give it "two thumbs-down."

Corduroy S   23 | 17 | 21 | $42
Sheraton Four Points Downtown, 1201 K St., NW (12th St.), 202-589-0699

■ "Hidden" "out of the way" on the second floor of the Four Points hotel is this "wonderful", "roomy" New American "surprise", whose unobtrusive location may explain why it lacks the "wider audience" that those who've "discovered" it say it "deserves"; it's worth checking out because "impressive" chef-owner Tom Power executes "simple" yet "gourmet" dishes based on the seasons (always on the menu, though, is his "spectacular" roasted chicken, which "puts mom's to shame").

Washington, DC | F | D | S | C |

Crisp & Juicy ꜱ | 21 | 5 | 12 | $11 |
Sunshine Sq., 1331G Rockville Pike (Congressional Ln.), Rockville, MD, 301-251-8833
Leisure World Plaza, 3800 International Dr. (Georgia Ave.), Silver Spring, MD, 301-598-3333
4540 Lee Hwy. (Woodrow St.), Arlington, VA, 703-243-4222
913 W. Broad St. (bet. Oak & Spring Sts.), Falls Church, VA, 703-241-9091

■ Most aptly named, this Peruvian chain is a "once-a-week" staple for scores of Beltway-area families who "couldn't live without" its "deliciously" "crisp and juicy" spit-roasted chicken; teamed with "tasty" yuca fries, black beans and rice and "divine" hot sauces, it adds up to a "very cheap", "sooo good" meal, though the exceedingly "plain" setting and "hard chairs" lead many to "take out."

Crystal Thai ꜱ | – | – | – | M |
Arlington Forest Shopping Ctr., 4819 Arlington Blvd. (Park Dr.), Arlington, VA, 703-522-1311

Best known for its seasonal soft-shell crab specialties, this "authentic" Arlington Thai earns customer loyalty with its other "consistently delicious" dishes too ("try the yummy Panang chicken" or the crispy whole fish); not only are the prices "reasonable", but the chandelier-lit digs are even somewhat "elegant" (albeit the tables are "a bit scrunchy").

Cubano's ꜱ | ▽ 18 | 16 | 17 | $23 |
1201 Fidler Ln. (Georgia Ave.), Silver Spring, MD, 301-563-4020

■ "Cheerful" and "festive", this "much needed" Cuban "addition" "brightens" the Silver Spring dining scene with "zesty", "authentic" (if "a little heavy") cooking; a "mix of neighborhood families and young professionals" digs into Cuban sandwiches (available till midday only – "a real shame"), "fabulous fried yuca", "excellent *ropa vieja*" and other nicely "spiced" "comfort foods", all "reasonably priced"; it may be "uneven", but its fans counter that "when it's on, it's great."

Da Domenico | 21 | 17 | 21 | $36 |
1992 Chain Bridge Rd. (Leesburg Pike), Tysons Corner, VA, 703-790-9000

■ Regulars at this Tysons Corner "power lunch" haunt "don't even bother to open" the Northern Italian menu; they know to order the "awesome" marinated veal chop, then sit back and be well taken care of by the "accommodating" staff and the "hospitable" owner ("we love Dom!"), whose "opera-singing" brother is an attraction in himself; it may get "a bit crowded", but "you'll always feel at home" in this "quaint" room, even if a few find it merely "so-so."

Daily Grill ꜱ | 17 | 17 | 18 | $27 |
1200 18th St., NW (M St.), 202-822-5282
Georgetown Inn, 1310 Wisconsin Ave., NW (N St.), 202-337-4900

Washington, DC F | D | S | C

(continued)
Daily Grill
Tysons Galleria, 2001 International Dr. (Chain Bridge Rd.), Tysons Corner, VA, 703-288-5100
▰ "Lots of business gets done" at these "mainstream" American "hangouts" where "classy happy-hour crowds" gather amid "clubby" surroundings for "good comfort food" including "hearty" chicken pot pie and a "killer" Cobb salad; while they're undeniably "popular", critics dismiss the "ordinary" fare and "haphazard" service and add that it's "a little expensive for a daily encounter."

David Greggory S   –|–|–| E
2030 M St. (21st St.), 202-872-8700
Talented toques David Hagedorn (ex Trumpets) and Greggory Hill (ex Gabriel) have created a spacious West End bistro that's quite an eye-catcher, with wraparound windows, glass decorations and a gorgeous bar; their collaborative New American menu offers imaginative takes on Southern, Mediterranean and Asian classics in appetizers, half portions and entrees, with whimsical touches (such as chocolate cake served with a ready-to-lick miniature whisk) to keep the foodies and trendies amused; in sum, this is sure to be a scene in no time.

da Vinci Ristorante S   –|–|–| M
Spring Field Mall, 6791-B Spring Field Mall (Spring Mall Rd.), Springfield, VA, 703-921-2500
This bistro's linen-clad tables, soft lamplight and ambitious Italian menu featuring pastas and seafood make it an unexpected find for Springfield shoppers and briefcase toters; a sporty bar and lunchtime offerings like panini and salads are more casual options.

DC COAST   25 | 24 | 23 | $45
Tower Bldg., 1401 K St., NW (14th St.), 202-216-5988
▰ "Electricity is in the air" at this "young power brokers'" pacesetter Downtown that boasts a "gorgeous" deco-style two-tiered space and a "fabulous" New American seafood-slanted menu "inspired by three coasts"; despite "unacceptable" noise (sit upstairs if you can), a "velvet-rope" vibe and tabs in the "luxury" stratosphere, followers promise that you'll have a "memorable" meal, because, after all, "food is the real star here."

Dean & DeLuca   19 | 13 | 13 | $16
3276 M St., NW (33rd St.), 202-342-2500 S
1299 Pennsylvania Ave., NW (13th St.), 202-628-8155
▰ At Georgetown's "gourmet express" – a "lively" cafe that owes its "exceptional variety" of "imaginative" New American "light fare" to its "DeLuxe" market annex – you'll spot "genteel" locals ("and their dogs") sunning on the "charming" piazza while enjoying a "delicious" bite; during

Washington, DC | F | D | S | C |

the summertime, the weekend brunch hour comes with live jazz, but note that the "indifferent" counter service and "Paris"-league prices are in effect year-round; N.B. there's a smaller branch Downtown.

Delhi Dhaba S | 19 | 11 | 16 | $16 |
4455 Connecticut Ave., NW (Yuma St.), 202-537-1008
7236 Woodmont Ave. (bet. Bethesda Ave. & Elm St.), Bethesda, MD, 301-718-0008
2424 Wilson Blvd. (Barton St.), Arlington, VA, 703-524-0008

■ What started out as a "good, cheap", cafeteria-style curry parlor near the Arlington Courthouse has branched out into "more restauranty" offshoots in Upper NW and Bethesda; stalwarts say all of them offer "authentic food at great prices", but skeptics who find them "mediocre" to begin with think that quality varies with the location.

Diner, The ●S | 16 | 17 | 16 | $16 |
2453 18th St., NW (bet. Belmont & Columbia Rds.), 202-232-8800

■ Filling a "major need" in Adams Morgan, this 24-hour "instant classic" with a "cool" retro style pulls in hordes of hungry, young hipsters round-the-clock; it's a "required stop" for post-clubbers, refueling them with all-American comfort eats like breakfast favorites, the "best" gravy fries and "world-class" shakes; the servers are "hardworking" but overburdened, leading wags to quip "good late-night food, but by the time you get it, it's morning."

Dish S | - | - | - | M |
The Rive Inn, 924 25th St., NW (bet. I & K Sts.), 202-338-8707

This compact, sophisticated Foggy Bottom hotel venue takes a fresh look at American classics like fried chicken and veggies and has a relaxing setting of warm woods and a mood-defining William Wegman diptych of a reclining weimaraner taking its ease; singles and tourists can dine sociably at the communal table (for eight) or at the bar, and it won't take long for Kennedy Center patrons to discover its smartly appointed tables.

District ChopHouse & Brewery S | 19 | 20 | 18 | $32 |
509 Seventh St., NW (bet. E & F Sts.), 202-347-3434

■ Just a toss away from the MCI Center, this "popular" "meat 'n' potatoes" palace set in a former bank really "hops" on game nights; fans hail it for its "blue-collar" American lineup of "big" beef, "onion rings stacked high" and "great handcrafted beers", delivered in a "lively" atmosphere (read: "unbearable din") at "cost-conscious" prices, but opponents rank it at the "lower end of chain steakhouses."

Dolce Vita S | 23 | 16 | 21 | $26 |
10824 Lee Hwy. (Main St.), Fairfax, VA, 703-385-1530

■ How sweet life would be if there were more "great neighborhood" "finds" like this "cozy" Fairfax Italian,

Washington, DC   F D S C

embraced for turning out "wonderful, smoky pizzas" and "lovely" pastas amid "clever" decorations and "romantic" serenades; then, maybe this "tight" room wouldn't be "packed shoulder-to-shoulder" at prime time, frustrating even the faithful with "forever" waits.

Dragon Chinese Restaurant S   – – – I
Festival at Muddy Branch Shopping Ctr., 227 Muddy Branch Rd. (Diamond Back Dr.), Gaithersburg, MD, 301-330-6222
Dim sum is served all day, every day, at this Northern Chinese whose tasteful interior makes it suitable for anything from a solo stop to family or business entertaining and belies its Gaithersburg shopping plaza location; best of all, its bilingual menu numbers and describes each of the nearly 100 authentic, well-priced dumpling, soup, noodle and small-plate choices, thereby encouraging experimentation while avoiding miscommunication.

DUANGRAT'S S   25 21 22 $28
5878 Leesburg Pike (Glen Forest Dr.), Falls Church, VA, 703-820-5775
■ "Classic" Thai food enhanced by "classy" touches – white tablecloths, "beautiful" flowers, chandeliers and "pleasing" waitresses in "colorful" native attire – continues to earn this "exotic" Falls Church "treasure" lavish praise; the menu offers "many wonderful", "fragrant" choices, most of them "heavenly", virtually guaranteeing that even "first-timers" will "love" this "visual and gustatory treat"; the only downside: it's "always crowded", despite its "out-of-the-way" location.

Dukem ● S   – – – I
1114 U St., NW (12th St.), 202-667-8735
Abuzz with a lively cross section of DC's large Ethiopian community, this New U gathering place provides a good introduction to that country's interestingly spiced stews, scooped up with spongy injera bread and eaten with the hands; it functions even more as a social center on weekends, when there's live entertainment, while on Sunday afternoons, it puts on a native coffee ceremony.

DuPont Grille S   – – – E
Jurys Washington Hotel, 1500 New Hampshire Ave., NW (19th St.), 202-939-9596
A people-watching perch with Mediterranean- and Asian-influenced American food is the story at this Dupont Circle hotel restaurant whose space was recast by the award-winning firm of Adamstein & Demetriou; expect a glass-enclosed pavilion and spiffy mango-and-black–accented space that promote see-and-be-seen sociability, and since he's a New Orleans Emeril alumnus, consider trying chef Cornell Coulon's daily gumbo.

vote at zagat.com

Washington, DC

F	D	S	C

Eat First ●S   21 | 8 | 16 | $18
609 H St., NW (6th St.), 202-289-1703

☑ Sinophiles "eat often" at this "plain" but "friendly" Chinese that relocated to another site in Chinatown two years ago, because it continues to deliver ("fast") a "fantastic selection of authentic" fare at "absurdly cheap" prices; there's still "no ambiance", but that hardly matters when the food is "as tasty as ever"; even if a few feel that some of the "magic" has been lost in the move, diehards who "welcome it back" urge it's "worth another try."

eCiti Restaurant & Bar ●   18 | 16 | 17 | $34
8300 Tyco Rd. (Leesburg Pike), Tysons Corner, VA, 703-760-9000

☑ Word is that this once hyper-"trendy" mingle-dine-and-dance scene in Tysons Corner is feeling the "high-tech bust"; while there is "less buzz" and more "pink slip" parties going on, a "smaller" crowd of followers still appreciates its "adventurous" New American menu and "renovated" warehouse digs; bears may dub it a "dot-bomb", but bulls retort at least there's "less pretense" in the house nowadays; N.B. the sushi bar is open until 1:30 AM.

El Golfo S   – | – | – | I
8739 Flower Ave. (Piney Branch Rd.), Silver Spring, MD, 301-608-2122

Formerly El Tazumel, this reinvigorated Silver Spring cantina angles for the interests of fin-fare fanciers with seviche and seafood versions of tacos, fajitas and enchiladas; the spacious setting evokes an imaginary Latin American Gulf Coast, making it convivial for families and groups.

Ella's Wood Fired Pizza   – | – | – | I
901 F St. NW (bet. 12th & 13th Sts.), 202-638-3434

Ed Hanson's (ex Sam & Harry's, Jaleo) spiffy Penn Quarter pizzeria gives expression to his 'do one thing right' sensibility with his restrained use of first-rate toppings, slow-rising dough (think several days) and state-of-the-art wood-fired oven; its menu is simple – a few interesting salads, antipasti, a roster of appealing pies and sandwich specials, all comfortably priced and served in attractive, cherry-stained wood and oiled-stone dining rooms and bar.

El Manantial S   – | – | – | E
Toll Oaks Village Ctr., 12050-A North Shore Dr. (Wiehle Ave.), Reston, VA, 703-742-6466

Roman murals and an elegant Mediterranean feel (retained from this restaurant's predecessor, the defunct Saint Basil) complement the French, Spanish and Italian dishes on the menu at this new arrival, located in a Reston shopping center; at lunch, its new owners (whose resumes include Taberna del Alabardero and La Côte d'Or Cafe) make good use of the pizza oven while also offering salads, quiches

Washington, DC

and serious entrees; dinnertime brings linen, dimmed lights and upscale meals.

El Mariachi S | – | – | – | I |
765C Rockville Pike (Wootton Pkwy.), Rockville, MD, 301-738-7177
"Visited regularly by sweaty runners", soccer moms with hungry players and lots of families, this "friendly", "tolerant" "neighborhood gem" on Rockville Pike is "always packed" with aficionados of "simple but sumptuous" Mexican and Salvadoran cooking; those who "return" often swear that "everything is authentic", "robust" and "inexpensive", making it a "real" "pleasure to eat here."

El Pollo Rico S⊄ | 25 | 5 | 15 | $11 |
2541 Ennalls Ave. (Veirs Mill Rd.), Wheaton, MD, 301-942-4419
932 N. Kenmore St. (Fairfax Dr.), Arlington, VA, 703-522-3220
■ "Finger-licking", "irresistible" "spit-roasted" chirpers sold at "prices so cheap you feel guilty" lure "Washingtonians of every stripe" to these Peruvian "queen of chicken" dives in Wheaton and Arlington; "nothing else can challenge" these "addictive" birds, but since "there's always a line and no good place to sit" (no booze, no frills and no plastic either), most opt for the "terrific takeout."

El Sol de Andalusia S | – | – | – | M |
838C Rockville Pike (Edmundson Dr.), Rockville, MD, 240-314-0202
At his new Rockville venue, ebullient Joaquin Serrano reprises the Moorish-accented decor and Spanish regional menu that earned him plaudits at his former Bethesda restaurant, Andalucia; here, Andalucian classics like zarzuela (seafood stew) and Seville-style duck (with sherry and olives) are enlivened by the owner's hospitality and the picturesque dining room.

Elysium S | ∇ 23 | 26 | 23 | $55 |
(aka Relais & Châteaux Morrison House)
Morrison House, 116 S. Alfred St. (bet. King & Prince Sts.), Alexandria, VA, 703-838-8000
■ When you sup amid the "old-money" appointments of this posh hotel dining room in Old Town, you're treated to a 'chef of your own' who comes to your table for a tête-à-tête before custom-designing your New American dinner courses based on seasonal, organic ingredients; whether or not you opt for the "perfectly matched" wine pairings, every "wonderful" morsel is presented with "exemplary care", making this "fabulous" "experience" one of a kind.

EQUINOX S | 25 | 21 | 23 | $49 |
818 Connecticut Ave., NW (I St.), 202-331-8118
■ Owners Todd and Ellen Gray and their "warmhearted" staff obviously "really like what they're doing" at this "superb" Regional American "centrally located" near the

Washington, DC | F | D | S | C |

White House, and they lend it "genuine" appeal; a recent James Beard award nominee, "talented" chef Todd showcases his "original", "sumptuous" seasonal dishes in a "tasteful", "comfortable" room, eliciting "huzzahs" from admirers, even if a minority "expects more from such hype."

Etrusco S | 22 | 22 | 20 | $43 |
1606 20th St., NW (bet. Q & R Sts.), 202-667-0047
◼ "Emulate the life of the pleasure-loving Etruscans" at this "buzzy", "beautiful" Dupont Circle "favorite" where chef-owner Francesco Ricchi does "marvelous things to ordinary ingredients", conjuring up the "earthy" "tastes of Italy" (with a focus on Tuscany) in such dishes as his "splendid" osso buco; though the kitchen can be "erratic" and the service likewise "dicey", partisans insist it's "worth the effort to try to hit it on the right night."

Evening Star Cafe S | 22 | 18 | 19 | $29 |
2000 Mount Vernon Ave. (Howell Ave.), Alexandria, VA, 703-549-5051
◼ "Personality" plus a "folksy, small-town" atmosphere sets the stage for a "grown-up" but "not too fancy" New American dining experience at this Del Ray "hangout"; it's a "neighborhood treasure", despite "spotty" service, attracting a loyal following that can choose seating in the "funky" (though "cramped") dining room, the "colorful" wine bar upstairs or out on the patio, a "welcoming" place to "watch the world go by."

Faccia Luna Trattoria S | 20 | 15 | 17 | $19 |
2400 Wisconsin Ave., NW (bet. Calvert St. & Observatory Ln.), 202-337-3132
823 S. Washington St. (bet. Green & Jefferson Sts.), Alexandria, VA, 703-838-5998
2909 Wilson Blvd. (Fillmore St.), Arlington, VA, 703-276-3099
◼ Hearth-baked "pizzas with pizzazz" and "good, cheap Chianti make up a great Saturday night" at these "reliable" Italian sources for "family-friendly", "cost-effective" dining; they're "not so fancy" inside, but the outdoor seating areas enhance their "breezy" ambiance, while the "harried" waiters display a "high tolerance for screaming children"; purists, however, who find it "not too exciting", "don't see what all the fuss is about."

Fadó Irish Pub ●S | 15 | 20 | 16 | $20 |
808 Seventh St., NW (bet. H & I Sts.), 202-789-0066
◼ Handy to the MCI Center, this "Disneyfied version" of a Dublin pub is "always packed" before and after a game; it's "beer first and everything else second" here, though its "hearty", "cardiac-arresting" Irish food does have its homesick fans; P.S. its "Monday-night trivia quiz is a cool way to be a nerd."

Washington, DC   F | D | S | C

Fahrenheit & Degrees S   _ | _ | _ | E
Ritz Carlton Georgetown, 3100 South St., NW (bet. K & M Sts.), 202-912-4110
The ritzy scene heats up at this new hotel restaurant in Georgetown: Fahrenheit, the main space, has antique brick walls and rich appointments that lend dignity to any-occasion meals off an Italian-influenced New American menu, while Degrees, the bar and lounge, features antipasti and seafood platters; those seeking to entertain in private should check out the 14-seat dining room here, inside a landmarked smokestack.

Fairfax Room ●S   _ | _ | _ | E
Westin Embassy Row, 2100 Massachusetts Ave., NW (21st St.), 202-293-2100
Once the site of the legendary Jockey Club (DC's version of NYC's '21' Club), this Embassy Row hotel venue now features a high-end New American–Continental menu of trendily packaged crowd-pleasers like seafood martinis and lobster risotto; the minimalist dining room, though, still retains a West Coast feel, while the wood-paneled lounge continues to be an inviting place for a drink and a bite by the fireplace; N.B. breakfast and lunch served seven days, dinner only on Fridays.

Faryab S   21 | 16 | 20 | $25
4917 Cordell Ave. (bet. Norfolk Ave. & Old Georgetown Rd.), Bethesda, MD, 301-951-3484
■ This Bethesda Afghan remains a "pleasant", "friendly" refuge brightened with homeland photos, artifacts and tapestries; it's a "warm" backdrop for a "delectable", "authentic" menu that makes it "easy to order something new" or stick with "delightfully spiced" favorites like its "world-class" lamb kebabs and "must-have pumpkin stew"; as if that weren't enough, it's also a "good value."

Felix S   20 | 21 | 18 | $32
2406 18th St., NW (bet. Belmont & Columbia Rds.), 202-483-3549
◪ "Hip", young things "slide into a martini and enjoy the upscale", "eclectic" New American menu and "campy James Bond" vibe at this slice of "SoHo" in Adams Morgan that's also known for its "excellent" kosher-style dinner every Friday (don't ask); many guests start or end their evening in the "chic" Spy Lounge next door (featuring "tasty tunes"), making this "swinging singles" scene "the place for a total evening's" worth of "fun."

15 ria S   _ | _ | _ | M
Washington Terrace Hotel, 1515 Rhode Island Ave., NW (Scott Circle), 202-742-0015
From the owners of NYC's Nobu and Tribeca Grill comes this fresh Contemporary American bistro in an intimate hotel just off Scott Circle; for pre-dinner sips, head to the

vote at zagat.com

Washington, DC | F | D | S | C |

retro-style bar, which specializes in high-end bourbons; the gently priced menu by chef Jamie Leeds can be sampled either in the casual, tree-shaded streetside cafe or the comfy boutique dining room; P.S. it didn't take long for her crisp-skinned roast pig Wednesday-night special to become a classic.

Filomena Ristorante S | 20 | 20 | 19 | $35 |
1063 Wisconsin Ave., NW (bet. K & M Sts.), 202-338-8800
■ The "pasta mamas" making "great ravioli" in the window of this Georgetown Italian set the stage for the "fun", "loud" "grandma's basement" scene in the dining room below, where every day a "generous", "too tempting" lunch buffet is offered at a bargain price; aside from the "homey" food, its "fantastic", over-the-top holiday decorations make it beloved by "kids" of all ages ("Washington personalities" too); P.S. the arrival of chef Enzo Febbraro (ex Centro) "could make it overcome its touristy" image.

Fin | – | – | – | M |
1200 19th St., NW (bet. M & N Sts.), 202-530-4430
Formerly Georgetown Seafood Grill, this Golden Triangle fish house sports a new, polished-steel-and-wood look and a recast mariner's menu encompassing a raw bar, sushi, small plates and entree-size piscatory pickings prepared any way you like (i.e. broiled, blackened, steamed, etc.); its inviting sidewalk cafe is sure to hook passersby for lunch and after-five socializing and people-watching.

Finemondo | – | – | – | E |
1319 F St., NW (bet. 13th & 14th Sts.), 202-737-3100
Rustic Italian chic defines this comfortable Downtown venue whose offerings run the gamut from happy-hour bruschetta to zuppa di pesce; the kitchen specializes in spit-roasted meats, poultry and fish, with traditional sauces and side dishes, while a private dining room reminiscent of a wine cellar completes the appealing package.

Finn & Porter ●S | – | – | – | E |
5000 Seminary Rd. (Quaker Ln.), Alexandria, VA, 703-379-2346
Swank business dining is the line at this mahogany-and-gold steak-and-seafood house in Alexandria's Mark Center featuring a clubby bar/lounge, plushly appointed dining areas, an exposed wine cellar and a terrace overlooking a geyser and pond; as its punning moniker suggests, it offers fresh fin fare (both classic American preparations and a sushi bar) along with a porterhouse-focused meat menu.

Fireflies S | – | – | – | I |
1501 Mt. Vernon Ave. (E. Nelson Ave.), Alexandria, VA, 703-548-7200
'Fresh, fast and fun' is the motto of this vibrant Del Ray Eclectic cafe that draws its name and culinary inspiration

Washington, DC F | D | S | C

from its ceramic hearth oven, which turns out pizza, roast chicken, grilled vegetables and baked pilafs (sandwiches, salads and eclectic entrees are also on the bill); order at the counter, choose a bottle from the wall of wines, seat yourself and watch the passing street scene until your food arrives (takeout also available).

Firefly S — | — | — | E
1310 New Hampshire Ave., NW (bet. N & 20th Sts.), 202-861-1310
Former Nora chef John Wabeck's passion for seasonal produce and boutique wineries rules at this intimate bistro below Dupont Circle; amid flickering lights, earth tones and witty woodland accents, the neighborhood can relax over New American dishes as interpreted by the toque who redefined bar food during his recent stints at Bar Rouge and Topaz Bar.

Firehook Bakery & Coffeehouse 21 | 14 | 15 | $11
3411 Connecticut Ave., NW (bet. Macomb & Newark Sts.), 202-362-2253 S
441 Fourth St., NW (bet. D & E Sts.), 202-347-1760 S
431 11th St., NW (E St.), 202-638-1637
3241 M St., NW (bet. Potomac St. & Wisconsin Ave.), 202-625-6247 S
215 Pennsylvania Ave., SE (bet. 2nd & 3rd Sts.), 202-544-7003 S
1909 Q St., NW (19th St.), 202-588-9296 S
912 17th St., NW (bet. I & K Sts.), 202-429-2253
555 13th St., NW (F St.), 202-393-0952
214 N. Fayette St. (bet. Cameron & Queen Sts.), Alexandria, VA, 703-519-8020 S
105 S. Union St. (King St.), Alexandria, VA, 703-519-8021 S
◪ Neighborhood-oriented and locally owned, this "friendly", "casual" chain of American bakery/coffeehouses "keeps Starbucks from taking over the world" with its "excellent selection" of "crusty" breads and "tempting" baked goods, along with its "gourmet" sandwiches, soups and salads; critics, though, note that expansion has its price – what was an "original" concept now has a "cookie-cutter" feel.

Five Guys S⌿ 24 | 8 | 15 | $9
4626 King St. (Beauregard St.), Alexandria, VA, 703-671-1606
107 N. Fayette St. (King St.), Alexandria, VA, 703-549-7991
7622 Richmond Hwy. (Fordson Rd.), Alexandria, VA, 703-717-0090
6541 Backlick Rd. (Old Keene Mill Rd.), Springfield, VA, 703-913-1337
◪ "Grease city" it may be, but "there are no better" burgers than those flipped at this "beyond-basic" Northern Virginia chain where the "big, sloppy" patties come "dripping with toppings" (don't forget the "awesome" made-from-scratch

Washington, DC | F | D | S | C |

fries); it's a "total dive" and you should "feel lucky if you find a place to sit", but "what a treat when all you want is a great" meal on a bun; P.S. voted the No. 1 Bang for the Buck in the Washington area, the chain has ambitious plans to add franchises in DC and suburban Maryland.

Fleming's S | 23 | 23 | 22 | $49 |
1960A Chain Bridge Rd. (International Dr.), Tysons Corner, VA, 703-442-8384

■ An "outstanding selection of wines by the glass" (more than 100) distinguishes this "contemporary" steakhouse chain with "good buzz"; it aims to entice with an "attractive" open layout, less masculine decor and a "non-smoking" policy, but the menu is quite traditional, highlighting "excellent" aged cuts like its signature porterhouse; faultfinders say it's "not quite Ruth's Chris or Morton's", but for that exact reason boosters appreciate it as a "refreshing change" of pace.

Florida Ave. Grill | 20 | 13 | 18 | $14 |
1100 Florida Ave., NW (11th St.), 202-265-1586

■ "Everything is fried, unapologetically fattening and good"-tasting at "DC's most famous diner", a Northwest soul food "institution" where folks from every walk of life have been coming in for years for "grits, biscuits, country ham and friendly AM life"; redolent with the "smell of old grease" and filled with Southern memorabilia, it's "a tradition worth preserving" proclaim the legions of loyalists that'd be "devastated" if it ever closed its doors.

Fontina Grille S | ▽ 19 | 20 | 19 | $28 |
King Farm Village Ctr., 801 Pleasant Dr. (bet. King Farm & Redland Blvds.), Rockville, MD, 301-947-5400

■ "Lively" and airy, this smart-looking Italian is "off to a good start" say settlers in this tony Montgomery County enclave of Rockville; the "cooking is adept" – from the crisp-crust pizzas and "fine" pastas to the "best" eggplant dishes and "interesting", updated specials – providing ample reasons for locals to dine near their new houses and office complexes.

Fortune S | 21 | 12 | 15 | $21 |
North Point Village Ctr., 1428 Reston Pkwy. (bet. Baron Cameron Ave. & Leesburg Pike), Reston, VA, 703-318-8898
6249 Arlington Blvd. (Patrick Henry Dr.), Seven Corners, VA, 703-538-3333

■ On weekends, the "chaotic parade of pushcarts" whizzing around an "amazing array" ("we always get too full before we've tried everything of interest") of "delicious dim sum" can be either an "overwhelming" sight or "such a blast", but appetites will be rewarded nonetheless at this pair of "hangar"-size Chinese emporiums in Northern Virginia;

Washington, DC

F | D | S | C

"come with a large group to share" the small plates, or visit later in the day for Hong Kong–style seafood specialties.

FOUR & TWENTY BLACKBIRDS S 26 | 21 | 23 | $44
650 Zachary Taylor Hwy. (Rte. 647), Flint Hill, VA, 540-675-1111
■ Nestled in the "scenic" Virginia foothills, this "delightful" New American "destination" is a "welcoming" country gem" "in the middle of nowhere", making it a "perfect getaway from DC"; though the "imaginative" gourmet menu changes every three weeks, you "can't go wrong" with any selection because everything is homemade, "very fresh" and "exceptional"; it's "well worth the drive", so "if you haven't taken the time to dine here, you need to reevaluate your priorities."

Franklin's S – | – | – | I
5123 Baltimore Ave. (Gallatin St.), Hyattsville, MD, 301-927-2740
Big and high-spirited, this yearling brings solid, largely American food – BBQ, salads and sandwiches, as well as pizzas and pastas – to a mostly barren stretch of Hyattsville; the whimsical touches in the multipurpose room reflect the sensibilities of owner (and former toy seller) Mike Franklin (don't miss browsing in his General Store next door).

Full Kee ●S 23 | 7 | 14 | $16
509 H St., NW (bet. 5th & 6th Sts.), 202-371-2233
5830 Columbia Pike (Leesburg Pike), Falls Church, VA, 703-575-8232
■ Novices should be "careful" – the food is "authentic" at this "spartan" Chinatown "mainstay" whose philosophy must be "if anybody will eat it, we'll cook it"; even if you're not so adventurous, you'll be more than satisfied with the "addictive shrimp dumpling soup" and other "astonishingly good" Cantonese choices, and if you go late (till 2 AM on weeknights, 3 AM weekends) you can catch off-duty chefs dining and unwinding; N.B. there's a Falls Church outpost.

Full Key ●S ▽ 21 | 7 | 14 | $16
Wheaton Manor Shopping Ctr., 2227 University Blvd. W. (Georgia Ave.), Wheaton, MD, 301-933-8388
■ A Chinese "soul food favorite", this "standby" is the "place to go" in Wheaton for the "best" Hong Kong–style noodle soups, fresh-made won tons "loaded with shrimp", "delicious" clams in black bean sauce and some "unusual" house specials, all priced "cheap"; "fast" food–like service may "scream carryout", but loyal customers don't much care because they "come here only for the food", and a recent remodel should make the setting more desirable.

Gabriel S – | – | – | E
Radisson Barcelo Hotel, 2121 P St., NW (21st St.), 202-956-6690
We didn't survey this Spanish near Dupont Circle, as it had planned to close temporarily for a major redo, but it changed

vote at zagat.com

Washington, DC | F | D | S | C |

its plans and continues to host an appreciative audience; still an "event" is its "lavish" Sunday brunch (centered around a whole "roast pig that's on the menu in heaven"), presented in a "cozy, tasteful" setting; it's "quieter on weeknights" and also worth a visit for its "flavorful" tapas, "innovative" Nuevo Latino dishes and "flights" of sherries; N.B. longtime chef Greggory Hill has left to open his own venue.

Galileo S | 26 | 23 | 24 | $58 |
1110 21st St., NW (bet. L & M Sts.), 202-293-7191
Laboratorio del Galileo
1110 21st St., NW (bet. L & M Sts.), 202-331-0880

■ Esteemed as the "Prada of Italian cuisine", this "rarified" "epicurean must" in the Golden Triangle is where DC players take their "best clients" for an "unmatched" "experience" orchestrated by Roberto Donna; for the "ultimate insider's dinner", book a table in the Laboratorio adjacent to the main room at Galileo, a private dining space with a state-of-the-art showcase kitchen, from which emerges a "spectacular", custom-designed series of 10–12 "complex" tasting courses "perfectly matched" with wines from the "divine" cellar.

Generous George's S | 17 | 15 | 16 | $16 |
3006 Duke St. (Roth St.), Alexandria, VA, 703-370-4303

◪ "Pandemonium" reigns at this "manic" Alexandria Italian parlor, a cavernous joint that caters to kids and "carb fiends" with its "kooky" decorations (think pink flamingos) and over-the-top menu of "big, yummy pizzas and pastas, or both together" in one dish; you better believe it's a total "assault on the senses", but if you're looking for somewhere to host a "birthday party for 10-year-olds, this is the place."

Georgia Brown's S | 22 | 22 | 22 | $38 |
950 15th St., NW (bet. I & K Sts.), 202-393-4499

■ "Check your heart at the door" at this "classy" Downtown "scene" with a clientele that epitomizes "chic" cultural diversity and then dig into "an embarrassingly large amount" of "clever" ("and rich") Low Country cooking "not like grandma used to make" ("give in to temptation and get those fried chicken livers"); when it gets "jammed", the service inevitably "slows" down, but there's "no other place like it"; P.S. the Sunday jazz brunch is an "awesome" display.

Geranio S | 22 | 19 | 20 | $37 |
722 King St. (bet. Columbus & Washington Sts.), Alexandria, VA, 703-548-0088

■ "Cozy", "dark" and "romantic", this "well-established" "charmer" set in a "quaint townhouse" in Old Town is a "real treat" for Italian food so "tasty" it'll "make you crave more"; supporters swear that "everything" on the "rotating" menu is "excellent" and the "professional" staff always "unobtrusive", making it a "delightful" place to take "that special someone."

Washington, DC   F | D | S | C

GERARD'S PLACE   27 | 22 | 24 | $63
915 15th St., NW (bet. I & K Sts.), 202-737-4445

■ "Tasteful and restrained", Downtown's most "Parisian" of places "wows" devotees with "fabulous", "imaginative" New French interpretations prepared with "finesse" (don't miss the "outstanding lobster"); it's "always among the best" destinations in DC thanks to chef-owner Gerard Pangaud's "exquisite" touch, "elegant" surroundings and "precise" (if "arrogant") service; it's "in a class by itself – too bad the prices are as well" sigh budget-minders.

Good Fortune ●S   21 | 13 | 16 | $19
2646 University Blvd. W. (bet. Georgia Ave. & Veirs Mill Rd.), Wheaton, MD, 301-929-8818

☑ The rolling dim sum carts on weekends make it way "too easy to order everything" in sight wail those addicted to this Wheaton Chinese's array of "expertly" made morsels (the lines form before noon, so better "go early"); considered one of the neighborhood's "best" Cantonese picks, it proves that "crowded", "dumpy" digs matter little when you "know how to cook a duck" like it does, though detractors feel it "waxes and wanes" too much.

Grapeseed S   21 | 18 | 19 | $38
4865 Cordell Ave. (Norfolk Ave.), Bethesda, MD, 301-986-9592

☑ "What fun!" cheer boosters of this "urbane", "intimate" Bethesda bistro that "creatively pairs" "interesting" New American appetizers with a "treasure trove" of wines by the glass in a "welcoming" atmosphere that "encourages a long, leisurely" stay; oenophiles "can't say enough good things" about this "great date spot", but faultfinders deem it "uneven" and caution that the "cost adds up" quickly.

Green Field Churrascaria S   19 | 16 | 18 | $29
1801 Rockville Pike (Randolph Rd.), Rockville, MD, 301-881-3397

☑ "Get really ready to eat" before going to this "sizzling" "*casa de carne*" in Rockville, where the set-price Brazilian barbecue deal begins with a trip to the extensive salad bar and hot food station (a "huge meal" right there), followed by an "endless" procession of servers who keep bringing skewers of "every kind of fire-roasted meat" to your table until you "roll yourself" out the door; skeptics, though, sniff "lots of food" but "mediocre quality."

Green Papaya S   21 | 22 | 20 | $28
4922 Elm St. (Arlington Rd.), Bethesda, MD, 301-654-8986

☑ Offering a "beautiful introduction to refined Vietnamese cuisine", this "tranquil" tropical fantasy in Bethesda gives traditional fare an "original" appeal ("love" the 'golden pancake' and "fantastic" sugarcane shrimp); the kitchen's "emphasis on fresh ingredients" allows the dishes' "true

Washington, DC | F | D | S | C |

flavors to shine through", but nitpickers feel that "as it's becoming more popular", it's becoming more "so-so."

Greenwood S | 19 | 19 | 15 | $44 |
5031 Connecticut Ave., NW (Nebraska Ave.), 202-364-4444
◪ Few local chefs seem to spark as much controversy as Carol Greenwood – her considerable "cult following" adores the artistic Upper NW venue where she puts together an "always surprising" New American bill of fare "based on what's seasonal", though they admit that enough "time can lapse between courses to take a nap"; foes, meanwhile, find her so "intolerant of any menu substitutions" ("the customer is never right" here) that they "wouldn't go back on a bet."

Grille 88 S | – | – | – | E |
1910 18th St., NW (bet. Florida Ave. & T St.), 202-588-5288
At this Dupont Circle locale for relaxed fine dining, cool blue tones and crisp white tablecloths provide the backdrop for a menu full of retro-inspired New American fare; look for classics, along with modish riffs on bar food like 'nachos', plus there's a piano bar for sophisticated live entertainment.

Grillfish S S | 19 | 17 | 17 | $30 |
1200 New Hampshire Ave., NW (M St.), 202-331-7310
◪ "Delish" and "easy", this "eccentric" seafood "concept" in the Golden Triangle "hits" the mark with "fresh" fish "simply" grilled (or, if you must, sautéed); neither the "wonderfully weird" "*Twilight Zone*" decor nor the "too enthusiastic" servers discourage youthful fin fanciers, but the "older" demographic finds it all just "bizarre", starting with the floor-to-ceiling mural behind the ornate stone bar.

Grill from Ipanema S | 20 | 18 | 18 | $29 |
1858 Columbia Rd., NW (bet. Belmont Rd. & 18th St.), 202-986-0757
■ "*Obrigado*" (thank you) "for the best local taste of Brazil" in Adams Morgan say admirers of this "buzzing" spot that mixes "killer caipirinhas" "worthy of Rio"; not only is a "great" "party" always going on, but it's the "place to go" for "authentic", "stick-to-your-ribs" food including "tasty" seafood stews and "interesting" dishes like "fried alligator."

Guajillo S | 19 | 13 | 15 | $20 |
1727 Wilson Blvd. (bet. Quinn & Rhodes Sts.), Arlington, VA, 703-807-0840
◪ Nothing "run-of-the-mill" about this small, "noisy" Mexican in Arlington – not its "unconventional bar specials" nor its "unusual" salsas, "incredible" seviche, "excellent" chicken mole and other "authentic" items ("definitely a cut above the standard"); service is "pleasant", if somewhat "unrefined", while a "playful" color palette perks up the simple decor.

Washington, DC   F | D | S | C

Gua-Rapo ◐S   ▽ 17 | 20 | 16 | $25
2039 Wilson Blvd. (Courthouse Rd.), Arlington, VA, 703-528-6500

■ When they want "something different" in Arlington's Courthouse district, the "chic crowd" saunters over to this "swanky" "see-and-be-seen" lounge with a blue-glass bar, settles into one of the "low", "comfortable sofas", orders "good specialty drinks" and nibbles on mix-and-match items from the Nuevo Latino menu; detractors, however, report that it's "still working out the kinks" while "trying desperately to be as trendy as Chi-Cha Lounge" in DC (run by the same owner).

Haad Thai S   22 | 17 | 19 | $20
1100 New York Ave., NW (11th St.), 202-682-1111
1472 N. Beauregard St. (Seminary Rd.), Alexandria, VA, 703-575-1999

■ "The little Thai that could" aptly describes these lunchtime staples "convenient" to Downtown business and the Mark Center in Alexandria, which "try hard and succeed" at satisfying surveyors with "wonderful", "authentically spiced" specialties; "lovely presentations", "fantastic" murals of faraway places, "prompt" service and "reasonable prices" only enhance the story; they're "always packed" during the day, but it's "easy to get a table at night."

Haandi S   24 | 17 | 21 | $25
4904 Fairmont Ave. (Old Georgetown Rd.), Bethesda, MD, 301-718-0121
Falls Plaza Shopping Ctr., 1222 W. Broad St. (Leesburg Pike), Falls Church, VA, 703-533-3501

■ Setting the Indian "standard" for many connoisseurs in the suburbs of Bethesda and Falls Church, this "terrific" traditional twosome with a "pretty-in-pink" color scheme "never lets you down" with its "tantalizing", "well-spiced" dishes (believe them when they tell you the lamb "vindaloo is hot") that "consistently" satisfy the "craving"; the less impressed, however, find the menu "unimaginative" and add that despite the staff's "genteel" manners, it can "feel like you're speed dining" here.

Hakuba S   ▽ 21 | 18 | 15 | $26
Kentlands Market Sq., 706 Center Point Way (Great Seneca Hwy.), Gaithersburg, MD, 301-947-1283

■ Though few out-of-area respondents know about this "tasteful", tranquil suburban sushi bar (which suits its tony Kentlands neighbors just fine), its admirers marvel that the fish is "so fresh we can't believe it's in Gaithersburg"; not only does it offer "some of the most original items in the DC area", but it also features a selection of "interesting" cooked dishes, as well as sake served (as it should be) in "your own cedar box."

vote at zagat.com

Washington, DC | F | D | S | C |

Hama Sushi S | ▽ 21 | 14 | 20 | $24 |
2415 Centreville Rd. (Sunrise Valley Dr.), Herndon, VA, 703-713-0088

■ Most Herndon regulars "check out the daily specials board for the freshest selections" at their local Japanese sushi spot, which offers "good quality and value for the money" in a "bright", if "uninspired", setting; a familiar "variety" of traditional cooked dishes is available too, presented with the same "warm" service, making this standby an easy pick for "day-to-day dining."

Hard Times Cafe S | 18 | 14 | 16 | $15 |
4922 Del Ray Ave. (Old Georgetown Rd.), Bethesda, MD, 301-951-3300
4738 Cherry Hill Rd. (Baltimore Ave.), College Park, MD, 301-474-8880
1021 Washington Blvd. (Cherry Ln.), Laurel, MD, 301-604-7400
Woodley Gardens, 1117 Nelson St. (Montgomery Ave.), Rockville, MD, 301-294-9720
1404 King St. (West St.), Alexandria, VA, 703-837-0050
3028 Wilson Blvd. (Highland St.), Arlington, VA, 703-528-2233
K-Mart Shopping Ctr., 428 Elden St. (bet. Herndon Pkwy. & Van Buren St.), Herndon, VA, 703-318-8941 ☽
Springfield Plaza, 6362 Springfield Plaza (Commerce St.), Springfield, VA, 703-913-5600 ☽
14389 Potomac Mills Rd. (Gideon Dr.), Woodbridge, VA, 703-492-2950 ☽

■ Sometimes the "proven pleasure" of a bowl of "great", "greasy" chili with a side of fried onion rings and a "cold beer" is worth the "serious heartburn risk", especially if downed in a joint with "character" like these American parlors with the "best" C&W jukeboxes around; skeptics, though, who sniff merely "serviceable", quip "one time was hard enough."

Harry's Tap Room S | - | - | - | M |
Marketplace Commons, 2800 Clarendon Blvd. (N. Fillmore St.), Arlington, VA, 703-778-7788

This handsome American brasserie, a Sam & Harry offshoot, taps into the rapidly upscaling Clarendon dining scene; look for a stylish, two-tiered setting with sweeping views of the neighborhood, large windows, mosaic and slate tiles, a fireplace, polished wood furniture and rich fabrics; the menu includes twin beef fillets sauced 11 different ways ($16.95) and steamed mussels galore, along with salads, burgers and modernized classic entrees.

Havana Breeze | 18 | 9 | 14 | $15 |
1401 K St., NW (14th St.), 202-789-0909

■ Providing a "refreshing" change from the power haunts and generic carry-out dives of the area, this "no-frills" Downtowner pleases the "office lunch" crowd with "real" Cuban sandwiches and other "down-home" fare that could

Washington, DC | F | D | S | C |

rival its Miami counterparts; though the place is a "dump" and "service isn't a priority", the eats "deliciously" explain "why Hemingway loved Cuba" so much.

Hee Been S | 22 | 14 | 19 | $23 |
6231 Little River Tpke. (Beauregard St.), Alexandria, VA, 703-941-3737
■ A home away from home for "Korean families and military veterans homesick for the food of Seoul", this Alexandria refuge promises a "fantastic experience" for novices too; though a "bilingual dictionary would be useful" for exploring the menu, you can't go wrong with the "terrific barbecue grilled to order at your table"; despite its "unattractive" surroundings, addicts are more than happy to sing "we been, we been and we won't stop"; N.B. sushi is available too.

Helix Lounge S | – | – | – | M |
Hotel Helix, 1430 Rhode Island Ave., NW (bet. 14th & 15th Sts.), 202-462-9001
Atmospheric to the nth degree, this edgy new lounge off the lobby of the boutique Hotel Helix in Logan Circle pays homage to pop art with its kaleidoscope of colors, silvery curtained nooks and modish settees; it's a smart backdrop for American comfort food given a contemporary tweak and tailor-made for sharing along with whimsical drinks (think a 'Ding Dong tini' garnished with an authentic junk-food specimen of the same name); N.B. come nice weather, check out the spectacularly lit patio with striped cabanas.

Heritage India | 25 | 23 | 21 | $33 |
2400 Wisconsin Ave., NW (Calvert St.), 202-333-3120
4931 Cordell Ave. (Old Georgetown Rd.), Bethesda, MD, 301-656-3373
■ "Lovely screens", historical photos and native handicrafts evoke the "refined" ambiance of a "wealthy Indian's private home" at this culinary ambassador in Georgetown, which "impeccably presents" "complex", "flavorful" fare that includes some "exquisite" dishes "not found" elsewhere (as does its unrated sibling in Bethesda); the cognoscenti regard it as a "wonderfully authentic" "jewel" but flaw-finders warn "watch out" for the "pushy" servers.

Hinode S | 20 | 16 | 19 | $25 |
4914 Hampden Ln. (Arlington Rd.), Bethesda, MD, 301-654-0908
134 Congressional Ln. (bet. Jefferson St. & Rockville Pike), Rockville, MD, 301-816-2190
11575 Old Georgetown Rd. (bet. Executive Blvd. & Rockville Pike), Rockville, MD, 301-881-7822
■ Utility players in the Montgomery County sushi league, these "reliable" Japanese fallbacks are valued by fans for their "bust-a-gut" lunch buffets, "fresh" fish and "nice 'cooked' sushi options", served in "family"-friendly environs; critics cite "plain", "uninspired" offerings and "distracted"

Washington, DC | F | D | S | C |

service; the new Old Georgetown Road outlet is unrated and offers teppan, where showman chefs cook at your table.

Hollywood East Cafe ◐ S | 25 | 10 | 19 | $19 |
2312 Price Ave. (Elkin St.), Wheaton, MD, 301-942-8282
◪ Get your taste buds ready for a real "adventure" at this Wheaton Chinese where visitors can find "authentic" renditions of their "favorite childhood dishes" or choose from a "long, exotic" menu of "intriguing" Cantonese "delights"; if the "miles" of specials seem overwhelming, the "helpful (if a bit gruff) staff will translate" for you; the digs are "gritty", but it's an "excellent value" for such "complex, sophisticated Hong Kong–style" cooking.

Hope Key ◐ S | 20 | 8 | 16 | $15 |
3131 Wilson Blvd. (Highland St.), Arlington, VA, 703-243-8388
◪ "The later the hour, the better the food" at this low-rent Arlington Chinese with "zero ambiance, whose "authentic" chow (notably "perfect shrimp, chicken and eggplant in a hot pot") is a "real belly-filler"; doubters may deem it "so-so", but at least you get a "ton of food for less $ than [the loose change] under your couch"; N.B. open till 1 AM on weeknights, 2:30 on weekends.

Hunan Lion S | 19 | 20 | 19 | $26 |
2070 Chain Bridge Rd. (Old Courthouse Rd.), Tysons Corner, VA, 703-734-9828
◪ "Consistently a cut above many other local Chinese restaurants", this Tysons Corner veteran is a "solid" place to "promptly" "satisfy your beef with broccoli craving" or enjoy other "well-prepared" standards from the extensive menu; while there may be "no surprises" here, regulars swear you "can't go wrong" with any of the dishes, which explains why it's recently "celebrated its 20th anniversary."

Hunan Palace S | ▽ 19 | 12 | 15 | $20 |
Shady Grove Shopping Ctr., 9011 Gaither Rd. (Shady Grove Rd.), Gaithersburg, MD, 301-977-8600
◪ "Plain" looking though it may be, this Gaithersburg Chinese is where "native Taiwanese go for their fix" (it's "one of the few places around that offer the true flavors" of that cuisine); though it features a broad, multiregional bill of fare, the best items are off the menu (including "great, fresh lobster and crab dishes"), which might clarify why those who don't persevere in ordering the most "authentic" selections judge the food "just fair."

Huong Que S | 24 | 15 | 22 | $22 |
(aka Four Sisters)
Eden Ctr., 6769 Wilson Blvd. (Roosevelt Blvd.), Falls Church, VA, 703-538-6717
■ "If you don't fall in love with the food (which you should)" at this "stellar" Falls Church Vietnamese, "you'll swoon

Washington, DC | F | D | S | C |

over the service from the beautiful sisters" (for whom it's nicknamed); they're "sweet" "ambassadors of their native cuisine and culture", and they'll "patiently" guide you through the "dauntingly long menu"; "fortunately, just about everything" is "sublime" (particularly the clay pot specialties), thus "it's hard not to want to work your way through it all", especially when the tabs are so moderate.

Il Cigno ▽ | 19 | 18 | 18 | $34 |
Lake Anne Plaza, 1617 Washington Plaza (N. Shore Dr.), Reston, VA, 703-471-0121

At its best for "alfresco dining" while "enjoying the view" of the jet fountain on Lake Anne, this "reliable" Reston Italian is also a "frequent stop" among the business crowd, which congregates over "solid, if unexciting", fare; the modish Mediterranean interior has been freshened, but the "lovely" terrace now sports a "huge" (and "controversial") tent, which "spoils" the outdoor experience for some.

Il Pizzico | 23 | 17 | 21 | $29 |
Suburban Park, 15209 Frederick Rd. (Gude Dr.), Rockville, MD, 301-309-0610

"From the greeting" to the "fresh herbs on the table" to the "high-quality" Italian cooking, "this place has style", in sharp contrast to its Rockville "strip-mall" exterior; headlining the menu are "simple", "wonderful" "homemade pastas", while the specials are always "inspired", delivered by "caring" waiters at a "more than fair price"; the only drawback: trying to nab a table in the "intimate" room.

Il Radicchio S | 17 | 14 | 15 | $22 |
223 Pennsylvania Ave., SE (bet. 2nd & 3rd Sts.), 202-547-5114
1801 Clarendon Blvd. (Rhodes St.), Arlington, VA, 703-276-2627

"Good for a filling meal for not too much money", this "no-nonsense" pair of Italian spaghetterias on Capitol Hill and in Arlington serves its purpose with "all-you-can-eat pasta" tossed with a "wide choice of sauces", "yummy, wood-fired pizzas" and "tasty salads"; though it's "not a place to take someone you want to impress" and the service can be, shall we say, "lazy", it works for many as an "informal" "standby."

Indique S | – | – | – | M |
3512-14 Connecticut Ave., NW (bet. Ordway & Porter Sts.), 202-244-6600

A chic design incorporating richly textured native fabrics, frescoes, lacquered inlays and antique furnishings forms the appealing backdrop for this two-tiered Cleveland Park Indian, an upscale offshoot of the popular Bombay Bistro restaurants; it features a sophisticated wine bar for sipping cocktails and sampling small plates, as well as an inviting dining room where an interesting menu of regional dishes offers both familiar favorites and unusual specialties.

Washington, DC | F | D | S | C |

INN AT LITTLE WASHINGTON S | 29 | 28 | 29 | VE |
Main & Middle Sts., VA, 540-675-3800

■ "Two perfectionists" – Patrick O'Connell and Reinhardt Lynch – treat "dining as an art form" at their "exquisite" Virginia country inn, and it shows, as this "unequalled star" has again been voted No. 1 for Food, Decor and Service in the Washington area; the owners have long made it their mission to ensure that "each guest enjoys the whole evening", from the moment they step into the "over-the-top" "fantasy" setting through every bite of the "magical" New American courses served by an "exceptional" staff; "could any meal be worth this much money?" – this one is.

International, The ●S | – | – | – | M |
Washington Plaza Hotel, 10 Thomas Circle, NW (bet. 14th St. & Massachusetts Ave.), 202-842-1300

The suave bar lounge in this Thomas Circle hotel classic features low-slung Biedermeier- and Bauhaus-inspired seating, various of-the-moment sips (including gold-dusted martinis) and eclectic sustenance ranging from caviar to quesadillas to a foie gras–enriched burger; just a few blocks from the White House and Downtown biz, it's a voguish venue for casual meetings of all sorts; N.B. opens at 4 PM.

i Ricchi | 25 | 23 | 23 | $49 |
1220 19th St., NW (bet. M & N Sts.), 202-835-0459

■ "Recreating Tuscany" in the Golden Triangle, this "classy" country villa is a "premier" "fine-dining establishment" showcasing "outstanding" Northern Italian fare – from the "obscenely good breads" to the "rich risotto" and "luscious" pastas to the wood-fired *bistecca alla Fiorentina* and "super" regional wines – in "fancy" environs tended to by "knowledgeable", if "stuffy", servers; those who "love" it "wish they could eat here every day", but dissenters who find it "overrated" concede that its occasional "slips" would likely be noticed less if the tabs "weren't so pricey."

Islander Caribbean S | ▽ 18 | 13 | 18 | $22 |
1201 U St., NW (12th St.), 202-234-4971

■ Trinidadian Addie Green, a "DC institution", presides over this "fun", festive Caribbean enclave on U Street, a bastion of "sophisticated island cooking"; order a "colorful, tropical drink" "with an umbrella", then sample an array of "tasty", "homemade" appetizers and entrees (including the "best plantains around" and "fabulous fish and stewed meats"), but better "get there an hour before you're hungry", as the joint operates in a decidedly leisurely manner.

Jaipur S | – | – | – | M |
9401 Lee Hwy. (Circle Woods Dr.), Fairfax, VA, 703-766-1111

As colorful as the Pink City for which it's named, this upscale Fairfax Indian reflects the noted culture and traditions of the capital of the northern state of Rajasthan with its brightly hued furnishings and rich cooking; inspired by the cuisine reserved for the ruling Moghuls (exemplified by such flavorful dishes as Jaipuri lamb), the varied menu also includes many other regional specialties.

JALEO [S] 23 | 21 | 19 | $29

480 Seventh St., NW (E St.), 202-628-7949
7271 Woodmont Ave. (Elm St.), Bethesda, MD, 301-913-0003

◪ What gives these "cool" "crowd-pleasers" in the Penn Quarter and Bethesda their "amazing staying power"? – more than 1,500 surveyors say it's their "upbeat" energy, "delectable" Spanish tapas that are "fun-to-share" ("every pick is better than the last", so have a "little of everything") and "superb" Iberian wines; of course, the "downside" of their raging success is the "frustrating" mob scene, though sidewalk seating offers some of the best viewing around.

Jean-Michel [S] 22 | 19 | 22 | $43

Wildwood Shopping Ctr., 10223 Old Georgetown Rd. (Democracy Blvd.), Bethesda, MD, 301-564-4910

◪ Jean-Michel Farret's Bethesda namesake is like that "slightly formal but congenial uncle, the one who taught you the proper way to hold a wineglass", the one who would know that these "traditional French dishes are done just right"; the "older" clientele appreciates the "reliable, high-quality" classics prepared here and feels right at home in the "genteel" quarters, so even if some fuss about "snippy" treatment, few can forgo that "unforgettable" soufflé.

Jefferson [S] ▽ 23 | 24 | 24 | $51

The Jefferson, 1200 16th St., NW (M St.), 202-833-6206

■ Considered by some insiders as the "ultimate power-lunch spot", this "cozy" hotel dining room keeps a low profile, though its "elegant" New American fare, "intimate nooks" and unobtrusive service are well known among the Capitol cognoscenti; its "hushed, historic" atmosphere also makes the formal afternoon tea a "treat", while sipping a cocktail in the urbane bar is a "very Washingtonian" thing to do; N.B. for special events and holidays, the kitchen recreates dinners from the Thomas Jefferson era.

Jeffrey's at the Watergate [S] 22 | 23 | 22 | $53

Swissôtel - The Watergate, 2650 Virginia Ave., NW (New Hampshire Ave.), 202-298-4455

◪ Despite hosting "too many Texans" (including Dubya), not to mention its location in a Nixon-era "landmark", this "sophisticated" Southwestern-flavored French hotel dining room near the Kennedy Center garners bipartisan support; followers champion the "interesting", "carefully prepared" dishes that pay tribute to the Lone Star State and the "lovely views of the Potomac River", but opponents find it too "impersonal."

Washington, DC | F | D | S | C |

Jerry's Seafood | 25 | 13 | 21 | $38 |
9364 Lanham Severn Rd. (¾ mi. east of Rte. 495, exit 20A), Seabrook, MD, 301-577-0333

■ Though the tables are now covered with tablecloths, nothing else has changed at this "friendly" Seabrook seafood house – to the great relief of its fans; still starring on the concise menu is the 'crab bomb', a "serious" 10-ounce cake made from the "best" jumbo lump meat, along with "wonderfully" "fresh" fish; wallet-watchers may quibble that given its "out-of-the-way" locale, the prices are too "high", but foodies promise it's "worth every penny."

Joe's Noodle House S | 18 | 8 | 13 | $15 |
1488C Rockville Pike (Twin Brook Rd.), Rockville, MD, 301-881-5518

■ Anticipate "many adventures on the menu" at this "no-frills" Rockville "find", whose "authentic" Chinese food (along with some Thai and Korean dishes) attracts a large Asian clientele, as well as locals looking for a "good, cheap" meal; the cooking's the "real deal" here, so don't expect the "spices" to be "toned down" for the American palate (take the chile pepper designations on the menu seriously); doubters, however, shrug "not as exciting as we thought it'd be."

Johnny's Half Shell S | 23 | 17 | 20 | $34 |
2002 P St., NW (bet. 20th & 21st Sts.), 202-296-2021

■ "Beautifully simple decor and simply great food" is the story at this "fresh and sassy" Dupont Circle seafood bistro whose "dreamy" "crispy oysters", inviting "little touches" (like the locally produced malt vinegar for the "great" fries) and "refreshingly casual" vibe have many admirers clamoring for a seat; nitpickers, on the other hand, find the portions "too small" and gripe that the "lovely lighting" doesn't do enough to dress up the "spare" setting.

jordans | - | - | - | E |
Ronald Reagan Bldg., 1300 Pennsylvania Ave., NW (13th St.), 202-589-1223

Downtown's "trendy" power player, Michael Jordan's New American fine-dining venture in the Ronald Reagan Building recasts Palomino Euro Bistro's bi-level circular space into a sophisticated lounge upstairs and a suave ("beige everywhere") dining room below; the kitchen turns out modernized meat and seafood classics; now that Michael Jordan has resigned from the Washington Wizards and left DC, his restaurant's future is in the air.

Kabob Palace ●S | ▽ 21 | 5 | 11 | $11 |
2315 S. Eads St. (23rd St.), Arlington, VA, 703-486-3535

■ Kebab lovers tailgate cabdrivers to this Crystal City pit stop for "excellent" skewers and other "super-good",

Washington, DC

| | F | D | S | C |

"authentic" Pakistani dishes; less palatial surroundings would be hard to find, but the "made-to-order" fare is a "bargain" and provides a culinary trip to "another world"; those who find the ambiance "not particularly welcoming", though, "get it to go."

Kanpai S
| – | – | – | M |

1401 Wilson Blvd. (N. Oak St.), Rosslyn, VA, 703-527-8400
Rosslyn residents and office workers are discovering this Japanese hideaway (entrance on N. Oak Street), which impresses with voguish decor and inviting outdoor tables; an extensive sushi selection, interesting appetizers and small plates offer lots of grazing possibilities, while heartier appetites can address seared-to-order fish or meat, katsu, tempura and stir-fry preparations.

Kazan
| 22 | 19 | 22 | $33 |

Cambridge Corner Shopping Ctr., 6813 Redmond Dr. (Chain Bridge Rd.), McLean, VA, 703-734-1960
■ "Warm and inviting", McLean's "Turkish delight" offers some of the "best" Mediterranean food around, and it's only enhanced by the owner's "personal touch"; look forward to "tasty" meze and "tantalizing" kebabs ("never had such juicy lamb" and "love the swordfish" too), served in an interior that's "attractive" enough "for a business lunch" or out on the year-round garden patio; factor in "courteous" service and "good-value" prices and it's easy to see why it's been an "old favorite" for decades.

Kaz Sushi Bistro
| 24 | 18 | 20 | $35 |

1915 I St., NW (bet. 19th & 20th Sts.), 202-530-5500
◪ Both "cutting-edge" and "traditional", this "artful" Japanese bistro in the Golden Triangle is renowned for its "exemplary sushi" and "original" "East meets West" "little dishes" based on "unusual pairings" (like the "decadent plum wine–infused duck foie gras"); though the decor's a bit "sparse", purists insist that's "the way it should be" so that "nothing distracts from the superb fish"; still, detractors feel it "doesn't live up to its stellar reputation."

KINKEAD'S S
| 27 | 24 | 25 | $51 |

2000 Pennsylvania Ctr., 2000 Pennsylvania Ave., NW (I St.), 202-296-7700
■ Voted yet again Washington's Most Popular restaurant, chef-owner Bob Kinkead's "winning" New American brasserie is lauded for maintaining its "high standards"; as Foggy Bottom's "power food" HQ, it's a "professionally run" "special-occasion" destination that delivers "absolutely astounding" seafood dishes and a "superior" wine list in a "supercharged atmosphere"; "a class act in all aspects", it's "hands down" one of the "best" establishments in the capital, even if "the elite" get "preferential" treatment.

Konami [S] ▽ 22 19 21 $27

8221 Leesburg Pike (Chain Bridge Rd.), Tysons Corner, VA, 703-821-3400

◪ In bustling Tysons Corner, this "convenient" neighborhood Japanese provides a "serene" refuge with its "pleasant" garden dining; the sushi is very "decent", though "not the best", but the prices are "reasonable" (the "box lunches" are a "great value") and the staff "young and eager."

Kramerbooks & Afterwords Cafe ◐[S] 17 15 15 $21

1517 Connecticut Ave., NW (bet. Dupont Circle & Q St.), 202-387-1462

◪ A "great hangout for the college and twentysomething crowd", especially on weekends (when it's open 24 hours), this "funky" Dupont Circle bookstore/cafe has long been a "DC favorite", offering groupies a "can't-miss combo of books, people-watching" and varied live entertainment; there is a "basic" American menu, but "don't expect great food", particularly at a place that serves cocktails by the pitcher; it's "always crowded" "late at night, so be prepared for a wait during that busy time."

Krupin's [S] 18 10 15 $18

4620 Wisconsin Ave., NW (bet. Brandywine & Chesapeake Sts.), 202-686-1989

◪ While longtimers "miss Mel", the retired founder of this Upper NW "time warp", his brother Morty is upholding the family tradition by presiding over some of DC's "best" Jewish-style provisions – matzo ball soup, corned beef and pastrami, and "smoked fish fresh from Brooklyn" – while trading "insults" with the customers; though it's "nostalgic" for some "lost New Yorkers", "disappointed" mavens sniff a mere "shadow of a real NY deli."

Kuna ▽ 22 17 21 $26

1324 U St., NW (bet. 13th & 14th Sts.), 202-797-7908

■ Italophiles marvel over the "unbelievably low prices for a pleasant dinner" at this "refreshing" "addition to the New U" scene, where the ever-changing menu "doesn't over-promise" but does deliver "farmhouse cooking at its best"; "hospitable" Mark Giuricich (the owner, "chief cook and dishwasher") cultivates a "personal" atmosphere and always manages to find a "minute to jam" with his patrons, who plead "we really like this place, but it's so small, so please don't tell anyone about it."

Kuzine [S] – – – M

302 King Farm Blvd., Ste. 110 (Frederick Ave.), Rockville, MD, 301-963-3400

From modest beginnings as a carry-out/sandwich shop in Rockville's King Farm enclave, this compact eatery has blossomed into a dining destination for hard-to-find Turkish,

Washington, DC F | D | S | C

Middle Eastern and Eastern European specialties; at night, when the lights are lowered, candles are lit and servers wait on the tables, the atmosphere is genteel – but the portions could still feed an army; N.B. beer and wine only.

LA BERGERIE S 25 | 22 | 24 | $49
218 N. Lee St. (bet. Cameron & Queen Sts.), Alexandria, VA, 703-683-1007

■ "Formal yet comfortable", this "understated" Old Town grande dame continues to "beautifully present" "refined" Classic French cuisine in a "timeless" setting; the menu is as "outstanding" as ever, but now it's been "enlivened" with some modern updates (don't worry, the "wonderful soufflés" are still available), while the "attentive", "professional" staff still tends to all details; long cherished by Alexandria's "old guard", it has been discovered in recent years by their offspring as a "sophisticated" way to "impress a date."

La Brasserie S 21 | 17 | 20 | $38
239 Massachusetts Ave., NE (bet. 2nd & 3rd Sts.), 202-546-9154

◪ See "senators at lunch, neighbors at dinner" at this "little bit of France" on Capitol Hill, where a "warm-weather" meal on the "flower-filled" terrace transports one to Paris; devotees are always happy to dine on its "very good" bistro renditions, but dissenters who find the fare "lackluster" ("once fine, now predictable") judge it "not worth the price."

La Chaumiere 24 | 23 | 23 | $42
2813 M St., NW (bet. 28th & 29th Sts.), 202-338-1784

◪ Reminiscent of a French country inn, this Georgetown Gallic is "a wintertime treat when the fireplace is roaring", but at any time of year visitors will be rewarded with rustic, "old-fashioned" cooking like "delicious" quenelles and "fantastic cassoulet", as well as "hard-to-find" dishes such as calf's brains and tripe; the few who find this old-guard favorite "stodgy" and "not inviting unless you're known" quip that the "warmth ends at the hearth."

La Colline 22 | 19 | 22 | $43
400 N. Capitol St., NW (bet. D & E Sts.), 202-737-0400

◪ Perennially a "safe bet for a business power gathering on Capitol Hill" or a "political fund-raiser", this "lobbyists' haunt" pleases with "dependable", "not too complicated" Gallic food, enough "space between tables" and smooth service; virtually everyone agrees that owner/"schmoozer"-in-chief Paul Zucconi is a "charmer", but some gourmands dismiss the "tired, boring" "French fare without flair."

La Côte d'Or Cafe S 22 | 21 | 21 | $45
6876 Lee Hwy. (bet. Washington Blvd. & Westmoreland Rd.), Arlington, VA, 703-538-3033

◪ One of the few upscale French options in Northern Virginia, this "welcoming" site is a "great place to celebrate"

vote at zagat.com

Washington, DC　　　　　　　　　　F | D | S | C |

or "just blow your diet in a spectacular way", satisfying with "delicious" cooking turned out in a series of "cute" "rabbit-warren" rooms; adding to the merriment is the "caring" owner, who "sings on occasion", but frugal sorts complain that it's too "pricey" considering the "hit-or-miss" dishes and "oddball" (read: "low-rent") Arlington location.

Lafayette S　　　　　　　　　　–|–|–| VE |
Hay Adams Hotel, 800 16th St., NW (H St.), 202-638-6600
From this legendary dining room in the Hay Adams Hotel, you can get a close-up view of the White House – that is, if you're not too busy scoping out the A-list clientele; reopened last year, with its timeless elegance fully restored, its New American menu (with a European accent) refreshed and its seasoned staff as poised and dignified as ever, this landmark powerhouse beckons anew.

La Ferme S　　　　　　　　　　22 | 24 | 22 | $45 |
7101 Brookville Rd. (bet. Taylor & Thornapple Sts.), Chevy Chase, MD, 301-986-5255
☑ "Though it feels dated", this "lovely" French farmhouse in Chevy Chase "delivers" "reliable" "country" fare in a room appointed with "beautiful" flowers and a fireplace or on the "delightful" terrace; the staff "treats" everyone "well", making it "comfortable" for its "wealthy" (predominantly "older") clientele; younger folk, however, frown upon the "unimaginative" cooking and "stodgy" ambiance.

La Fourchette S　　　　　　　　　21 | 18 | 20 | $35 |
2429 18th St., NW (bet. Columbia & Kalorama Rds.), 202-332-3077
☑ Supping at this veritably French bistro in Adams Morgan is "like having dinner with family – and the family is glad you're there"; it's "quaint", "cramped, loud and rushed, but somehow it all combines to form a lively canvas for great, authentic French cuisine", which explains why it's been a "solid" "favorite for more than 20 years."

La Madeleine　　　　　　　　　16 | 16 | 13 | $17 |
French Bakery & Café S
3000 M St., NW (30th St.), 202-337-6975
7607 Old Georgetown Rd. (Commerce Ln.), Bethesda, MD, 301-215-9142
Mid-Pike Plaza, 11858 Rockville Pike (Montrose Rd.), Rockville, MD, 301-984-2270
500 King St. (Pitt St.), Alexandria, VA, 703-739-2854
Bailey's Crossroads, 5861 Crossroads Center Way (Columbia & Leesburg Pikes), Falls Church, VA, 703-379-5551
1833 Fountain Dr. (bet. Baron Cameron Ave. & New Dominion Pkwy.), Reston, VA, 703-707-0704
1915C Chain Bridge Rd. (Leesburg Pike), Tysons Corner, VA, 703-827-8833
☑ Heavy traffic at these "faux" French bakery/cafes signals that there's a "lot to be said about a reliable chain that serves

Washington, DC | F | D | S | C |

fresh bread with marmalade as a free attraction" to begin a "hearty" meal, provides a "comfortable" place for socializing and is priced "reasonably"; on the other hand, there's less to be said about the "controlled pandemonium" of the cafeteria lines and the "disorganized" help.

La Miche | 23 | 20 | 22 | $45 |
7905 Norfolk Ave. (St. Elmo Ave.), Bethesda, MD, 301-986-0707
◪ When rookie chef-owner Jason Tepper took over this "charming" bit of provincial "France in Bethesda", he pledged to keep preparing the "great" bourgeois "classics" exactly the way the "high-brow, blue-hair" clientele likes them; while he's smart enough not to fix what isn't broken (retaining the "dependable" kitchen crew and "gracious" staff), he offers more seafood choices with updated sauces; N.B. the post-*Survey* change may outdate the above Food score.

Landini Brothers S | 20 | 18 | 19 | $36 |
115 King St. (Union St.), Alexandria, VA, 703-836-8404
◪ "Pretend the host" at this "roomy" Old Town Italian fixture "has been your best friend for over 20 years – everybody does" (from movers and shakers to "tourists"), and it's easy to do so because the staff is so "jovial"; the "clubby" feel ("downstairs is the place to be") and traditional "home cooking" win it many friends, though bashers dismiss it as a "trap" and only go with "out-of-town guests whose tastes aren't too discriminating."

Landmark, The S | – | – | – | M |
Melrose Hotel, 2430 Pennsylvania Ave. NW (bet. 24th & 25th Sts.), 202-955-6400
'Elegant comfort cuisine' is the byword at this recently revamped West End hotel dining room, where updated American classics – shepherd's pie, fish 'n' chips, roasted chicken – are served in relaxed yet formal surroundings; its 'library' bar offers clubby intimacy for informal meetings, while its outdoor sidewalk seats are prized, by locals and tourists alike, for after-work sipping and scoping.

L'AUBERGE CHEZ FRANÇOIS S | 28 | 27 | 28 | $59 |
332 Springvale Rd. (Beach Mill Rd.), Great Falls, VA, 703-759-3800
■ A "magical" "pleasure from apéritif to soufflé", this "truly special" Country French "treat" set on "lovely" bucolic grounds in Great Falls has "epitomized" "romantic" dining for generations; in "cozily" rustic quarters whose "charm can't be beat" and in the "glorious" garden, an "informed" but "not snotty" staff brings to table "hearty", "outstanding" Alsatian dishes; despite the "reservations hassle", the "experience as a whole" is so "superb" that you're sure to "leave feeling tingly" all over.

L'AUBERGE PROVENÇALE [S] 25 | 26 | 25 | $66

13630 Lord Fairfax Hwy. (Rte. 50), Boyce, VA, 540-837-1375

◪ "French country dining with a Virginia hunt country address" is the appeal of this "delightful escape" set in a "lovely", antique-filled manor house circa 1753 that "oozes charm" and "easy elegance"; devotees laud the "rich" dishes and "polished" service and recommend an "overnight stay" in the inn (if only to "get the fantastic breakfast"), but a "disappointed" minority feels it "doesn't live up to its reputation"; N.B. now serving Sunday brunch.

Lauriol Plaza [S] 21 | 21 | 17 | $25

1835 18th St., NW (T St.), 202-387-0035

◪ "Packed nightly", this "fun" Dupont Circle East "hot spot" hosts a perpetual Latin "fiesta" attended by the "beautiful, young people" (as well as "suburbanites cashing in on the [free] parking") who soak up the scene on the "irresistible" rooftop deck; the "wait" is "ridiculous" ("you could get a law degree in the time it takes to get a table on the weekend"), but aficionados praise the "tasty" Mexican-Spanish-Cuban dishes and "sneakily strong margaritas", clearly willing to endure all to join the action.

Lavandou [S] 21 | 19 | 19 | $38

3321 Connecticut Ave., NW (bet. Macomb & Ordway Sts.), 202-966-3002

◪ Bringing "a ray of Provençal sunshine" to Cleveland Park, this "intimate" "neighborhood" bistro pleases with its "full-flavored" French fare and "pretty" decorative touches; habitués advise that it's "best to go" "for lunch" or early on "weekday evenings", when it's "quieter" and the service is less "rushed", but critics who object to "heavy-handed seasoning" at any time dub it "more of a Lavandon't."

LEBANESE TAVERNA [S] 23 | 18 | 20 | $26

2641 Connecticut Ave., NW (bet. Calvert St. & Woodley Rd.), 202-265-8681

Congressional Plaza, 1605 Rockville Pike (Congressional Ln.), Rockville, MD, 301-468-9086

Pentagon Row, 1101 S. Joyce St. (Army Navy Dr.), Pentagon City, VA, 703-415-8681

5900 Washington Blvd. (McKinley Rd.), Arlington, VA, 703-241-8681

◪ "Friendly and inviting", this "wonderful" family-run chainlet is a "must stop on the ethnic dining circuit" due to its "delicious", "properly garlicky" Middle Eastern cooking; its broad menu and Lebanese sampler platters work for groups, kids and "picky eaters" alike, service is "cordial" and the tabs "won't break the bank", but some surveyors feel that as it expands, the dishes are starting to taste "a little prefab" while the service is becoming "slower"; a user-friendly wine list adds another touch.

Washington, DC   **F | D | S | C**

Legal Sea Foods   19 | 16 | 18 | $32
2020 K St., NW (bet. 20th & 21st Sts.), 202-496-1111
704 Seventh St., NW (bet. G & H Sts.), 202-347-0007 **S**
Montgomery Mall, 7101 Democracy Blvd. (I-270), Bethesda, MD, 301-469-5900 **S**
2301 Jefferson Davis Hwy. (23rd St.), Arlington, VA, 703-415-1200 **S**
Ronald Reagan Washington Nat'l Airport (Terminal C), Arlington, VA, 703-413-9810 **S**
Tysons Galleria, 2001 International Dr. (Chain Bridge Rd.), Tysons Corner, VA, 703-827-8900 **S**

◪ Schools of supporters rave about the "straightforward New England–style seafood" served by this Massachusetts-based chain, notably its "great chowdah, fried clams and raw bar"; critics, however, carp about what they call "basic food at above-basic prices" dished out in a "corporate"-feeling atmosphere, but even they concede that "if you can't make it to Boston, this mass-production operation can fill the need."

Le Gaulois **S**   23 | 20 | 20 | $36
1106 King St. (bet. Fayette & Henry Sts.), Alexandria, VA, 703-739-9494

◪ "Just what a French bistro should be" according to its loyal coterie, who seek out this Old Town "sleeper" for its "deep menu of classic dishes and seasonal treats" (the cassoulet is always a "standout") at a "good" value, "civilized" dining by the "fireplace" and "pretty garden"; while last winter's ownership change puts a question mark after its ratings, a longtime sous-chef remains, as does that Gallic "attitude."

Le Petit Mistral **S**   22 | 17 | 20 | $43
6710 Old Dominion Dr. (Chain Bridge Rd.), McLean, VA, 703-748-4888

◪ McLean's "cozy French retreat" is a "bustling, intimate" "storefront" whose "haute" bistro fare reflects a "lot of care in the preparation"; devotees cherish it as "a *petit* treasure" and especially tout the "great" weekday lunch and early-dinner prix fixe "values", but a few detractors maintain that its "success has bred indifference in the food and service."

Le Refuge   23 | 19 | 20 | $39
127 N. Washington St. (bet. Cameron & King Sts.), Alexandria, VA, 703-548-4661

◪ With enough "genuine" French cafe "ambiance to satisfy any Francophile", this Old Town "favorite" is a "wonderfully quaint" place to savor "traditional, satisfying" bourgeois cooking; habitués expect to have "their neighbor's elbow in their plate" (these quarters are "claustrophobic") and take the "rushed" pace in stride, but critics sniff it "hasn't had a new idea since the '80s."

---

vote at zagat.com

Le Relais [S] 25 | 23 | 23 | $52

Seneca Square Shopping Ctr., 1025-I Seneca Rd. (Georgetown Pike), Great Falls, VA, 703-444-4060

◪ A "dream come true" for sophisticated Northern Virginia suburbanites, this "dressy" Great Falls French "treasure" "stylishly" showcases "marvelous" dishes that "taste as good as they look", along with a "fabulous wine list", in "beautiful, contemporary" surroundings; though prices are on the "regal" side, its affluent clientele is willing to pay for "top quality" (despite an occasional "ragged" performance), especially when chef Yannick Cam is in the kitchen.

Les Halles ☾ [S] 19 | 17 | 17 | $37

1201 Pennsylvania Ave., NW (12th St.), 202-347-6848

◪ "Legitimately French", this "convivial" "late-night" Downtown meat market pulls off the "authentic brasserie" look, providing a "charming" backdrop for "comforting classics" like hanger steak with nearly "perfect pommes frites" and monthly regional specialities; it's "fun" to watch the walking "scenery" from the sidewalk tables, but you better "bring patience" (and a "megaphone") and brace yourself for "Parisian snobbery."

Le Tarbouche 23 | 24 | 22 | $40

1801 K St., NW (18th St.), 202-331-5551

■ "Intriguingly" appointed with a luminous blue-hued, tent-ceilinged dining room, "romantic nooks" and a "sexy", "candlelit" bar, this K Street "scene" is a "beautiful", "exotic" place for a rendezvous; the "bold" yet "refined" Nouvelle Mediterranean dishes, based on "unusual spices and ingredients", are presented "with style" by a "polite" staff, making for a "really interesting diversion."

Le Tire Bouchon – | – | – | E

4009 Chain Bridge Rd. (Main St.), Fairfax, VA, 703-691-4747

Classic Gallic traditions are honored at this charming Fairfax City upstart owned by Jacques de Lorme and Huseyin Kansu (veterans of long-closed Le Lion d'Or and Le Pavillon); expect white tablecloths, upscale appointments, elegant traditional dishes, a choice wine list and old-fashioned service with flourishes like tableside flambées.

Levante's [S] 17 | 17 | 16 | $26

1320 19th St., NW (Dupont Circle), 202-293-3244
7262 Woodmont Ave. (Elm St.), Bethesda, MD, 301-657-2441

◪ Off Dupont Circle and in Bethesda, this pair of popular gathering spots looks to the Levant for its "expansive" Mediterranean menu, bright blue-and-yellow color scheme and "lively" sidewalk seating; the "fun little pizzas" called pides are crowd-pleasers, but "everything else is quite dull", the interior is "distractingly noisy" and the service runs "hot and cold"; the bottom line according to many: "if you can't sit outside, don't bother."

Library Lounge [S] — – – – E

St. Regis, 923 16th St., NW (K St.), 202-879-6900
The clubby elegance of this hotel restaurant two blocks from the White House lends dignity to any business or social dealing; the dining room (once the site of Lespinasse) is as stately as ever but now features a New American menu with such dishes as NY strip steak and pasta with seafood; N.B. presently, dinner is served only in the bar/lounge.

LIGHTFOOT [S] — 22 26 21 $38

11 N. King St. (Market St.), Leesburg, VA, 703-771-2233
◩ Housed in a "gorgeously restored bank" in Leesburg, this "roomy yet private"-feeling New American cafe shows off chef/co-owner Ingrid Gustafson's "deft touch" with the "freshest ingredients" (she runs a farmer's market), which results in "serious food out in the boondocks"; "somewhat chilly" service notwithstanding, gourmands are happy to "indulge in some top-notch, albeit a bit pricey", courses.

Little Saigon [S] — ▽ 23 13 18 $22

6218B Wilson Blvd. (Patrick Henry Dr.), Falls Church, VA, 703-536-2633
◩ Falls Church's Vietnamese community knows about the "absolutely authentic" cooking at this "hole-in-the-wall" near the Eden Center, even if others have yet to discover it; the "interesting" menu runs the gamut from "great jicama rolls" to "excellent fish", offering countless good-"value" possibilities that make it easy to overlook the lack of decor.

Little Viet Garden [S] — 20 15 17 $20

3012 Wilson Blvd. (Garfield St.), Arlington, VA, 703-522-9686
◩ "Twinkly lights" around the "festive" garden patio help make Clarendon's young gentry "forget that it's surrounded by busy streets" at this buzzing Vietnamese venue; at a "good price", customers get "fresh food that isn't too heavy" ("love the lemongrass chicken" and "good" spring rolls), but skeptics who find it "a bit hit-or-miss" "wonder why there are few Vietnamese customers" here.

Local 16 [S] — – – – M

1602 U St., NW (16th St.), 202-265-2828
Ruby tones, gleaming wood and vintage punk-rock photos along with a moderately priced seasonal Middle Eastern–influenced New American menu signal that this smart-looking U Street start-up means to elevate the neighborhood dining scene; upstairs, a spacious roof deck and a loungey space further enhance its prospects as a cool destination for drinks on the fly or a sit-down meal.

Louisiana Express Co. [S] — 20 9 16 $19

4921 Bethesda Ave. (Arlington Rd.), Bethesda, MD, 301-652-6945
◩ Proving that folks will "gladly sit on straight-back chairs" in "shanty" digs for a "quick dose" of "yummy" Bayou

cooking that "packs a punch" (notably the "goody, goody gumbo"), this low-down spot is "unlike anything else in Bethesda" and "you won't mistake it for something by Emeril" either; amenities are few, but it delivers a "bargain taste of Louisiana."

Luigino [S] 21 19 20 $36

1100 New York Ave., NW (bet. 11th & 12th Sts.), 202-371-0595

◩ Italian food mavens "don't dismiss" this citizen of the red, white and green just because it's so convenient to Downtown goings-on and looks a bit "antiseptic" from the sidewalk; inside is an "enjoyable lunch spot (it's much less lively at dinner)" where one can "sit by the window and watch the passersby" while dining on "wonderful" pastas (if you're eating alone, you'll feel "comfortable" at the convivial counter); a few dissenters, however, report food as "uneven" as the service.

Luna Grill & Diner [S] 18 16 17 $19

1301 Connecticut Ave., NW (N St.), 202-835-2280
4024 28th St. S. (Quincy St.), Arlington, VA, 703-379-7173

◩ "Diner food with aspirations" is what to expect at this pair of "cool" American eateries off Dupont Circle and in Arlington, where the dishes range from "greasy to organic", as exemplified by its "addictive" sweet potato fries; its young and hungry regulars advise "sticking with the blue- or green-plate specials", slung by servers who are "cute", "cocky" or "characters" (or all of the above), but critics cavil that "nothing quite tastes as it sounds" on the menu.

MAESTRO 27 28 28 $69

Ritz-Carlton Tysons Corner, 1700 Tysons Blvd. (International Dr.), Tysons Corner, VA, 703-917-5498

■ Open two years, this "exquisite" "gourmet heaven" at Tysons Corner's Ritz-Carlton is already a "top contender" in the "fine-dining" stakes; "genius chef" Fabio Trabocchi, who dares to "take risks", orchestrates a "world-class" "symphony of Italian flavors" from a "gorgeous open kitchen" that only "adds to the evening entertainment"; enhanced by a "luxuriously" appointed space and an "impeccable" staff, it adds up to an "ultimate dining performance" that's "worth every penny" of admission.

Maggiano's Little Italy [S] – – – E

5333 Wisconsin Ave., NW (Western Ave.), 202-966-5500
Tysons Galleria, 2001 International Dr. (Rte. 123), Tysons Corner, VA, 703-356-9000

At these spirited nostalgia-themed Italians, gut-busting family-style portions of pastas, fish and top-quality steaks are served on red-checked tablecloths in bustling rooms; their prime business district locations, in Tysons Corner and Chevy Chase, attract an upscale clientele, so it's no surprise that their private rooms host prominent events.

Majestic Cafe [S] 23 | 21 | 21 | $36

911 King St. (Patrick St.), Alexandria, VA, 703-837-9117

◪ "Chef Susan McCreight Lindeborg does it again", this time in Old Town, where she has "re-created an atmospheric" art deco–style cafe from the "WWII" era; it's a "chic" spot to "be seen in" while partaking of "some of the classiest" Southern-accented New American cooking "you'll ever have" (save room for the "fabulous" old-fashioned layer cake), and fans want to "eat every meal here."

MAKOTO [S] 27 | 24 | 25 | $53

4822 MacArthur Blvd., NW (U St.), 202-298-6866

■ Anticipate a "genuine Japanese experience" at this "peaceful little enclave" in the NW Palisades, designed for those "willing to be adventurous" (after removing their shoes); while the prix fixe menu offers a "great introduction for the novice", presenting a series of "tiny jewels", sushi connoisseurs swoon over the "sweet" morsels of raw fish that are "fresh beyond description"; legions attest that this is "as good as any place in Tokyo, at one third the price."

Malaysia Kopitiam [S] 21 | 11 | 19 | $21

1827 M St., NW (bet. 18th & 19th Sts.), 202-833-6232

◪ "A fascinating blend of Chinese and Indian" influences, among others, characterizes the "spicy appeal" of Malaysia, and at this "dumpy" Golden Triangle basement, the dishes "explode with scents and flavors"; the "caring", hospitable hosts want you to love their native cuisine, so follow their recommendations, or just point to what looks "interesting" in the "great picture-book menu"; enthusiasts insist that "everything is good" and pretty "cheap", thus it's hard to go wrong.

Mamma Lucia [S] 19 | 12 | 17 | $22

4916 Elm St. (bet. Arlington Rd. & Woodmont Ave.), Bethesda, MD, 301-907-3399

Olney Village Mart, 18224 Village Mart Dr. (Olney-Sandy Spring Rd.), Olney, MD, 301-570-9500

Federal Plaza, 12274-M Rockville Pike (Twinbrook Pkwy.), Rockville, MD, 301-770-4894

14921 Shady Grove Rd. (Medical Center), Rockville, MD, 301-762-8805

◪ When you need to feed an SUV-load of "suburban" tykes "cheap and fast", these Montgomery County Italians "get the job done" with "decent" NY-style pizzas and "hearty", "surprisingly tasty" pastas; sure, they're usually "crowded" and "noisy" and the service can be "haphazard", but they're an "easy, satisfying" pick for a "casual" meal.

M & S Grill [S] 19 | 19 | 19 | $32

600 13th St., NW (F St.), 202-347-1500

◪ "Lunch reservations are hard to get" at this "clubby" Downtown grill because its "private booths", "comfortable"

Washington, DC   F | D | S | C

seats and "business" ambiance set just the right tone for the office crowd; though the service is "spotty", the American menu is "varied" and relatively "reasonably" priced, while the happy-hour bar-food deals and "even better martinis" make it equally marketable in the evening.

Mannequin Pis S   23 | 16 | 19 | $40
18064 Georgia Ave. (Olney-Sandy Spring Rd.), Olney, MD, 301-570-4800

☑ For a "touch of Brussels" in Olney, fans seek out this "small", "hard-to-find" bistro, which "proves that Belgian cuisine can give French a run for its money" (consensus is, the former "wins hands down in the beer category"); you may well agree after "scarfing" down its "mouthwatering mussels" (prepared in 15 different ways) and pommes frites, though foes denounce "inconsistent" dishes served in "cramped", "chaotic" digs.

MARCEL'S S   26 | 25 | 25 | $58
2401 Pennsylvania Ave., NW (24th St.), 202-296-1166

■ Robert Wiedmaier's "brilliant", "inventive" Flemish dishes tweaked with a French flair (the "boudin blanc is incredible") and "lavishly presented" have earned him a devoted following at this "plush", "sophisticated" West End "star" that may "look stuffy, but isn't" (and steps have been taken to address complaints that it's "accoustically challenged"); he and his "courtly" crew woo guests with "tip-top wine selections", "great" live music nightly in the bar and even complimentary "limousine service to and from the Kennedy Center", while still keeping the focus "on the food."

Mar de Plata ●S   21 | 16 | 20 | $34
1410 14th St., NW (bet. P St. & Rhode Island Ave.), 202-234-2679

☑ A "welcome face on 14th Street" for Studio and Source Theatre ticket-holders, as well as Logan Circle denizens, this "warm, friendly" Spanish "find" features a simple setting but "provocative" tapas and seafood specialties; detractors, however, find the food and atmosphere "dull" and feel the staff "doesn't seem to care", adding that the "prices are pretentious for the area."

Market St. Bar & Grill S   20 | 19 | 20 | $38
Hyatt Regency Reston, 1800 Presidents St. (Market St.), Reston, VA, 703-709-6262

☑ "Better than average hotel food" is the word on this Reston fallback; everyone agrees that the New American menu is "inventive", but whereas fans say it's "pleasant", foes counter it "doesn't always succeed" ("it tries too hard to be clever") and that combined with "inconsistent" service, it adds up to "mediocre fine dining"; P.S. the "live jazz" on weekends is worth checking out.

Washington, DC F | D | S | C

Mark's Duck House ●S | 22 | 9 | 16 | $23
Willston Ctr. I, 6184A Arlington Blvd. (Patrick Henry Dr.), Falls Church, VA, 703-532-2125
■ One of the "most authentic Hong Kong–style" restaurants in Northern Virginia, this Falls Church Chinese "dive" is patronized by knowledgeable "food lovers" (a "healthy majority" of whom are Asian), who gather to "discover exotic dishes" (ask for translations of the Chinese language listings) and to seek comfort in favorites like "delightful dim sum", "awesome Peking duck" and "excellent roast pig"; "don't expect a high-end setting, just great" fare.

Mark's Kitchen S | – | – | – | I
7006 Carroll Ave. (Laurel St.), Takoma Park, MD, 301-270-1884
In Takoma Park, this funky "local favorite" run by committed, "kid-friendly" people offers an "unlikely but delightful menu" of American and Korean diner food, from a grilled-cheese-and-bacon sandwich and spinach salad to the "best kimchi" and teriyaki chicken (it's a "vegetarian delight" too); "not only is the food delicious, but it really feels like it's good for me", though it has become so discovered that some regulars "don't even dare try to get in for Sunday breakfast."

Matchbox S | – | – | – | M
713 H St., NW (bet. 7th & 8th Sts.), 202-289-4441
Flaming red and stacked three stories high around a glowing brick oven, this sliver-thin Chinatown start-up is earning early buzz for its notably thin-crust pizzas and casual-chic vibe; still, it won't be long before the locals discover that its compact Contemporary American kitchen also produces seriously interesting salads, sandwiches and entrées that are several notches above the usual tavern fare.

Matisse S | 20 | 22 | 19 | $44
4934 Wisconsin Ave., NW (Fessendon St.), 202-244-5222
■ "Lovely" and "romantic", this Upper NW New French–Mediterranean is considered a virtual standout given its location in a "part of town" with many sophisticated diners but "few good places" to eat; while nobody disputes its "understated elegance", doubters who reserve judgment call it "potentially wonderful" – citing "decor that's better than the food", "service on the too neighborhood-y" side and "Downtown-fancy" prices.

Matuba S | 22 | 14 | 19 | $25
4918 Cordell Ave. (Old Georgetown Rd.), Bethesda, MD, 301-652-7449
2915 Columbia Pike (Walter Reed Dr.), Arlington, VA, 703-521-2811
■ "Dependable" and "unpretentious", this long-running Japanese twosome in Bethesda and Arlington makes sushi an everyday family affair, presenting "well-made" selections in "child-friendly", "feel-like-home" surroundings; the

Washington, DC F | D | S | C

menu also offers a wide range of traditional cooked dishes and "good lunch-box specials", all at "reasonable" prices, but the cognoscenti sniff "volume over quality."

Maxim – | – | – | E
1725 F St., NW (bet. 17th & 18th Sts.), 202-962-0280
Infused with "old-world elegance", this "hospitable" two-year-old transports guests to Eastern Europe with its "interesting" Russian and Georgian specialties (including "amazing" broiled sturgeon and beef stroganoff) and exclusive regional wines; the convivial bar is a happy-hour fixture, while on Friday and Saturday nights, when the musicians tune up and the crowd hits the dance floor, the "international" clientele shows Downtown how to party.

MCCORMICK & SCHMICK'S S 21 | 21 | 20 | $37
1652 K St., NW (bet. 16th & 17th Sts.), 202-861-2233
7401 Woodmont Ave. (bet. Montgomery Ln. & Old Georgetown Rd.), Bethesda, MD, 301-961-2626
11920 Democracy Dr. (bet. Discovery & Library Sts.), Reston, VA, 703-481-6600
Ernst & Young Bldg., 8484 Westpark Dr. (Leesburg Pike), Tysons Corner, VA, 703-848-8000
■ Thirtysomethings socialize at the bar at these popular seafood houses over happy hour, while business meals are dignified by "old-school" dark-wood-and-brass environs and curtained booths; "afishionados" praise the kitchen's "sure hand" with "fresh" fish and the "fabulous" oysters, but critics crab that the operation is more "production-line than custom-order" and caution about a "hectic" pace and "sometimes hyper waiters."

Mediterranee 23 | 18 | 22 | $35
3520 Lee Hwy. (Monroe St.), Arlington, VA, 703-527-7276
■ Tucked away in Cherrydale, this "homey" French-Mediterranean is "surprisingly popular" due to its "generous servings" of "high-quality" dishes and "VIP treatment" for all guests; "from the street, you'd never guess what a charming place" it is inside – brightened with colorful curtains, tablecloths and dried flowers – leading devotees to urge "try it", because this is one "terrific neighborhood place" and a "great" value to boot.

Meiwah S 22 | 18 | 19 | $24
1200 New Hampshire Ave., NW (M St.), 202-833-2888
■ Geared to the City Center's worker bees, this "busy" business-class Chinese is a "semi-fancy" "staple" that's a satisfying lunch option thanks to its broad menu of "distinctive" dishes with lots of "vegetarian picks"; fans recommend it as a "good place to experiment with unusual foods", but purists decry it as a "no-chopsticks" kind of place ("unless you ask for them") with "bland" chow; Chevy Chase will get an outlet in summer 2003.

MELROSE [S] 26 | 24 | 25 | $53

Park Hyatt Washington, 1201 24th St., NW (M St.), 202-955-3899

■ "Efficient for lunch, delightful for dinner", this "light and airy" "special-occasion" destination in the West End is an "oasis of calm", soothing with an "impressive" fountain-bedecked patio and "thoughtful" service; "talented" chef Brian McBride "does equally well cooking for a table of two or for a banquet", turning out "fabulous" New American fare; to the many fans who can't wait to "dine and dance the night away" on weekends, this "class act" "belies the hotel restaurant curse."

Mendocino Grille & Wine Bar [S] 22 | 20 | 21 | $41

2917 M St., NW (bet. 29th & 30th Sts.), 202-333-2912

◪ California reveries are fulfilled at this modish, open-to-the-street Georgetown "gem" where "superbly chosen" "flights" of West Coast wines hook up with "innovative", "appealing" New American dishes suitable for a laid-back lunch or "romantic" dinner, especially now that its new owner, Eli Hengst (ex Tryst and The Diner), is using seasonal and organic products to complement its "excellent" list and, with luck, addressing complaints that at "peak times" it can be hard to "hear across the table."

Meskerem ◐ [S] 22 | 19 | 18 | $23

2434 18th St., NW (bet. Belmont & Columbia Rds.), 202-462-4100

◪ "Scooping up" "subtly spiced" savory stews with "spongy" injera bread is a "fun" "adventure" at this mainstream Ethiopian "escape" in Adams Morgan, where diners "eat with their hands"; many favor the "colorful, upper-level" space with low, cushioned seats or the window perches, both of which allow for prime "people-watching", but wherever your table, you'll be served by "beautiful", "helpful" waitresses (who may not "speak English well"), even if opponents "don't see what the fuss is about."

Meze ◐ [S] ▽ 19 | 18 | 17 | $24

2437 18th St., NW (bet. Belmont & Columbia Rds.), 202-797-0017

◪ "Cheap grazing and chic people-gazing" draw in the "beautiful people" at this "hip" late-night two-year-old in Adams Morgan; it's a "stylish", "sophisticated" haunt with "tasty" Mediterranean–Turkish tapas (plus a few entrees) and an "excellent" martini menu, but those who proclaim it "mediocre all around" feel that it "isn't yet up to snuff."

Mezza9 [S] ▽ 21 | 20 | 20 | $37

Hyatt Arlington, 1325 Wilson Blvd. (Nash St.), Arlington, VA, 703-276-8999

◪ A "great place to get to know someone" or to "seal" a business deal, this "peaceful", often "overlooked" Rosslyn hotel dining room pleases with an "interesting" Med menu full of "flavorful" "little dishes to share", while in the morning

Washington, DC F | D | S | C |

breakfast is "presented with all the niceties", including "fresh-squeezed orange juice"; still, demanding types find it "not so exciting", especially for the price.

Mie N Yu S — | — | — | E |
3125 M St., NW (31st St.), 202-333-6122
Nightclub entrepreneur John Boyle's (Nation) exotic new Georgetown venture features eye-popping decor inspired by the Silk Road that includes a Turkish tent room, a Moroccan bazaar, netted private booths, a baroque dragon-themed lounge and a chef's table in a bird-cage suspended between two floors, not to mention a must-see unisex basement bathroom; its eclectic American menu takes second place.

Mimi's American Bistro ◑ S | 18 | 20 | 20 | $28 |
2120 P St., NW (bet. 21st & 22nd Sts.), 202-464-6464
◪ Offering a "good" meal and "campy" cabaret "for the price of one", this Mediterranean-flavored New American "gathering place" off Dupont Circle showcases a "talented" performing staff that "livens up" the joint with "show tunes" while serving your meal; boosters swear that somehow the "gimmick" works – as long as you're in the mood for "loud" singing and boisterous high jinks – but party-poopers grouch that the "novelty can't overcome the boring food."

Minh S — | — | — | I |
2500 Wilson Blvd. (Cleveland St.), Arlington, VA, 703-525-2828
A multinational clientele fills the tables at this young Clarendon Vietnamese that garners good buzz thanks to its extensive menu of fresh, authentic dishes, served in a softly lit room that's as suitable for a business deal as a date.

Mirage Kabob & Sweets Café S — | — | — | I |
5916 Leesburg Pike (Glen Forest Dr.), Falls Church, VA, 703-845-1600
Those drawn by the Middle Eastern confections at Falls Church's defunct Samadi Sweets have reason to cheer, since the new owner, Harshan Yavari, who has remodeled the storefront into an open, airy cafe, has retained the Lebanese pastry chef to make the same mouthwatering desserts, which are now served with fragrant Iranian tea or Turkish coffee; the rest of the menu is Persian, including affordable kabobs and rice, salads, sandwiches and special country dishes.

Mi Rancho S | 19 | 15 | 18 | $20 |
19725A Germantown Rd. (Middlebrook Rd.), Germantown, MD, 301-515-7480
8701 Ramsey Ave. (Cameron St.), Silver Spring, MD, 301-588-4872
◪ Amigos say that the "homestyle" Mexican food featured at this "bustling" pair in Germantown and Silver Spring is prepared with a "lot of heart", from the "standout" fajitas to the "so good *carne asada*"; "cheery" and "appropriately

Washington, DC F | D | S | C

tacky", it's an "unpretentious" place that's "friendly to kids" and "reasonably priced", but fusspots are "not impressed."

Moby Dick ⊄   21 | 7 | 13 | $13
1300 Connecticut Ave., NW (N St.), 202-833-9788
1070 31st St., NW (bet. K & M Sts.), 202-333-4400 S
7027 Wisconsin Ave. (Leland St.), Bethesda, MD, 301-654-1838 S
105 Market St. (Kentlands Blvd.), Gaithersburg, MD, 301-987-7770
12154 Fairfax Towne Ctr. (W. Ox Rd.), Fairfax, VA, 703-352-6226 S
6854 Old Dominion Dr. (Chain Bridge Rd.), Tysons Corner, VA, 703-448-8448 S

◾ "Looking for great kebabs?" – then sail over to one of these "no-nonsense", "eat 'n' run" Persian "dives" that are praised for their "fantastic" "fresh-baked bread", "delicious" hummus, "juicy" skewers and "awesome daily specials"; some find that the "family atmosphere of years past now seems more institutionalized" as outlets multiply and spruce up their decor, but plenty of addicts remain convinced that this is "about as good as it gets for fast, fresh", "cheap" grub.

Mon Ami Gabi S   – | – | – | M
7239 Woodmont Ave. (Bethesda Ave.), Bethesda, MD, 301-654-1234
SRO since day one, this handsome, spacious French bistro evokes the Champs-Elysées with its belle epoque details and elegant rolling wine carts; the menu brims with well-priced Gallic classics (including seafood platters and four versions of steak frites), while its prime Bethesda Row location guarantees a scene, especially on the sidewalk cafe.

Mondo Sushi S   – | – | – | M
Pentagon Row, 1301 S. Joyce St. (Army Navy Dr.), Pentagon City, VA, 703-418-0003
Cool vibes permeate this futuristic white-on-white sushi spot on Arlington's Pentagon Row, strikingly appointed with slanted walls, recessed panels of graphics and a sleek steel bar replete with stools on hydraulic lifts; locals can thank the folks responsible for Dragonfly, Local 16 and other trendy clubs for bringing Downtown sensibilities and late hours (till 2 AM Thursday–Saturday) to their suburban mall, not to mention serious Japanese fare starring spicy rolls.

Monocle   16 | 18 | 20 | $35
107 D St., NE (1st St.), 202-546-4488
◾ Say what you will about this "aging" institution and its "ordinary" American food, but where else can you see "nearly as many senators as at a State of the Union address" and eavesdrop on history being made while eating lunch?; of course, you may feel like an "outsider" in this "clubby"

vote at zagat.com

Washington, DC

F | **D** | **S** | **C**

enclave, but just "say hi to Bob the bartender", order the "decent crab cakes" and settle in for some of the "best" people-watching in town.

Montmartre S
23 | 20 | 20 | $39

327 Seventh St., SE (Pennsylvania Ave.), 202-544-1244

■ At their "delightful addition to Capitol Hill", Bistrot Lepic alumni Stephane Lezla and Christopher Raynal add a Gallic accent to prettied-up quarters in a onetime post office; the "skillful" kitchen turns out "delicious" bistro classics as well as updated interpretations, enriching the neighborhood scene and helping its many new *amis* dining at its outdoor tables pretend that Pennsylvania Avenue runs through the Left Bank.

Morrison-Clark Inn S
24 | 24 | 23 | $48

Morrison-Clark Inn, 1015 L St., NW (bet. 11th St. & Massachusetts Ave.), 202-898-1200

◪ With its "lovely presentations", "charming Victorian drawing room feel" and "attentive" ways, this New American hotel restaurant Downtown promises a "blissfully sedate", "grown-up" experience; to its enchanted coterie, it's "always a special place" to visit, but faultfinders report a "mixed performance."

MORTON'S, THE STEAKHOUSE S
24 | 21 | 23 | $53

3251 Prospect St., NW (Wisconsin Ave.), 202-342-6258
Washington Sq., 1050 Connecticut Ave., NW (L St.), 202-955-5997
1631 Crystal Sq. Dr. (bet. 15th & 18th Sts.), Arlington, VA, 703-418-1444
Reston Town Ctr., 11956 Market St. (Reston Pkwy.), Reston, VA, 703-796-0128
Fairfax Sq., 8075 Leesburg Pike (Aline Rd.), Tysons Corner, VA, 703-883-0800

■ Virtually synonymous with "great steaks", "mean" martinis and fine cigars, this national chain of prime "porterhouse palaces" exemplifies the "glorification of excess", hauling out steaks of such "monster size" that you may feel like you're in a "*Honey, I Shrunk the Kids*" sequel; well-hoofed carnivores who are members of the "boys' business club" sigh that the "tender" "beef is pure heaven", though a surprising number confess that the "unbelievable" Godiva cake is the "real reason" they come.

Mr. K's S
23 | 23 | 24 | $44

2121 K St., NW (bet. 21st & 22nd Sts.), 202-331-8868

◪ "Ceremonious, leisurely and elegant", this haute Chinese relic on K Street is an "over-the-top" "anachronism" that's guaranteed to "amaze" guests; while a majority still considers it the "Cadillac of the cuisine", foes yawn that it's just like "yesterday's newspaper", though even they concede that it might be worth it just for the "coffee brewed at your table via a fascinating mad scientist's contraption."

Murasaki [S] – | – | – | M

4620 Wisconsin Ave., NW (Brandywine St.), 202-966-0023

Upper NW sushi fanciers quickly discovered this "modest but pleasant" place that fashions "pristine" raw fish into interesting creations; Japanese diplomats and business types can also choose from a broad range of traditional appetizers, noodles and tempura dishes, while seriously adventurous eaters can request off-menu specialties (some featuring internal organs and other unfamiliar ingredients).

Myanmar [S] ∇ 21 | 9 | 18 | $18

7810 Lee Hwy. (Hyson Ln.), Falls Church, VA, 703-289-0013

■ Treating curious appetites to a rare opportunity to sample Burmese cooking, this "tiny", family-run place in Falls Church has an "excellent" menu that lists more than 100 dishes ("what a variety!"); deftly integrating hot, sour, salty, bitter and sweet tastes, the dishes add up to an "unusual" and satisfying meal; in sum: "sweet smiles + great value = great find."

Mykonos Grill [S] 21 | 21 | 20 | $30

121 Congressional Ln. (Rockville Pike), Rockville, MD, 301-770-5999

◪ Escape to the "Aegean Islands" at this sunny re-creation of a Hellenic cafe just off Rockville Pike, where the "pretty" setting provides an "evocative" (if "somewhat artificial") backdrop for "good" traditional Greek food and welcoming hospitality; despite some quibbles about "uninspired" cooking, most of its suburban "neighbors" appreciate this "reasonably priced" option.

Nam's of Bethesda [S] 20 | 16 | 20 | $25

4928 Cordell Ave. (Old Georgetown Rd.), Bethesda, MD, 301-652-2635

■ "Delicate" soups, "tasty" pho and "mouthwatering" grilled fish are just some of the "authentic", "wholly pleasurable" menu choices at this "quiet Vietnamese retreat" in Bethesda; the "courteous" servers make "helpful recommendations" about the "well-seasoned" specials and the tables are "nicely spaced", resulting in an "all-around good experience" that merits a return visit.

Nam Viet [S] 22 | 12 | 18 | $21

3419 Connecticut Ave., NW (bet. Macomb & Porter Sts.), 202-237-1015

1127 N. Hudson St. (Wilson Blvd.), Arlington, VA, 703-522-7110

■ "Years of eating experience confirm the remarkable consistency" of these Vietnamese veterans in Cleveland Park and Arlington, which comfort with "down-to-earth" cooking including "rich pho" soups, "delicious rice noodles with subtle sauces" and "crispy red snapper that'll thrill the whole table"; granted, the digs are "lackluster", but

Washington, DC F | D | S | C

the "wonderful" food compensates, even if a few nitpickers find it "Americanized."

Napa Thai S — | — | — | M
4924 St. Elmo Ave. (Norfolk Ave.), Bethesda, MD, 301-986-8590
Though it's named after the Thai word for 'sky' (the walls are covered with images of faraway galaxies) and not the Napa Valley, the "pleasant patio" at this attractive Bethesda two-year-old does give it a certain "California" feel; the "excellent" menu, however, is fairly traditional and offers a "wide variety" (don't miss the "best chicken and coconut milk soup" or the "incredible deep-fried or steamed whole fish"), plus the service is "accommodating" and "polite."

Nathans S 17 | 18 | 17 | $34
3150 M St., NW (Wisconsin Ave.), 202-338-2000
◪ Georgetown's "classic", "well-polished" saloon hosts a grown-up bar scene up front and a "dark and mysterious" back room, which provides the local gentry with a "perfect rendezvous" to conduct business or romance; regulars, who have long been content with the "solid" American pub grub (especially the "good" burgers), say that the "upgraded" steakhouse menu is "igniting sparks of flavor", which may appease those who deem this "tradition" "undistinguished."

Nectar S — | — | — | E
824 New Hampshire Ave., NW (bet. H & I Sts.), 202-298-8085
Tucked away in Foggy Bottom and adorned with eye-catching photographs of luscious produce, this chic boutique space provides sophisticated, market-driven Contemporary American cuisine for Kennedy Center ticketholders and tourists desiring dishes prepared with restraint and complemented by select wines and elegant desserts; N.B. its hideaway bar and inner courtyard seem perfectly cast for a romantic rendezvous.

Negril ∇ 18 | 8 | 14 | $13
2301G Georgia Ave., NW (Bryant St.), 202-332-3737
18509 N. Frederick Ave. (Travis Ave.), Gaithersburg, MD, 301-926-7220
Mitchellville Plaza, 12116 Central Ave. (Landover Rd.), Mitchellville, MD, 301-249-9101
965 Thayer Ave. (Georgia Ave.), Silver Spring, MD, 301-585-3000
◪ West Indian expats and Jamaican food "addicts" satisfy their cravings with the "homey meat patties and peas 'n' rice", "great" jerk, curried chicken and other Caribbean comfort foods prepared at this "simple", self-serve quartet; the digs aren't much to look at (other than the "hand-painted tables" at the Gaithersburg outlet), but the portions are so generous you'll have "enough for lunch the next day."

Neisha Thai [S] 22 20 20 $25
Culmore Plaza, 6037 Leesburg Pike (Glen Carlyn Rd.), Bailey's Crossroads, VA, 703-933-3788
7924LB Tysons Corner Ctr. (Chain Bridge Rd.), McLean, VA, 703-883-3588
◪ Designed to "break into your shopping-mall coma", these suburban Siamese twins with a "creative license" spin "trendy" riffs on the standards (think "awesome passion beef" and "tangy" tilapia with lime) amid "cave-like" environs; while bashers tag them "Thai light" for "watered-down curries", supporters retort the food is "yummy", "they make you feel welcome" and "there's never a wait."

New Fortune ◐ [S] 22 14 15 $21
16515 S. Frederick Ave. (Westland Dr.), Gaithersburg, MD, 301-548-8886
■ "Packed on Sundays" with large parties sampling its "authentic" dim sum (available daily), this "cavernous" Hong Kong–style banquet hall in Gaithersburg sends out "more rolling carts than you know what to do with", steered by "friendly" servers who "get excited when you pick something exotic"; at lunch and dinner, expect an enormous, "interesting" menu starring "unusual" seafood specialties and, perhaps, entertainment from the "karaoke" performers and "wedding parties" that are often present.

New Heights [S] 24 22 22 $46
2317 Calvert St., NW (Connecticut Ave.), 202-234-4110
◪ "Artistic" and "adventurous", this "light-filled" Woodley Park "favorite" makes guests feel they're dining on the "cutting edge – even though it's been around forever"; savor "delicious new takes" on New American dishes paired with "well-chosen" wines and served by an "informed" staff in a "lovely", "serene" room (downstairs, "stunning woodwork" marks one of the "most beautiful bars in the city"); while there are some "disappointments", most believe it "reaches new heights each time."

Neyla [S] 22 24 20 $36
3206 N St., NW (Wisconsin Ave.), 202-333-6353
◪ "Dramatic in an *Arabian Nights*" way, this "trendy" Mediterranean scene in Georgetown is alive with attractive thirtysomething "urbanites" sharing "winning" Lebanese-style meze, sipping "fun" mango martinis and soaking up the "sensuous" atmosphere at either the convivial communal table or in the "Casbah"-like dining room; though the noise level is akin to a "747 taking off", the service is "gracious" and the courtyard is one of the most pleasant around.

Nick & Stef's Steakhouse 20 19 19 $46
MCI Ctr., 601 F St., NW (6th St.), 202-661-5040
◪ Appreciated for its "sophisticated" "elegance", this MCI Center steakhouse is a palace of meat that even a

"vegetarian could love"; while its dry-aged rib-eye is "fine", the "refreshingly" "inventive sides" ("blue cheese mashed potatoes, sautéed spinach with shallots") and "divine Caesar salad" nearly steal the show; critical carnivores, however, find it a "mite" "pricey" for the quality and caution that it can get awfully quiet here on non-event nights.

Nick's Chophouse ▽ 20 | 22 | 18 | $45

700 King Farm Blvd. (bet. Rockville Pike & Shady Grove Rd.), Rockville, MD, 301-926-8869

◩ Early settlers "welcome" this citified fine-dining venture to their Montgomery County enclave; dressed up with elaborate floral arrangements, the "bright", airy room is a comfortable place to dine on "good", if "pricey", steaks, veal chops and fish, also available in the "great" lounge; though it's so far "inconsistent" (it "needs some work"), patrons are optimistic that it'll grow up to be "a keeper."

Niwano Hana [S] ▽ 20 | 16 | 20 | $24

Wintergreen Plaza, 887 Rockville Pike (Edmonston Dr.), Rockville, MD, 301-294-0553

◩ Sharply divided camps war over this Rockville Pike Japanese, with proponents praising its "fresh" sushi, "innovative rolls and tofu dishes", as well as its genuine "hospitality" and "good value", while opponents complain that the "menu is limited" and "not very authentic"; even so, the fact that it's usually "jammed" should be an indication of its merits.

Nizam's [S] 22 | 17 | 21 | $33

Village Green Shopping Ctr., 523 Maple Ave. W. (Nutley St.), Vienna, VA, 703-938-8948

◩ "Real" doner kebab (available on Tuesdays and Friday–Sunday) is the leading "star" at this bright Turkish fixture, though the "tasty" meze is equally "worth" a pilgrimage around the Beltway to Vienna; diplomats and world travelers join locals in the ornate rooms for "dependably delicious" specialties delivered by a "professional" team, easily forgiving minor flaws like the "crowded tables."

Noodles & Company [S] – | – | – | I

7320 Baltimore Ave. (bet. Hartwick & Knox Rds.), College Park, MD, 301-779-5300

177 Kentlands Blvd. (Great Seneca Hwy.), Gaithersburg, MD, 301-926-5901

Main Street Mktpl., 10296 Main St. (Old Lee Hwy.), Fairfax, VA, 703-218-4400

Pentagon Row, 1201 S. Joyce St. (Washington Blvd.), Pentagon City, VA, 703-418-0001

Speedy dining gets a global twirl at these spiffy shopping-center eateries (outposts of a Boulder, CO–based chain); choose from a family-friendly roster of international noodle dishes, salads and soups, all of which can be customized

Washington, DC | F | D | S | C |

with meat, shrimp, tofu or veggies and downsized for kids, then order at the counter and wait for your meal to be brought to your table; beer, wine and organic juices are also available.

NORA | 25 | 23 | 24 | $53 |
2132 Florida Ave., NW (bet. Connecticut & Massachusetts Aves.), 202-462-5145

◪ "Eat luxuriously and don't feel guilty" at Nora Pouillon's "outstanding" New American quartered in a "charming" carriage house above Dupont Circle; her "feel-good" ethic – create "beautiful" dishes based on "first-rate" "organic" products – is not only beneficial "for both your health and the environment", it also results in a "memorable" "feast"; even though a "senator may well be at the next table", the staff will "make you feel like the center of attention", though foes don't buy the "arrogantly" PC philosophy.

Nouveau East S | – | – | – | M |
Ballston Common Mall, 671 N. Glebe Rd., Ste. 1248 (Wilson Blvd.), Arlington, VA, 703-807-4088

In Arlington, this Asian bistro conquers its pedestrian Ballston mall location with futuristic decor and an ambitious menu offering Japanese, Chinese and Indochinese cuisines, along with fusiony riffs on American steak and seafood favorites; all-day table service and $1 sushi deals at happy hour add to its drop-by appeal, as does its multipurpose layout replete with dual dining bars.

OBELISK | 27 | 22 | 26 | $60 |
2029 P St., NW (bet. 20th & 21st Sts.), 202-872-1180

◪ For gourmands who love food and wine, this "exquisite" Dupont Circle Northern Italian "treasure" is home to "36 of the best seats in town"; the "superb" five-course prix fixe menu changes daily, but it's always "thoughtfully" conceived and combines an "element of surprise along with authentic" touches; though the seating is a bit "tight" and a few beaus feel that the decor is akin to an "old flame that could use some new makeup", the "first-rate" service team really "cares about doing it right."

Occidental S | 22 | 23 | 22 | $45 |
Willard Plaza, 1475 Pennsylvania Ave., NW (14th St.), 202-783-1475

◪ At this Downtown "political version of Sardis" in NYC, "VIP" photographs on the walls illustrate its motto 'where statesmen dine', while "belle epoque" appointments lend a "classy, historic" resonance to the ambiance; by most accounts, the New American menu is a "match" for the "attentive" (if "stuffy") service, but even if some think the tab is "not worth it", watching the comings and goings of power brokers from the patio is a most enjoyable way to pass the time.

OCEANAIRE SEAFOOD ROOM [S] 23 | 23 | 22 | $47

1201 F St., NW (bet. 12th & 13th Sts.), 202-347-2277

◪ With all of that genre's "excesses", this "sleek '30s-style" Downtown American provides the equivalent of a "steakhouse experience for fish" lovers, showing off "bird bath"–big martinis, "super-size" entrees, a single side dish that's "enough for four" people and flaming desserts; fin fanatics are hooked by the "up-to-date" menu ("great" crab cakes and oysters), welcoming this "alternative in a city swimming" with beef barns, but dissenters object to the too "slick" "commercial" feel and Titanic prices.

Olazzo [S] – | – | – | M

7921 Norfolk Ave. (Cordell Ave.), Bethesda, MD, 301-654-9496

Roberto and Riccardo Pietrobono's engaging Bethesda storefront Italian epitomizes a family-run operation – while Riccardo prepares hearty, homestyle dishes from heirloom recipes in the kitchen, his brother Roberto oversees the dining room, which is enlivened by family photos and memorabilia and a trompe l'oeil brick fireplace glowing in the corner (it's really a DVD) that was crafted by their dad; N.B. its prices are friendly to families too.

Old Angler's Inn [S] 21 | 24 | 20 | $51

10801 MacArthur Blvd. (Clara Barton Pkwy.), Potomac, MD, 301-365-2425

◪ Bosky "summer evenings under the stars", along with cocktails by the blazing fire in the wintertime, have nurtured countless "romances" over the years at this "quaint" Great Falls "hideaway"; while the New American menu can't rival the "picturesque" setting, admirers laud the "fine" surprise tasting menus, but detractors deem the food and service "indifferent" and note that the upstairs dining room is quite "charmless."

Old Ebbitt Grill ◐ [S] 20 | 22 | 20 | $33

675 15th St., NW (bet. F & G Sts.), 202-347-4801

◪ "Who knows which Cabinet secretary will stop by for lunch" at this handsome "must-see" "legend" Downtown; a "powerhouse" at breakfast too and a "tradition" late at night at its four bars, this is a "classic" saloon with "brass and wood everywhere" and "well-prepared" all-American food on the menu; though spoilsports hiss "tired and touristy", with way "too many Republicans" in the house, you "can't get more DC" than here.

Old Glory All-American BBQ [S] 18 | 16 | 17 | $22

3139 M St., NW (bet. 31st St. & Wisconsin Ave.), 202-337-3406 ◐

6208 Multiplex Dr. (bet. Lee Hwy. & Rte. 28), Centreville, VA, 703-266-4066

◪ Clamorous collegians "craving BBQ" crowd this open-to-the-street Georgetown crib for its "solid ribs" slathered

Washington, DC F | D | S | C

with a "pick-your-own" housemade sauce and other "hearty" grub; after the meal, belly up to the vintage carved bar (stocked with 79 varieties of bourbon), hauled up from Memphis and reputedly the same one where Elvis tucked into some 'cue, and chat with the "great bartenders"; N.B. there's a newer, unrated outpost in Centreville.

Olives | 23 | 22 | 20 | $44
World Center Bldg., 1600 K St., NW (16th St.), 202-452-1866
◪ Just a few blocks from the White House, this multi-tiered "'in' place with an uptown feel" is Todd English's "stylish" tribute to contemporary Mediterranean cooking; the downstairs space is "beautiful" (and quieter), but "all the twentysomethings" head to the "hip upstairs" level, where solo diners can snag a seat at the bar facing the exhibition kitchen; though the "original" menu and "models"/servers get mixed reviews, few sniff at the "world-shattering warm chocolate cake."

Oodles Noodles | 20 | 15 | 17 | $19
1120 19th St., NW (bet. L & M Sts.), 202-293-3138 S
4907 Cordell Ave. (bet. Norfolk Ave. & Old Georgetown Rd.), Bethesda, MD, 301-986-8833
◪ "Consistently good" and "healthy fast food" leaves customers "feeling full but not stuffed" at these Asian noodle houses in the Golden Triangle and Bethesda; despite "long lines", "crowded" seating and an "impersonal you come, you eat, you leave" atmosphere, wallet-watchers proclaim it a no-brainer – "big portions" and "lots of variety for not much cash"; N.B. the DC location, now known as Nooshi, serves sushi as well.

Oriental East S | ▽ 20 | 9 | 15 | $19
1312 East-West Hwy. (Colesville Rd.), Silver Spring, MD, 301-608-0030
◪ "Extraordinary dim sum" choices still turn this Silver Spring Chinese into a "madhouse" on weekends despite its post-*Survey* relocation to larger quarters in a spiffy shopping center nearby; dinnertime is less hectic and the meal is nearly as "good – if you order right", meaning ask for the translated Chinese specialty menu and don't settle for the "same old Cantonese options"; expect, however, "gruff" treatment at any time.

Ortanique | ▽ 22 | 23 | 21 | $40
730 11th St., NW (bet. G & H Sts.), 202-393-0975
◪ "Fabulously" decorated with tropical hues and a colorful saltwater aquarium, this "beautiful", romantic two-tiered space Downtown exudes "great" island atmosphere (as does salsa dancing on Friday nights); "equally as exotic" as the setting is its Nuevo Latino 'cuisine of the sun' (think Bahamian black grouper with a citrus sauce), which helps fill an "underserved" Caribbean niche in town; it's young,

Washington, DC

Oval Room | 22 | 23 | 23 | $46 |
800 Connecticut Ave., NW (bet. H & I Sts.), 202-463-8700

This "elegant" New American's "sparkling new" decor causes Democrats to quip that the "transition is better here than in the Oval Office" nearby (referring to its major redo after the last presidential election); its strategic location, as well as a staff that "makes you feel like a player" and a patio wherein "to see and be seen", pulls in the "power lunch" crowd, and "if you're in the mood to dress up" for dinner, "this is your place"; as for the food, partisans approve of the ever "exciting" menu, but some opponents veto it as too "variable."

PALENA | 25 | 23 | 22 | $60 |
3529 Connecticut Ave., NW (Porter St.), 202-537-9250

At their "refined" Cleveland Park venue, Frank Ruta's seasonal New American dishes (inspired by the cuisines of France and Italy) "awaken taste buds you didn't even know existed", while Ann Amernick's "fabulous" desserts are legendary; everything is "painstakingly prepared" (read: "slowly") and served in a "serene" room by a staff that's either "attentive" or "forgetful" (depending on the night); all in all, most can't wait to "return"; N.B. more casual gourmet cafe fare is now available at the bar and on the patio.

PALM S | 24 | 20 | 23 | $51 |
1225 19th St., NW (bet. M & N Sts.), 202-293-9091
1750 Tysons Blvd. (International Dr.), Tysons Corner, VA, 703-917-0200

Locus of the definitive "power lunch", this "rough-and-tumble" chain is famed for its "outstanding" NY strip steaks and "amazing lobsters", as well as its "frenetic pace" and customer "abuse" (our "waiter kept us laughing all night"); while it's true that "regulars" and "VIPs" are pampered with "especially nice treatment" at the Golden Triangle branch and the Tysons Corner outlet (a "romper room") draws "tons of kids", if you think of the place as a "caricature of itself", "it's a kick."

Panino | ▽ 24 | 21 | 22 | $42 |
9116 Mathis Ave. (Sudley Rd.), Manassas, VA, 703-335-2566

"Don't be put off" by its "blue-collar" "strip-mall" locale, because inside this "unexpected spot" the kitchen turns out "first-rate" Northern Italian cooking; it's a "real find" for "fine" dining in "handsome" environs, and the entire experience is so "wonderful" that supporters are convinced it's the "best Manassas has to offer."

Washington, DC   F | D | S | C

Panjshir   ▽ 24 | 14 | 19 | $23
924 W. Broad St. (West St.), Falls Church, VA, 703-536-4566
224 Maple Ave. W. (Lawyers Rd.), Vienna, VA, 703-281-4183 S

■ Among Northern Virginia's "best" and most accessible ethnic options, this pair of Afghan "gems" is a "favorite for guests timid about exotic" foods; based on familiar ingredients like lamb, rice and pumpkin and "mild in spiciness", the "downright good" dishes are turned out in a "low-key" storefront setting by "affable" folks at such budget-friendly prices that it's easy to dine here "a lot."

Paolo's S   18 | 18 | 17 | $29
1303 Wisconsin Ave., NW (N St.), 202-333-7353 ☉
Reston Town Ctr., 11898 Market St. (Reston Pkwy.), Reston, VA, 703-318-8920

◪ "Prime" locales make these "trendy" Cal-Ital cafes in Georgetown and Reston "buzzing" "hangouts" that are best enjoyed out on the "lively" patio ("fine" "people-watching"); the "superb" giveaway breadsticks and olive dip are "worth filling up on", which is a good thing because there can be a "wait" for your "decent" pasta, pizza or salad to arrive; though most find them an "easy" pick, critics dismiss the "predictable" menu and "amateur" service.

Parkway Deli S   20 | 10 | 19 | $17
Rock Creek Village Shopping Ctr., 8317 Grubb Rd. (East-West Hwy.), Silver Spring, MD, 301-587-1427

◪ Montgomery County mavens are convinced that this "mensch-like" Silver Spring "mecca" is where lox-and-eggs seekers "want to be on Sunday mornings"; upholding deli tradition, the "irreverent" help also dishes up "grandma's chicken soup", "latkes with sour cream" and all the other "classic" Jewish "comfort foods"; most give it a "grade of B", though because it's in the "wrong area code", it can't possibly live up to its detractors' fond "NYC" memories.

Pasta Mia   24 | 14 | 14 | $20
1790 Columbia Rd., NW (18th St.), 202-328-9114

◪ "Worth" the "hellacious" wait to end up with a "delicious food coma and five days of leftovers", this idiosyncratic Adams Morgan Italian has cultivated a loyal following that simply craves its "unbelievable" "homemade" pastas; note, however, that it's "cramped", with "no frills" and a "temperamental" staff (which fully believes that "good food takes time, so if you don't have it, go somewhere else"), and even diehards admit that they "would never tolerate being treated like cattle anywhere else."

Pasta Plus S   24 | 13 | 20 | $26
Center Plaza, 209 Gorman Ave. (bet. Rtes. 1 & 98), Laurel, MD, 301-498-5100

■ As its name suggests, this "terrific" "hidden treasure" in suburban Laurel features not only "fabulous", "authentic"

vote at zagat.com

Washington, DC

pastas but also "great pizzas" and "down-to-earth" Italian entrees; it's "run by a friendly gentleman [from Abruzzi], who knows his business", and the "lines out the door" at his labor of love are "testimony" to his "marvelous" effort; N.B. having his brother (who ran the much-missed Mare e Monti in Bowie) oversee the kitchen adds another real bonus.

Peacock Cafe S | 21 | 19 | 19 | $25
3251 Prospect St., NW (bet. Potomac St. & Wisconsin Ave.), 202-625-2740

"Coveted" for its sidewalk tables that allow "great" scoping of the Georgetown street scene, as well as for its "casual" "California" vibe, this "airy", "stylish" New American cafe provides "fresh, light" nourishment to a "Euro" yuppie crowd; some "snubbed" surveyors may bash this "wanna-be" for serving dishes that "fall short", but plenty of regulars "know the day of the week by its soup schedule."

Peking Gourmet Inn S | 25 | 15 | 21 | $28
Culmore Shopping Ctr., 6029 Leesburg Pike (Glen Carlyn Rd.), Falls Church, VA, 703-671-8088

Clearly, the Bush presidency isn't hurting business at this "bustling" veteran Chinese in Falls Church, a destination long associated with Republican Administrations ("check out the political photos on the wall"); it's "well known" for its "phenomenal" Peking duck and specially grown garlic sprouts, but supporters urge first-timers to try other dishes as well (like the "crispy" Szechuan beef) because they're commendably "different from the standard fare" found elsewhere.

Penang S | – | – | – | M
1837 M St., NW (19th St.), 202-822-8773

In the Golden Triangle business district, this "attractive" Malaysian offers something different for lunchtime and after-work meetings with its menu focused on the "interestingly" "sweet and spicy" blend of Southeast Asian, Chinese and Indian influences that marks its native homeland's cuisine and the seductive lighting and lounge-like seating that give it a supper club feel.

Perry's S | 20 | 22 | 16 | $32
1811 Columbia Rd., NW (Biltmore Rd.), 202-234-6218

Summertime sushi under the stars on the "awesome" rooftop deck at this "hip" Adams Morgan "scene" used to be as much about watching the "pretty people" as dining on "creative" Asian fusion cuisine or "acceptable" sushi – that is, until consulting chefs John Cochran and Sidra Forman (ex Ruppert's) upgraded the seasonal, eclectic fare; downstairs are comfy couches and a "funky" bar, but brace yourself for "attitude" everywhere; P.S. the "risqué" "drag queen brunch" on Sundays is a "must-do."

Persimmon [S] 25 | 19 | 22 | $43

7003 Wisconsin Ave. (bet. Leland & Walsh Sts.), Bethesda, MD, 301-654-9860

◪ Recently enlarged and still "beautiful", this Bethesda New American "find" "aims for understatement and achieves it"; the kitchen deftly delivers "finely crafted" dishes that are "delicious" and "different", including some of the "best fish around"; boosters believe it "outshines its competition" in town, but exacting types who feel it "needs some oomph" think that it's "pricey for what you get."

Pesce [S] 24 | 15 | 19 | $38

2016 P St., NW (bet. Hopkins & 20th Sts.), 202-466-3474

◪ The "chef knows how to cook fish" at owner Regine Palladin's "informal" seafood bistro near Dupont Circle, where "sparkling fresh" fish and "ingenuity, not attitude", rule (the daily selections on the chalkboard reflect the "best" the market has to offer); the "exposed brick" setting is as "charming" as ever, and a handsome polished bar provides a most "welcome" waiting area; still, a few crab about "close quarters" and a sometimes "hurried" atmosphere.

Pesto Ristorante [S] – | – | – | M

2915 Connecticut Ave., NW (Cathedral Ave.), 202-332-8300

A touch of Italy transforms the former Mrs. Simpson's site in Woodley Park into a smart-looking neighborhood bar and restaurant with a well-priced menu of Italian favorites; its streetside patio attracts passersby on the way to the National Zoo, while the cozy atmosphere inside encourages rainy-night rendezvous, and overseeing all is gregarious owner Vincenzo Belvito.

Petits Plats [S] 21 | 19 | 21 | $41

2653 Connecticut Ave., NW (Calvert St.), 202-518-0018

◪ Francophiles find "great charm" and "accomplished" "traditional" fare at this "easy-on-the-eyes" bistro with a beguiling sidewalk cafe on Woodley Park's restaurant row; "warm" and "vibrant", it captures that certain French feel that "many shoot for but miss", and even if the dishes are "a bit inconsistent", the menu offers "many high points" – from "delightful appetizers" to "amazing salads" to "fantastic crème brûlée."

P.F. Chang's China Bistro [S] 20 | 20 | 18 | $26

White Flint Mall, 11301 Rockville Pike (Nicholson Ln.), Rockville, MD, 301-230-6933

Tysons Galleria, 1716M International Dr. (Chain Bridge Rd.), Tysons Corner, VA, 703-734-8996

◪ "Chinese with pizzazz" is what you can expect at this "glitzy", "hyper"-paced chain where the stagey "mood" lighting and "eye appeal" add an "interesting twist" to the familiar; the fare is "tasty", especially the "flavorful" lettuce wraps, and the atmosphere "fun", which explains why it's

Washington, DC F | D | S | C

"always crowded", even though most diners recognize that this is "not real Chinese" food; foes, however, snipe that the concept is "wearing thin."

Pho 75 S⃠   22 | 8 | 16 | $13
1510 University Blvd. E. (New Hampshire Ave.), Langley Park, MD, 301-434-7844
771 Hungerford Dr. (Mannakee St.), Rockville, MD, 301-309-8873
1721 Wilson Blvd. (Quinn St.), Arlington, VA, 703-525-7355
3103 Graham Rd. (Arlington Blvd.), Falls Church, VA, 703-204-1490
382 Elden St. (Herndon Pkwy.), Herndon, VA, 703-471-4145

◪ For the "ultimate comfort food on a cold day", order a "beyond-hearty" bowl of pho (aka "Vietnamese penicillin") at this "no-frills" chain, a "complex, flavorful" concoction of broth, noodles, vegetables and meat that "fills you up" without weighing you down; available in a number of "permutations" (the "thin-sliced eye-round is always a safe choice"), it's ladled up "briskly" and "inexpensively" but with "no smiles."

Pike's Restaurant ◐S   – | – | – | I
(aka Pike's Pizza)
4111 Columbia Pike (George Mason Rd.), Arlington, VA, 703-521-3010

Though some locals frequent this late-night Arlington joint for its namesake pies, those in-the-know urge "forget the pizzas, try the *saltenas*" (hard-to-find Bolivian pastries filled with spicy chicken or meat); it's a different world here, especially on weekends, when it's "mobbed" by the Bolivian community, which enjoys a "noisy" good time dining on native specialties like chicharrón, fried pork chunks and beef stew while musicians play lively tunes from their homeland.

Pizzeria Paradiso S   25 | 15 | 18 | $21
3282 M St., NW (bet. 32nd & 33rd Sts.), 202-337-1245
2029 P St., NW (bet. 20th & 21st Sts.), 202-223-1245

■ Paradise found rhapsodize acolytes of this "civilized" Dupont Circle pizzeria's "heavenly" wood-fired pies – the "best in DC" – made with a "crisp, light" crust and topped with all sorts of "scrumptious" "goodies" (its "great sandwiches and salads are only a bonus"); aside from the "long" prime-time "wait", most surveyors "come with high expectations" – and they're fully "met"; N.B. the new, brick-walled Georgetown branch, with stylish bar and wood-burning ovens, answers prayers for more seating.

Portabellos S   – | – | – | M
Cherrydale Shopping Ctr., 2109 N. Pollard St. (Lee Hwy.), Arlington, VA, 703-528-1557

Virginia native Bill Hamrock fills Cherrydale's contemporary-dining void with this New American located on the site last occupied by Pasha Cafe; dishes like its signature portobello

Washington, DC

F D S C

mushroom stuffed with vegetable ratatouille are served in a comfortable, simply decorated space that's equally suitable for a casual bite after work or a festive dinner.

Poste S — | — | — | E

Hotel Monaco, 555 Eighth St., NW (bet. E & F Sts.), 202-783-6060
Chicly transformed, the former General Post Office's magnificent mail-sorting room makes a plush rendezvous for visitors to the lately opened Penn Quarter Spy Museum; entrances in the Hotel Monaco lobby and via the Parisian-style Eighth Street courtyard give way to several airy, skylit settings in which diners can peruse the ambitious New American menu from its new young chef, Joseph Comfort.

PRIME RIB 27 | 26 | 26 | $57

2020 K St., NW (bet. 20th & 21st Sts.), 202-466-8811
■ Surprisingly "snazzy" for a lobbyists' lair, this "high-class" K Street powerhouse is nearly as famed for its "wonderful" crab imperial as for its "melt-in-your-mouth" prime rib and "reasonably" priced fine wines; amid "gleaming" lacquered walls and "fresh flowers" all about, "gentlemen and ladies" are cosseted with "royal treatment"; though some find the ambiance a bit "stuffy", most appreciate its ageless appeal and advise when you want to "feel like a character in a '50s movie", dress up (jacket and tie required) and come here.

Primi Piatti 22 | 20 | 20 | $42

2013 I St., NW (bet. 20th & 21st Sts.), 202-223-3600
◪ Favored for both a "high-powered lunch" and "corporate entertaining in the PM", this "sophisticated" trattoria brings Italy to Foggy Bottom; the "A-list" settles itself in the "attractive" indoor/outdoor dining space and "thoroughly enjoys" the "first-rate" pastas, "good" veal chop and "fresh fish" specials, but malcontents fault "unremarkable" yet "overpriced" dishes and "spotty", "uppity" service.

Prince Michel S ∇ 26 | 24 | 27 | $65

Prince Michel Vineyards, Rte. 29 S. (bet. Culpeper & Madison), Leon, VA, 540-547-9720
■ Offering a "relaxing", "lovely" "respite" on the way to Charlottesville, this petite winery showcase in "rural" Leon pairs the vineyard's "wonderful" choices with an "elegant" French menu; throughout the operation, there's an obvious "attention to detail" by a "superb" staff that "strives to please", making a trip "worthwhile", and if you "combine a meal with a stay" in one of the luxurious suites, you'll be assured of a "lovely weekend"; N.B. closed at press time for renovations and scheduled to reopen in August 2003.

Queen Bee S 20 | 11 | 17 | $21

3181 Wilson Blvd. (Washington Blvd.), Arlington, VA, 703-527-3444
◪ The interior has recently been spiffed up, but it's the "delectable" Vietnamese cooking at this "dingy" Clarendon

Washington, DC | F | D | S | C |

dowager that "keeps people coming back" for more of the "best" spring rolls; many still regard it as a "favorite" "standby", but former friends who feel it's "not what it used to be" say there are now "too many better choices" around.

Rabieng S | 25 | 17 | 20 | $25 |
Glen Forest Shopping Ctr., 5892 Leesburg Pike (Glen Forest Dr.), Bailey's Crossroads, VA, 703-671-4222

■ Billed as nearby Duangrat's less fancy (and "less expensive") "country cousin", this "amazing" Bailey's Crossroads Thai is equally distinguished for its "exciting variations" on the standards, delivering "unusual regional dishes" as well as an "innovative" take on Siamese "street food" at its weekend dim sum brunch; there's "never a dull moment" on the plate, making it "worth the big lines."

Rail Stop S | 21 | 17 | 19 | $34 |
6478 Main St. (Fauquier Ave.), The Plains, VA, 540-253-5644

◪ At this citified "country oasis" in The Plains, the pink-jacket gentry, "tourists" out for a drive and "real-life locals" gather in the "understated", rustic quarters and out on the terrace for a "solid" American repast; most find it a "charming" place to stop, but some laid-back souls resent being "rushed" over a "perfectly average" meal.

Raku S | 20 | 19 | 16 | $25 |
1900 Q St., NW (19th St.), 202-265-7258
7240 Woodmont Ave. (Elm St.), Bethesda, MD, 301-718-8681

◪ Boasting "cool" new wave decor, "hip" vibes and "scenic sidewalk cafes", these self-described Asian diners off Dupont Circle and in Bethesda keep the faithful coming with their "something-for-everyone" "finger foods" ("a wonderful adventure in eating"); fans think the concept is an "ingenious idea", but foes dub it "fusion confusion" (they "manage to make simple foods unappealing") and warn of a "meltdown when it gets crowded."

Ray's The Steaks S | – | – | – | M |
Colonial Village, 1725 Wilson Blvd. (Rhodes St.), Arlington, VA, 703-841-7297

Chef-owner Michael Landrum (aka Ray) came up with a straightforward business plan for his American bistro in Arlington: give customers what they want – charbroiled steaks and market-catch seafood – and add on thoughtful touches like hot-from-the-oven bread; in contrast to the homespun cooking, the whitewashed quarters with an open kitchen are rather stripped down, but that just allows diners to focus on the food; clearly, his idea is working.

Red Hot & Blue BBQ S | 19 | 14 | 16 | $20 |
Grove Shopping Ctr., 16811 Crabbs Branch Way (Shady Grove Rd.), Gaithersburg, MD, 301-948-7333
677 Main St. (Rte. 216), Laurel, MD, 301-953-1943

Washington, DC   F | D | S | C

(continued)
Red Hot & Blue BBQ
6482 Landsdowne Ctr. (Beulah St.), Alexandria, VA, 703-550-6465
3014 Wilson Blvd. (Highland St.), Arlington, VA, 703-243-1510
4150 Chain Bridge Rd. (Rte. 236), Fairfax, VA, 703-218-6989
Bellwood Commons Shopping Ctr., 541 E. Market St. (Plaza St.), Leesburg, VA, 703-669-4242
8366 Sudley Rd. (Irongate Way), Manassas, VA, 703-367-7100
1600 Wilson Blvd. (Pierce St.), Rosslyn, VA, 703-276-7427

◪ When you need a "barbecue fix", this Memphis-style chain of pig palaces is "quick and inexpensive" and replete with the "appropriate" decor (read: "cheesy") for down 'n' dirty "messy" eating; many are satisfied with the "tasty" ribs and pulled pork ("good, solid flavors") teamed with "all the right sides" (willingly braving "indigestion" for the "great", "greasy" onion loaf), but disgruntled connoisseurs quip "no cigar."

Red Sage ●S   21 | 23 | 19 | $39
605 14th St., NW (F St.), 202-638-4444

◪ At the upstairs chili bar (known as Border Cafe) at this "funkadelic" Southwestern fantasy, Downtown dot-pros tuck into a "fast" lunch "with a kick" and "blow off steam" after work; serious business is done on the "lower level", which ("over-the-top" decor notwithstanding) "oozes mellow sophistication"; a post-Survey chef change installed Michael Greenstein (ex Cape Cod's Chillingsworth), revitalizing the Contemporary American fare and making it a food enthusiast's destination; N.B. closed Sundays from July 4–Labor Day.

Renato S   19 | 15 | 18 | $36
10120 River Rd. (Falls Rd.), Potomac, MD, 301-365-1900

◪ "Potomac's rich and famous" "drop in" at this "pricey" Italian "staple" to "see their neighbors and enjoy good pasta, chicken and fish" dishes (the signature penne Norma is "delicious"); "regulars" who regard it as "our home away from home" are "treated very well", but be forewarned that if you're an unknown, you might be made to "feel like a second-class" citizen.

Restaurant 7   – | – | – | E
8521 Leesburg Pike (Springhill Rd.), Tysons Corner, VA, 703-847-0707

Artfully crafted bar/bistro and fine-dining settings and wide-ranging New American menus accommodate most occasions and appetites at this ambitious Tysons Corner enterprise; it's awash in marble, granite, cherrywood, mosaics and rich fabrics and boasts most every gastronomic accoutrement, from a wood-burning pizza oven to a dramatic glass-walled wine room – all designed to lure the area's techies and business high-rollers.

Washington, DC | F | D | S | C |

Restaurant 2941 S | – | – | – | E |
2941 Fairview Park Dr. (Arlington Blvd.), Falls Church, VA, 703-270-1500
Contemporary fine dining in Northern Virginia takes on new dimensions at this spacious, sophisticated venue with a seasonal American menu that reflects chef Jonathan Krinn's work with Gerard Panguad (Gerard's Place) and at Gramercy Tavern in NYC; few locales offer such picturesque prospects as this one does from its posh tables and terrace (overlooking Fairview Lake), and private entertaining is enhanced by waterfall and garden views.

R.F.D. Washington S | – | – | – | M |
810 Seventh St., NW (bet. H & I Sts.), 202-289-2030
The regional food and drink of the Chesapeake Bay is the focus of this new American bistro (a spin-off of DC's legendary Brickskeller) that has turned the Chinatown site last occupied by Coco Loco into a spacious outlet for sampling beers and brew-based dishes such as mussels steamed in lager, which can be washed down with your choice of 30 drafts or 270 bottles.

Rhodeside Grill S | 16 | 14 | 16 | $22 |
1836 Wilson Blvd. (Rhodes St.), Arlington, VA, 703-243-0145
☑ "Unassuming on the outside", this Courthouse-area bar with a "strong neighborhood feel" features "Hopper-like scenes of Arlington and a wacky mural on the back wall" inside, providing an artistic backdrop for "creative", if "a bit erratic", bar dining and a few New American dishes that "can surprise you" (the shrimp and grits in "spicy gravy" is "awesome").

Rico y Rico | ∇ 19 | 21 | 19 | $41 |
Rio Entertainment Ctr., 9811 Washingtonian Blvd. (Sam Eig Hwy.), Gaithersburg, MD, 301-330-6611
☑ This "pretty", airy rendezvous replete with a waterside patio and periodic live harp music is Gaithersburg's "Saturday night date" restaurant; not only does it feature contemporary International dishes with "style" (especially the Spanish-type tapas), but it boasts an "excellent wine program", though foes feel it "needs to work out some problems with the menu" and the service.

Rio Grande Cafe S | 21 | 17 | 18 | $23 |
4919 Fairmont Ave. (Old Georgetown Rd.), Bethesda, MD, 301-656-2981
231 Rio Blvd. (Washingtonian Blvd.), Gaithersburg, MD, 240-632-2150
4301 N. Fairfax Dr. (Glebe Rd.), Arlington, VA, 703-528-3131
Reston Town Ctr., 1827 Library St. (New Dominion Pkwy.), Reston, VA, 703-904-0703
☑ Hungry hordes fortify themselves with "great chips", "smoky" salsa and "out-of-this-world" swirlies during the

Washington, DC F | D | S | C |

"long wait" for a table at these wildly "popular" cantinas; once seated, they dig into "dependable" Tex-Mex standards (notably the "area's best fajitas") served at a "decent" price by a "kid-friendly" staff; though it may be a "chain", amigos say it has "its act down", but detractors are turned off by the "zoo-like" atmosphere.

Ristorante La Perla S — | — | — | VE |
2600 Pennsylvania Ave., NW (26th St.), 202-333-1767
Hand-painted tiles, a fountain, friezes and other plush appointments set the tone at this Italian fine-dining spot at the gateway to Georgetown; the formal setting is warmed by chef-owner Vittorio Testa's ebullience and the rich recipes that earned him a devoted following at his previous venue in McLean; a private dining room, with panoramic Potomac river views, is both inviting and impressive – like having your own palazzo for the night.

Ristorante Murali — | — | — | E |
901 Ninth St., NW (I St.), 202-371-0681
1101 S. Joyce St. (Washington Blvd.), Pentagon City, VA, 703-415-0411 S
Romantic murals of Venice (in Virginia) and ancient Rome (in DC) dominate these ornate Italians outfitted with plush appointments that evoke their heritage; classic antipasti, pastas and entrées can be sampled in a variety of settings – in Downtown's Victorian mirrored lounge or at its dressy tables, and in the Pentagon City branch's airy dining room, in the courtyard 'piazza' or at its open kitchen counter, where patrons can check out cooks rolling noodles, made in-house every day.

Ritz-Carlton, The Grill (Pentagon City) S 24 | 25 | 24 | $52 |
1250 S. Hayes St. (bet. Army Navy Dr. & 15th St.), Pentagon City, VA, 703-412-2760
■ There's "not an 'i' left undotted" at this "elegant" New American–Continental hotel dining room in Pentagon City, where one goes "to be pampered and not rushed"; its "quiet, classy" surroundings are "quite conducive to conducting both serious love or serious business" over lunch or dinner, while its formal afternoon tea and "elaborate" Sunday brunch provide "terrific" excuses to "get together" with friends; a few windows wouldn't hurt, but nothing's perfect.

Ritz-Carlton, The Grill (Washington, DC) S 20 | 25 | 21 | $53 |
1150 22nd St., NW (bet. L & M Sts.), 202-835-0500
◪ Exemplifying the "Ritz-Carlton's effortlessly elegant style", this New American grill in the West End is as "beautiful" as you've come to expect from such a prestigious hotel chain; as for the food, however, the consensus is that it's generally "good, if not truly outstanding" (though the

Washington, DC | F | D | S | C |

"superb" Sunday champagne brunch buffet garners praise), leading skeptics to conclude "all style, little substance."

Robert's S | – | – | – | M |
Omni Shoreham Hotel, 2500 Calvert St., NW (Connecticut Ave.), 202-756-5300
"Elegant yet comfortable", with soft lights, mirrored walls and a "terrace with a view of the beautifully landscaped grounds", this spacious New American hotel dining room in Woodley Park may not be that well known, but those who have visited it recommend its "interesting" menu, "exceptional" resort-like setting and "moderate prices."

Rocklands S | 22 | 11 | 15 | $17 |
2418 Wisconsin Ave., NW (Calvert St.), 202-333-2558
4000 Fairfax Dr. (Quincy St.), Arlington, VA, 703-528-9663
◼ "Why heat up your grill" when you can get "bone-sucking good" BBQ ("made like they care"), as well as "great" Texas corn pudding, the "best" baked beans and even some "unusual" "fixings", ready to go from this Georgetown pit?; if you're in the Arlington area, there's a sit-down outpost tucked away inside the CarPool billiards parlor, which offers "tunes, pool and pick-up possibilities" along with the ribs.

Roof Terrace at the Kennedy Center S | 17 | 21 | 18 | $43 |
Kennedy Ctr., 2700 F St., NW (bet. New Hampshire & Virginia Aves.), 202-416-8555
◼ "Convenient" for an event at Kennedy Center, this rooftop New American lets you "check out the monuments" while you sup; even if the "passable" dinner menu doesn't "live up" to the "spectacular view", the Sunday brunch is "terrific", with guests trooping though the kitchen and piling up their plates along the way; N.B. closed at press time for renovations but expected to reopen in September 2003.

RT's S | 23 | 14 | 20 | $32 |
3804 Mt. Vernon Ave. (Glebe Rd.), Alexandria, VA, 703-684-6010
◼ "Tons of character", "lots of hustle and bustle" distinguish this "time-warp" saloon in Alexandria, where the "solid" kitchen turns out "fabulous" New Orleans–style cooking (especially seafood like "awesome Jack Daniel's shrimp") that's heavy on "rich sauces"; fusspots may gripe that it can take a "long time to get your calories here", but if you want a taste of what this town once was, this is the place.

RUTH'S CHRIS STEAK HOUSE S | 24 | 23 | 23 | $49 |
1801 Connecticut Ave., NW (S St.), 202-797-0033
724 Ninth St., NW (H St.), 202-393-4488
7315 Wisconsin Ave. (Elm St.), Bethesda, MD, 301-652-7877
2231 Crystal Dr. (23rd St.), Crystal City, VA, 703-979-7275
◼ At this "classy" temple of meat, they sure know how to put the "sizzle" in steak, so prepare to "sink your teeth into"

Washington, DC | F | D | S | C |

a "wonderfully" "decadent" "hunk of beef"; "dressing up seems right" in such a luxurious atmosphere (suitable for business entertaining and "special occasions" alike), but critical carnivores feel the experience doesn't "rate the hype or the prices" (though they don't seem to complain if "the company is paying"); P.S. the Crystal City venue affords a "breathtaking view" of DC sparkling with lights.

Saigon Asia S | – | – | – | I |
3811 N. Fairfax Dr. (bet. Glebe & Nelson Rds.), Arlington, VA, 703-243-5454
Warm and inviting, this newcomer brings an interesting menu of traditional Vietnamese and nouveau Asian dishes to Arlington's Virginia Square; the attractive, mahogany-accented interior features charming touches like rickshaws turned into wine carts, while in the kitchen chef Vu Anh Nguyen (father of proprietor Jessica Tonthat, who also owns Saigon Saigon) gives grilled meats and fish a fusion flair.

Saigonnais S | 22 | 15 | 19 | $24 |
2307 18th St., NW (bet. Belmont & Columbia Rds.), 202-232-5300
■ You'll find all the familiar "favorites" ("excellent spring rolls", "tasty lemongrass beef") plus more at this "small, comfortable" Adams Morgan Vietnamese with dishes made from "high-quality ingredients"; let the "super-friendly owner" help you choose "something new to try" from the "varied" menu that reflects Saigon's cosmopolitan culture.

Saigon Saigon S | – | – | – | M |
Pentagon Row, 1101 S. Joyce St. (Army Navy Dr.), Pentagon City, VA, 703-412-0822
Offering a sliver of serenity amid the new Pentagon Row sprawl, this Vietnamese pleases the eye with soothing tones, unusual accent pieces and soft lighting, while pleasing the palate with mostly traditional country-style dishes (with "good flavors") complemented by daily specials and a few fusion touches such as steak flambéed in a Cabernet sauce.

Sakana | 23 | 15 | 18 | $27 |
2026 P St., NW (bet. 20th & 21st Sts.), 202-887-0900
◪ An open "neighborhood secret" shared by Dupont Circle's old guard and "Gen Y" is the "excellent" sushi prepared at this easy-to-miss basement Japanese; in a "small room that feels like Tokyo", "entertaining chefs" please the cognoscenti with "non-Americanized" raw-fish selections, along with "wonderful seaweed salad", "yummy bento boxes" and "interesting" specials, though detractors conclude "good but not worth going out of your way."

Saki ◐ S | – | – | – | M |
2477 18th St., NW (bet. Belmont & Columbia Rds.), 202-232-5005
This ultra-sleek Asian grill and lounge brings the technology, space-age decor and relaxed seating found in Europe's

Washington, DC F | D | S | C

trendiest clubs to the 18th Street strip in Adams Morgan; its menu of small-plate selections, sushi and sashimi is as cutting-edge as the kinetic lighting (panels on the wall and atop a bar are constantly changing color) and the nightly DJ music ranging from acid rock to future funk, broken beat and hip-hop.

Sakoontra S ▽ 21 | 20 | 19 | $23
Costco Plaza, 12300 Price Club Plaza, Bldg. C (W. Ox Rd.), Fairfax, VA, 703-818-8886

■ "Colorful" and "playful", this "friendly" Fairfax Thai charms youngsters with the tuk-tuk "buggy" (brought over from Bangkok) parked inside the front door while satisfying their elders with "consistently good" food at a "decent" price; boosters swear that everything on the extensive menu is "great", but they especially "love the duck salad."

Sala Thai S 19 | 15 | 18 | $22
3507 Connecticut Ave., NW (Ordway St.), 202-237-2777
2016 P St., NW (bet. 20th & 21st Sts.), 202-872-1144
4828 Cordell Ave. (Wisconsin Ave.), Bethesda, MD, 301-654-4676
2900 N. 10th St. (Washington Blvd.), Arlington, VA, 703-465-2900

■ Earning a cult following with "out-of-the-ordinary" dishes filled with "big tastes" (a request for 'Bangkok hot' is taken seriously), this Thai quartet is a "treat" according to fans but "nothing special" to minority foes; while the menu is similar at the four branches, the settings are very different – the "subterranean" Dupont Circle flagship has a *Twilight Zone* feel, the Arlington outlet is "nice" in a suburban way; the Cleveland Park yearling is modish and the new Bethesda locale (formerly Andaman) is spare and avant-garde.

Sam & Harry's 24 | 22 | 24 | $50
1200 19th St., NW (bet. M & N Sts.), 202-296-4333
8240 Leesburg Pike (Chain Bridge Rd.), Tysons Corner, VA, 703-448-0088

■ For most locals, this pair of hometown steakhouses is "the class of its class", and they'll choose it every time over the chain beef barns because the atmosphere is "less pretentious" and you'll always "encounter interesting people" at the bar; while the Golden Triangle cornerstone still pulls in a "power" crowd, the Tysons Corner offshoot is now just a bit "quieter after the dot-com bust", but both are known for "mouthwatering" prime cuts backed by an "awesome wine" cellar and "smart" service – making special events even more so.

Saveur S – | – | – | E
2218 Wisconsin Ave., NW (Calvert St.), 202-333-5885
This "charming" Upper Georgetown bistro continues to be a "good date place", even if the proprietors need to "work

Washington, DC

F | **D** | **S** | **C**

out some kinks"; as for the New French–Californian menu, reports are that many of the dishes – notably bouillabaisse, rack of lamb with garlic mousseline and tuna with miso sauce – are a "pleasant surprise", while the chocolate fondant is simply "unbelievable."

Savino's Cafe & Lounge —|—|—|M

1 Dupont Circle (New Hampshire Ave.), 202-872-1122
Savino Racine (Finemondo, Primi Piatti) introduces Dupont Circle to sophisticated cafe/lounge dining with a modern Italian menu and cocktails with exotic ingredients (like 24K gold dust) and blush-worthy names; amid various svelte settings, sippers and suppers can listen to Racine's collection of unusual world music while state-of-the-art acoustics (adjustable for each table) let them whisper sweet nothings or hold meaningful conversations.

Sea Catch 21|21|19|$42

Canal Sq., 1054 31st St., NW (M St.), 202-337-8855
■ "Enchanting" summertime dining on a deck overlooking the C&O barge canal hooks in schools of fans at this "civilized" retreat in Georgetown; the seafood menu stars "fresh", "well-prepared" fish, plus there's a "spectacular" raw bar and "good happy-hour deals"; admirers consider it an "excellent choice" for grilled fin fare, and while skeptics carp about "too casual" service and too upscale pricing, locals cool out on summer evenings in its courtyard.

SEASONS S 25|26|26|$57

Four Seasons Hotel, 2800 Pennsylvania Ave., NW (28th St.), 202-944-2000
■ "Elegant in every respect", this "especially attractive" hotel dining room in Georgetown "maintains the high standards of the Four Seasons"; appointed with every "luxurious" detail, it promises "a wonderful experience" – from the "relaxing" ambiance to the "comfortably spaced tables" to the "impeccable" service; the "toque sits well" on chef Doug Anderson, whose New American menus are "imaginative" and "superb", and who has made the Sunday brunch more "incredible" than ever; a recent $2 million renovation created dramatic special-event settings.

Sequoia ☾S 16|24|16|$35

Washington Harbour, 3000 K St., NW (30th St.), 202-944-4200
■ "Who can resist dining outdoors overlooking the Potomac River in the summertime?" ask defenders of this "overpriced hangout" that's "always overrun" with thirtysomethings "looking for someone" at sunset, as well as "tourists" joining the action; clearly, the "uninspired" American menu is merely an "afterthought", but that doesn't deter the many whose main objective is to "people-watch" and take in the "unbelievable" "view."

vote at zagat.com

Washington, DC F | D | S | C

Sesto Senso 20 | 18 | 18 | $35
1214 18th St., NW (bet. Jefferson Pl. & M St.), 202-785-9525
◪ A "high Euro-chic quotient" may explain why this "trendy club" below Dupont Circle doesn't register more strongly on foodies' radar screens, but insiders attest that the Northern Italian menu is "authentic" and "surprisingly affordable" ("don't miss the grilled calamari" or "excellent pastas"); "good for business lunches" during the day, it "turns into Mr. Hyde in the evenings", with a "hip" "bar scene" and "late-night dancing" on the weekends.

701 S 23 | 23 | 23 | $45
701 Pennsylvania Ave., NW (7th St.), 202-393-0701
■ For a "great swanky night out" in the Penn Quarter, replete with "caviar and champagne" at its svelte new raw bar and "quiet jazz", it's hard to beat this "perpetual" New American favorite where "elegant is done right"; patrons are treated like "grown-ups" in a "sophisticated" setting that permits conversation while dining on "tasteful" dishes served by a "knowledgeable" team; delivering "true value for the quality", it "rarely disappoints."

Seven Seas ◐S 21 | 12 | 17 | $24
Federal Plaza, 1776 E. Jefferson St. (bet. Montrose Rd. & Rollins Ave.), Rockville, MD, 301-770-5020
◪ "Ask for the red menu, which has all the good Chinese stuff" (including Taiwanese specialties), advise those in-the-know about this modest Rockville Asian; you can be assured that the "whole fish dishes are terrific" because you can see the ingredients swimming in the tanks, but the more "unusual" seafood selections are worth "trying" too (sushi is also available at dinner); critics, however, gripe that the "seedy" digs "need a face-lift" and caution that service isn't as "organized as it should be."

1789 S 26 | 25 | 25 | $53
1226 36th St., NW (Prospect St.), 202-965-1789
■ Much, much more than just a "place to take your visiting parents", this "inviting" Federal period piece in Georgetown provides "formality" "without intimidation"; "genius" chef Ris Lacoste deftly "blends" old and new seasonal American recipes into "top-notch" renditions (her "superb" rack of lamb makes sure that "food is the star of the show" here), while the "outstanding" staff "goes out of its way for guests"; it's a "splurge", but the prix fixe menus are a "steal."

Shula's Steak House S 20 | 18 | 18 | $46
Wyndham City Center, 1143 New Hampshire Ave., NW (M St.), 202-828-7762
Tysons Corner Marriott Hotel, 8028 Leesburg Pike (Old Gallows Rd.), Tysons Corner, VA, 703-506-3256
◪ Owned by Don Shula, the most winning coach in NFL history, these beefy players are "macho" "shrines" that

Washington, DC | F | D | S | C |

score with "too large portions" of "competently" prepared certified angus steaks; boosters approve of the "well-appointed" space, decorated with memorabilia from his Dolphins days, but opponents pass on the hokey hand-"painted football menu" and pre-game show of raw meat.

Signatures — | — | — | VE
801 Pennsylvania Ave., NW (9th St.), 202-628-5900
A Penn Quarter lair for lawyers, lobbyists and legislators, this handsome haunt is abuzz from morning till late at night – especially since chef Morou Ouattara (ex Red Sage) added his bold imprimatur to its New American menu featuring seasonal and luxury ingredients and fashionable sushi (which can be delivered to your door); N.B. the moniker refers to its noteworthy collection of historical memorabilia, many signed, all for sale.

Simply Fish S — | — | — | M
1700 Fern St. (Kenwood St.), Alexandria, VA, 703-998-6616
Fish shadows swimming up the wall and a fanciful mermaid mural dress up this sprightly marine-blue Alexandria seafooder where fin fanciers can choose a fish ($14–$16), a cooking method (sautéed, steamed, grilled, broiled or blackened) and, if desired, one of 10 eclectic toppings, which range from Thai coconut curry to Argentine chimichurri; there are also plenty of starters, side dishes and choices for vegetarians and carnivores, all developed by consulting chef Christie Velie (ex Cafe Atlantico).

Siné ●S — | — | — | M
1301 S. Joyce St. (Army Navy Dr.), Arlington, VA, 703-415-4420
Located on Arlington's newly minted Pentagon Row (next to the Pentagon City Mall), this handsome, spacious establishment provides a number of settings – convivial bars, alcoves and booths, a pair of patios, even fireside tables – in which to hoist a glass (expect a wide selection of brews and malts); for ballast, the kitchen turns out hearty English-Irish specialties such as shepherd's pie, beer-battered fish 'n' chips and nachos spun with a Celtic twist (they're made with fried potatoes).

Singh Thai S — | — | — | I
2311 Wilson Blvd. (N. Wayne St.), Arlington, VA, 703-312-7118
The owners of this modish, bite-size Courthouse Thai camouflage the firepower of their assertively seasoned food with welcoming smiles and a serene salmon setting; the combination of highly flavored fare and moderate prices should give the neighborhood something to sing about.

Skewers/Cafe Luna S 20 | 16 | 18 | $20
1633 P St., NW (bet. 16th & 17th Sts.), 202-387-7400
◼ Two restaurants in one, this "indispensable" Dupont Circle East staple gives diners an option: head upstairs if

Washington, DC

you're in the mood for "good" kebabs and other "healthy, tasty" Middle Eastern dishes that are suitable for "sharing", served in quarters that are a little "cramped" but long on atmosphere; or stay on the ground floor if you're looking for "quick, fresh" Italian fare like pastas and pizzas; either way, you'll find "interesting people to watch."

Smith & Wollensky ◐ S — 21 | 20 | 21 | $48
1112 19th St., NW (bet. L & M Sts.), 202-466-1100
■ Situated on "angus alley" in the Golden Triangle, this "consistently good" Big Apple import appeals to a somewhat "younger" (in spirit, anyway) crowd with its "beautiful cuts" of prime meat, "excellent" wine list and "try-harder" ethic; the "grill has all the cholesterol, at a cheaper price", making it an "informal alternative to the rather stuffy dining room side", while the sidewalk cafe is "wonderful" in clement weather.

Smith Point ◐ — - | - | - | M
1338 Wisconsin Ave., NW (O St.), 202-333-9003
An underground find (in more ways than one), this Georgetown basement hideaway was designed with Nantucket in mind (it's named after a beach on that island) – an inspiration reflected in its flagstone patio-like setting, casual schedule (open Wednesday–Saturday nights) and chef David Scribner's ever-changing farm-fresh American menu; though it's still a sleeper, the word is spreading.

Sorak Garden S — ▽ 22 | 16 | 13 | $27
4308 Backlick Rd. (Little River Tpke.), Annandale, VA, 703-916-7600
■ "One of the better places in the area for Korean food", this spacious, "affordable" Annandale standby features a "great variety" of "tasty", "authentic" dishes including BBQ kalbi, bulgoki and bibimbop; supporters say it's a "lovely food experience", but foes complain about "slapdash" service.

South Beach S — - | - | - | M
7904 Woodmont Ave. (bet. Fairmont & St. Elmo Aves.), Bethesda, MD, 301-718-9737
Pastel colors and art deco motifs make a festive backdrop for "gracious" chef-owner John Richardson's "fresh and airy" Miami beachhead in Bethesda; just as "lively" as the setting is his "creative" menu inspired by the cuisines of Florida and Cuba; in addition to street-level dining, there's an upstairs lounge that features colorful drinks, flavorful bites and salsa dancing (on Sundays), making it one of the "hottest" late-night scenes around.

Spezie — 22 | 20 | 19 | $39
1736 L St., NW (bet. Connecticut Ave. & 18th St.), 202-467-0777
■ This "worthy" entry in DC's "already crowded field of modern Italians" "showcases" owner Enzo Livia's (Il Pizzico)

Washington, DC F | D | S | C

"range" as a chef; at lunchtime, Golden Triangle lawyers and lobbyists congregate over "delicious pastas" in an "elegant" space with lots of elbow room; though there's "nothing really surprising on the menu", advocates say "that doesn't detract from the pleasure of dining here", but faultfinders feel "there's room for improvement."

Spices S — 20 | 17 | 18 | $25
3333A Connecticut Ave., NW (bet. Macomb & Ordway Sts.), 202-686-3833
■ Reopened after a mod makeover (a "major improvement"), this "sexy" Cleveland Park "hot" spot offers something "Asian for everybody" – from "yum yum" noodles and stir-fries to curries and sushi – and the "assortment" is so "diverse" you "won't run out of things" to try; "be prepared to sit too near" your neighbors, though, and beware that the "engaging" servers can quickly get "overburdened."

Starfish Cafe S — – | – | – | M
539 Eighth St., SE (bet. C & D Sts.), 202-546-5006
Warm and welcoming, this Capitol Hill rookie brings an "upscale" note to a burgeoning area near the Shakespeare Theatre with its "attractive" tiled bars, exposed brick and colorful art; the "ambitious" seafood-slanted menu ranges from scallop and salmon ceviche to cornmeal-crusted sea bass, making it a "good place to graze."

Starland Cafe S — 18 | 17 | 20 | $30
5125 MacArthur Blvd., NW (bet. Arizona Ave. & Dana Pl.), 202-244-9396
■ Coming up with some "interesting ideas in a contemporary setting", this "relaxing" New American in the Palisades provides an appreciated dining option – whether it be a "pleasant" lunch on the terrace or an "imaginative" Friday night dinner (try the "flavorful" fish) accompanied by "live music" – to a "mix" of young families, yuppies and their elders; though some say it's "nothing special", others retort, with few other options, "it's all it has to be."

Sushi-Ko S — 25 | 17 | 20 | $35
2309 Wisconsin Ave., NW (south of Calvert St.), 202-333-4187
■ A "Washington classic", this "memorable" Upper Georgetown Japanese "challenges your taste buds" with "still squirming" sushi and "divine" omakase meals "intelligently paired" with fine French wines; aesthetes are "disappointed" by the "stripped-down" decor ("not a good mood-setter"), but the majority embraces it as a "standard"-bearer.

Sushi Taro S — 24 | 20 | 20 | $32
1503 17th St., NW (P St.), 202-462-8999
■ Reputedly the "pick of the Japanese press corps" (and also favored by its Embassy staff), this "busy" Dupont Circle

Washington, DC F | D | S | C

East traditionalist is well respected for its "succulent sushi" (choose from a "wide selection of critters"), "fine tempura" and other "delicious entrees"; whether you sit at the long sushi bar, at a sunny window seat or in the tatami room, the "authentic" experience is like "visiting Tokyo but at a much more reasonable" price.

Sweet Basil S   23 | 19 | 22 | $29
4910 Fairmont Ave. (bet. Norfolk Ave. & Old Georgetown Rd.), Bethesda, MD, 301-657-7997

■ Definitely not "ho-hum" Thai, this "sweet" "star" on the Bethesda scene takes a "light", "creative" approach to its native cuisine, exemplified in "nontraditional" dishes like its signature grilled rack of lamb with tamarind sauce and "terrific" chicken curry pot pie; the surroundings are modern yet "not too slick", providing a compatible backdrop for the "delicately seasoned" dishes and leaving admirers eager to return "again and again."

Sweetwater Tavern S   21 | 19 | 20 | $26
14250 Sweetwater Ln. (Multiplex Dr.), Centreville, VA, 703-449-1100
3066 Gatehouse Plaza Dr. (bet. Gallows Rd. & Rte. 50), Merrifield, VA, 703-645-8100
45980 Waterview Plaza (Loudon Tech Dr. & Rte. 7), Sterling, VA, 571-434-6500

■ At these "congenial" cowboy country–themed brewpubs (the "beer sampler is a must") in Northern Virginia, "value-conscious" diners stampede in for "tasty" Southwestern favorites like hickory-smoked babybacks, "drunken" rib-eye steak and the "great chocolate waffle dessert"; popularity notwithstanding, detractors find the menu "predictable", the noise "deafening" and the service too "fast-paced."

Tabard Inn S   22 | 23 | 21 | $38
Hotel Tabard Inn, 1739 N St., NW (bet. 17th & 18th Sts.), 202-331-8528

■ "Quirky, charming" and filled with "funky antiques", this Dupont Circle "delight" is as much "about mood" as the "creative" New American food; the courtyard is a "refreshing hideaway" and the dining room is a "genteel" haven, but many "particularly cherish" "rendezvousing" by the "roaring fire" in the lounge while "drinking wine, eating cheese and making the world a better place"; those not smitten, however, snipe about "tired", "uneven" food that's "less than inspiring."

TABERNA DEL ALABARDERO   25 | 26 | 25 | $52
1776 I St., NW (18th St.), 202-429-2200

■ "Old-world Spain comes alive" at this "gorgeous" "standout" near the World Bank, where "you can be romantic or all business" and still have a "memorable" meal; at the bar, the "international elite sips wine and eats

Washington, DC | F | D | S | C |

tapas", while earthy regional dishes and contemporary updates are served "with flair" in the "sumptuous" dining rooms by a "pampering" staff; N.B. its new top toque, Enrique Sanchez, worked closely with now-retired chef Josu Zubikarai in its kitchen and is expected to maintain the same high standards.

Tachibana S | 25 | 16 | 19 | $32 |
6715 Lowell Ave. (Emerson Ave.), McLean, VA, 703-847-1771

■ "Die-hard fans fill the sushi bar" at this "unaffectedly unstylish" McLean Japanese known for its "impressive variety" of "high-quality" selections (check the specials, but don't miss the "best" spicy tuna or scallop roll); the "sashimi lunch is invariably fresh, generously sliced" and more than fairly priced, plus the kitchen turns out "consistently good" cooked dishes, which compensates for the sometimes "indifferent" service.

Tako Grill S | 23 | 17 | 19 | $28 |
7756 Wisconsin Ave. (Cheltenham Dr.), Bethesda, MD, 301-652-7030

■ In Bethesda's increasingly cosmopolitan dining hub, this established "neighborhood" favorite continues to please connoisseurs with its "fresh" sushi and sashimi, but it's the other Japanese specialties – "excellent" tempura, nabeyaki and especially the "unique" robatayaki (grilled vegetables, fish or meats) – that draw a wider audience; while a few fear that "overpopularity has taken its toll", most feel that it has actually "improved" over the years.

Tandoori Nights S | – | – | – | M |
106 Market St. (Kentlands Blvd.), Gaithersburg, MD, 301-947-4007

Fanciful murals, svelte appointments, a modish bar and a menu of healthfully prepared Indian favorites distinguish this "classy" new addition to the cosmopolitan Kentlands Market Square dining mix; choices abound for meat lovers and vegetarians alike, presented in an upscale atmosphere that works for both socializing and business, leading locals to proclaim it a "don't miss."

Taqueria Poblano S | ▽ 23 | 14 | 19 | $17 |
2400B Mt. Vernon Ave. (Oxford Ave.), Alexandria, VA, 703-548-8226
2503 N. Harrison St. (Lee Hwy.), Arlington, VA, 703-237-8250

■ "Colorful and cheerful", this "family"-friendly Del Ray Mexican outpost is "full of charm"; "fantastic" tacos and other "delicious" "California-style" items reflect the LA-raised owner's commitment to "authenticity" and quality; though the compact quarters can get "too crowded", the dining is "delightful in the summertime, when you can sit outside" in the sidewalk cafe; the cleverly designed Arlington spin-off has more elbow room.

vote at zagat.com

Tara Thai [S] 21 | 20 | 19 | $24

4828 Bethesda Ave. (bet. Arlington Rd. & Woodmont Ave.), Bethesda, MD, 301-657-0488
9811 Washingtonian Blvd. (Sam Eig Hwy.), Gaithersburg, MD, 301-947-8330
12071 Rockville Pike (Montrose Rd.), Rockville, MD, 301-231-9899
4001 Fairfax Dr. (bet. Quincy & Randolph Sts.), Arlington, VA, 703-908-4999
7501E Leesburg Pike (Pimmit Dr.), Falls Church, VA, 703-506-9788
226 Maple Ave. W. (bet. Lawyers Rd. & Nutley St.), Vienna, VA, 703-255-2467

◪ "Radioactive" "under-the-sea" decor and "pretty plates" are the eye-catching attractions at these wildly popular Thai mainstays whose "well-priced", "solid" fare provides a "satisfying experience" for the "masses"; critics may knock their success, citing "sanitized" flavors and a "rushed" "fast-food" feel, but the heavy traffic gives them some credibility.

Taste of Morocco [S] – | – | – | M

3211 N. Washington Blvd. (Wilson Blvd.), Arlington, VA, 703-527-7468

An "intimate" refuge in Clarendon near "otherwise drab Wilson Boulevard", this "charming" Moroccan "transports guests to Casablanca" with its comfortable seating on pillowed banquettes, congenial belly dancer and "yummy" food (especially the "savory" couscous and b'steeya); it's "reasonably priced" and worth "checking out."

Taste of Saigon [S] 24 | 17 | 20 | $26

410 Hungerford Dr. (Beall Ave.), Rockville, MD, 301-424-7222
8201 Greensboro Dr. (International Dr.), Tysons Corner, VA, 703-790-0700

■ Providing an "oasis" of "comfort" in "sterile" suburban office parks in Rockville and Tysons Corner, this Vietnamese twosome "feeds you well and treats you well"; its distinctive black-pepper sauce "on anything" is so "delicious" that addicts can't bring themselves to "experiment with the rest" of the "huge", "wonderful" menu; it's a "superb value" too.

X **Teaism** 19 | 17 | 15 | $16

800 Connecticut Ave., NW (H St.), 202-835-2233
400 Eighth St., NW (D St.), 202-638-6010 [S]
2009 R St., NW (Connecticut Ave.), 202-667-3827 [S]

◪ "Stress relief" is dispensed at this trio of "Asian-esque" teahouses, which function as "college coffeehouses for post-post-grads, only with no coffee" available; instead, expect "huge mugs of satisfying chai" and a limited menu of "interesting" small plates and bento boxes presented in "coolly" "rustic" settings "best" visited during "off-times" if you're seeking a "soul-cleansing" break; nitpickers, though, quibble "a little too light on the service that would make for a truly tranquil place."

TEATRO GOLDONI 24 | 25 | 22 | $50

1909 K St., NW (bet. 19th & 20th Sts.), 202-955-9494

◪ At this "sophisticated", "eye-catching" "carnival" on K Street, chef-owner Fabrizio Aielli promises the "'in' crowd" a "full evening of entertainment", showing off his "artistic", Venetian-inspired Nuovo Italian cooking (his lobster risotto is "amazing") and regional classics in a "gorgeous", "theatrical" space decorated with a wall of vintage masks and colorful glass panels that pay homage to Harlequins; fans applaud this "feel-good" "star", but critics pan it as "hit-or-miss", reserving special barbs for the "pretentious" service.

Temel [S] ▽ 24 | 19 | 21 | $28

3232 Old Pickett Rd. (Old Lee Hwy.), Fairfax, VA, 703-352-5477

■ "Let's keep this one a secret" plead those in-the-know about this "hidden jewel" tucked away in a nondescript Fairfax "strip mall" ("another case of don't judge a book by its cover"); it's a "real surprise" for "delicious, authentic" Turkish meals served in an "attractive, comfortable" space (replete with "relaxing" waterfalls) by "hospitable" people at a "good value."

Tempo [S] 23 | 19 | 22 | $38

4231 Duke St. (Gordon St.), Alexandria, VA, 703-370-7900

◪ Some of the "best fine-dining for the money" can be had at this Alexandria "winner" where "imaginatively prepared" Italian (with a touch of French) "classics" are presented in a "converted gas station"; despite the "noisy" acoustics and occasionally "overwhelmed" service, "regular customers feel really appreciated" and just "love" the "unpretentious" ambiance.

TENPENH 25 | 25 | 23 | $45

1001 Pennsylvania Ave., NW (10th St.), 202-393-4500

◪ "Atmosphere and attitude" reign at one of Downtown's most glamorous "destinations", a pastiche of Pan-Asian visuals and victuals where the "beautiful people" are part of the show; don't think for a second, though, that the food is secondary, because Jeff Tunks' crew will "astonish" your taste buds with his "clever, creative" plays on the cuisines of Thailand, Vietnam, China, the Philippines and beyond, presenting his dishes as works of "art" on a plate; still, holdouts hoot "too bad you can't eat hipness."

Terrazza 22 | 19 | 21 | $41

2 Wisconsin Circle (Western Ave.), Chevy Chase, MD, 301-951-9292

◪ "Hidden away" on the terrace level of a Friendship Heights office building, this "spacious" Northern Italian caters to discriminating palates with the "best" grilled calamari, "great" pumpkin agnolotti and "first-rate" saltimbocca;

Washington, DC | F | D | S | C |

the unconverted, however, feel that "something's flat" about some of the dishes and caution that while there's "lots of room", it gets "loud" fast if "large parties" are present.

T.H.A.I. ⓢ | 23 | 21 | 21 | $24 |
Village at Shirlington, 4029 28th St. S. (Randolph St.), Arlington, VA, 703-931-3203

◪ At this eye-catching Thai in Shirlington, the "modern" design, theatrical lighting and bold colors form an "arty" backdrop for the kitchen's "inventive", "spicy" plates; though traditionalists may shake their heads, partisans insist that the "truly beautiful dishes taste as good as they look" and give kudos too to the "sweet staff that aims to please"; P.S. the "big bowl lunch special is a bargain."

Thai Basil ⓢ | ▽ 19 | 15 | 19 | $22 |
14511 Lee Jackson Memorial Hwy. (Airline Pkwy.), Chantilly, VA, 703-631-8277

■ "Hard to find but well worth the effort", this "authentic Thai surprise south of Dulles airport" in Chantilly justifies the journey with its "consistently" "fine" dishes ("try the curries" and what may be the definitive version of pad Thai), some of which are "not found on menus" elsewhere; though the digs are a little "plain", they're brightened up by artifacts from the homeland.

Thai Farm ⓢ | - | - | - | I |
800 King Farm Blvd. (Redland Blvd.), Rockville, MD, 301-258-8829

Sprouting amid the townhouses in Rockville's King Farm development, this stylish Thai seedling reflects savvy spadework by management formerly connected with Sakoontra (in Fairfax, VA); its stylish design – an imaginative, painted backdrop of verdant fields – heralds a vegetarian-friendly menu with uncommon salads, stir-fries without fish sauce and a versatile menu where most items can be prepared with veggies only or with beef, poultry or fish.

Thaiphoon ⓢ | 19 | 17 | 16 | $23 |
2011 S St., NW (20th St.), 202-667-3505
Pentagon Row, 1301 S. Joy St. (Pentagon Row Pl.), Pentagon City, VA, 703-413-8200

◪ "Exciting as a good first date" and "crowded as Bangkok", this "slick" Thai bistro above Dupont Circle (and its unrated Pentagon Row young sister) seduces with "urban" "energy" and a "well-designed" space, not to mention its "extensive", "satisfying" menu; the DC locale's detractors, though, don't like getting "squeezed" into a "closely packed table", nor the "hurry-up attitude", and deem the dishes "underwhelming."

Thai Tanic ⓢ | - | - | - | I |
1326A 14th St., NW (bet. N St. & Rhode Island Ave.), 202-588-1795

Off Logan Circle in DC's little Theater District, this sparkly Thai youngster plays to a diverse audience of ticket-holders,

Washington, DC F | D | S | C

artistic types, urban pioneers and recently arrived local gentry with agreeably priced standards like curries, stir-fries and noodle and rice preparations; its witty presentations, playful moniker, theatrical decor and interesting people-watching ensure an entertaining meal.

Thanh Thanh S ▽ 22 | 17 | 21 | $19
11423 Georgia Ave. (University Blvd.), Wheaton, MD, 301-962-3530

■ Achieving pure "depths of flavor", this Vietnamese "treasure" in Wheaton "will change your whole sense of what fish" should taste like after one bite (also a must is the "memorable crispy quail" and "phenomenal pho"); "charming" and unassuming, not even a "small language barrier" detracts from the "pleasant" experience, making it a "great", "cheap" "escape" that's "so not DC."

That's Amore S 16 | 15 | 17 | $27
1699 Rockville Pike (Halpine Rd.), Rockville, MD, 301-881-7891
15201 Shady Grove Rd. (Research Blvd.), Rockville, MD, 301-670-9666
46300 Potomac Run Plaza (Cascades Pkwy.), Sterling, VA, 703-406-4900
Danor Plaza, 150 Branch Rd., SE (Maple Ave.), Vienna, VA, 703-281-7777

◪ "Mega-size" platters of Southern Italian food (with "garlic in everything") dished up *famiglia* style (individual portions are available too) plus handy suburban locales make these "festive" (or "hectic") "mass-market" halls useful for "family" dining; while they attract heavy traffic, though, gourmands shrug the "food didn't make me feel the love."

Thyme Square S 19 | 18 | 18 | $28
4735 Bethesda Ave. (Woodmont Ave.), Bethesda, MD, 301-657-9077

◪ A "cheery" pit stop for cyclists and other "healthy types", this New American "vegetarian's dream" just "off the bike path" in Bethesda features a "wide range" of "interesting" dishes based on organic ingredients and wholesome cooking techniques (no deep-frying, for example); for all its good intentions, however, many find the preparations too "erratic" ("either delicious or a dud") and the service "eager" but rather "untrained", leading sympathizers to "want it to be better than it is"; a juice bar has recently been added.

Timpano Italian Chophouse S 18 | 18 | 18 | $32
12021 Rockville Pike (Montrose Rd.), Rockville, MD, 301-881-6939

◪ "Sinatra would feel right at home" at this "dark" "Las Vegas"-in-the-suburbs Italian steakhouse in Rockville that's filled with martini sippers and swing-night strutters (third Thursdays); while many concede that the food is

Washington, DC | F | D | S | C |

"pretty good", sticklers caution that there's "more ambiance than authenticity" (expect a "theme-park feel") at work at this "wanna-be."

Tivoli | 22 | 19 | 21 | $37 |
1700 N. Moore St. (Wilson Blvd.), Rosslyn, VA, 703-524-8900
☒ "Year after year", a mature audience in Rosslyn has regarded this "step back in time" as a "comfortable friend" thanks to its "consistently well-served" Continental and Northern Italian dishes, "fine European" pastries and award-winning wine list; though the "rich" fare may be "a diet-destroyer" and the room a bit "dated", loyalists insist it's an "often overlooked" "treat" for a "traditional" meal.

Toka Cafe ● | – | – | – | E |
1140 19th St., NW (M St.), 202-429-8652
White-on-white color treatments, reflective surfaces and cleverly sculpted spaces transform the basement setting of this Golden Triangle upstart into a stylish place replete with a glowing blue bar that's ideal for after-work socializing, while the Asian-tinged American menu offers something a little different from the other eateries nearby.

Tono Sushi S | 19 | 14 | 19 | $26 |
2605 Connecticut Ave., NW (Calvert St.), 202-332-7300
☒ "If you're on a budget, go for the soups" or the "great bento box lunch" deal at this "laid-back" Woodley Park Japanese, which is also known for preparing the "best" soft-shell crab roll; detractors admit to "decent sushi at a decent price" but find it "boring all around", though the "outdoor seating" may be its "redemption."

Tony & Joe's Seafood Place S | 15 | 20 | 15 | $32 |
Washington Harbour, 3000 K St., NW (30th St.), 202-944-4545
☒ "Wear Prada" if you go to this "singles'" see-and-be-seen scene set on the banks of the Potomac, which boasts a "delightful location" with a "fantastic view of the harbor"; on Friday nights in the summertime, it's like a "frat party with heels and ties", and though "they could do better" in the way of the seafood menu and the service, it doesn't seem to matter much to those focused on the "waterfront setting" and people-watching.

Tony Cheng's S | 20 | 14 | 17 | $25 |
619 H St., NW (bet. 6th & 7th Sts.), 202-842-8669
☒ "Throngs of white-collar types flock to this fun" all-you-can-eat Mongolian BBQ near the MCI Center at lunchtime and compete to see "who can load their bowl the highest"; groups and kids find the concept a "hoot", but serious eaters head to the "upstairs seafood restaurant" where they feel the daily dim sum is the "real star of the venue"; despite "cheesy" decor, this is a "piece of old Chinatown" that should be seen "before it disappears."

Topaz Bar [S] ▽ 20 | 24 | 19 | $26

Topaz Hotel, 1733 N St., NW (bet. 17th & 19th Sts.), 202-393-3000

◪ Providing a "trendy" backdrop, with "cool" (or "odd") mood lighting that shifts from iridescent red to blue to green, this "hip" lounge attracts the "somewhat young" to Dupont Circle; the Asian-flavored New American menu highlights "adventurous small plates" (make that "tiny" dishes) that are a "mix of awesome and so-so", but many "would go again" just for the "inventive" cocktails.

TOSCA [S] 26 | 24 | 23 | $53

1112 F St., NW (bet. 11th & 12th Sts.), 202-367-1990

◪ Downtown's "rising star" is this "svelte" showroom where chef Cesare Lanfranconi (ex Galileo) masterminds "fabulous" Northern Italian fare that achieves a "refined" "balance of traditional and contemporary" styles, with many dishes inspired by his native Lombardy; his tasting menu is particularly "heavenly" and the "sophisticated" dining room is a place to feel oh so "Cary Grant", but it's "still finding its way" and a few discordant notes can be detected in what a few term "arrogant" service; N.B. try the chef's table in the kitchen.

Tower Oaks Lodge [S] – | – | – | M

2 Preserve Pkwy. (bet. Tower Oaks Blvd. & Wootton Pkwy.), Rockville, MD, 301-294-0200

A woodland preserve in Rockville is the backdrop for this new American from the Clyde's Restaurant Group; Native American and sportsmen's collectibles and accoutrement fill four large rooms, whose transporting Adirondack ambiance extends from the commodious booths, carved tables and massive fireplaces to the wicker rockers on the front porch (overlooking a fish pond) – overall, a must-see extravaganza.

Tragara [S] 21 | 20 | 21 | $45

4935 Cordell Ave. (bet. Norfolk Ave. & Old Georgetown Rd.), Bethesda, MD, 301-951-4935

◪ This "special-occasion" Northern Italian in Bethesda serves the likes of osso buco to a wealthy clientele who appreciate the "upscale" menu, "fancy" surroundings and "private party" expertise; as dissenters see things, the kitchen is getting "tired" while the staff is busy "trying to look elegant rather than be elegant", but a recent renovation may improve their opinion.

Trattoria Liliana – | – | – | M

4483 Connecticut Ave., NW (bet. Albermarle St. & Windom Pl.), 202-237-0893

Liliana and Maurice Dumas' warmhearted welcome, homestyle dishes from their native Liguria (along with their favorite regional Italian dishes) and local talent John Hutson's vibrantly colored, imaginative interior with rich

Washington, DC | F | D | S | C |

fabrics, artful mirrors and window greenery have turned this Van Ness storefront into a smart neighborhood delight; N.B. save room for mouthwatering gelati and other desserts.

Tropics | – | – | – | M |
Germantown Commons Shopping Ctr., 13016 Middlebrook Rd. (Germantown Rd.), Germantown, MD, 301-972-9300
Tropical motifs evoke West Africa and the Caribbean at Vittorio and Vivian Weeks' Germantown bistro where authentic African-Caribbean fare, unusual beers, live music, readings and dancing (on weekends) draw a cosmopolitan crowd from around the beltway; its daily specials (most under $11), which feature exotic ingredients in uncommon preparations, offer a chance for gastronomic exploration.

Tryst ●S | 16 | 20 | 13 | $15 |
2459 18th St., NW (bet. Belmont & Columbia Rds.), 202-232-5500
■ For lattes at breakfast, "chunky sandwiches" at lunch, the "city's best chai" in the afternoon or cocktails during the "meat market" action at night, this "funky" coffeehouse is the "perfect social hangout" in Adams Morgan ("if you can tolerate the smoke"); nobody – "including the staff" – is "in a hurry" here, so sink into a "beat-up sofa" or perch on a "stool at the counter" and settle in for a spell.

Tuscarora Mill S | 23 | 22 | 21 | $34 |
Market Station, 203 Harrison St., SE (Loudoun St.), Leesburg, VA, 703-771-9300
■ "Tuskies", as it's affectionately called by Leesburg's "'in' crowd", is a little "like *Alice's Restaurant*" in that "you can get anything you want" to eat or drink – "lite plates", American "comfort food scaled up", "wonderful" "wine flights (great fun)", "very good beers" – all "dependably" "splendid"; "interestingly" quartered in a "charming", "beautifully" restored grain mill, it's rustic in a tony way, with a "warm" atmosphere, and "worth the drive."

2 Amys S | 22 | 14 | 17 | $22 |
3715 Macomb St., NW (Wisconsin Ave.), 202-885-5700
■ Peter Pastan's (of Obelisk renown) "very special" Italian gift brings wood-fired artisanal pies (crafted per standards set by the Verrace Pizza Napoletana trade association) to this sunny, tiled venue in Northwest DC; his "dedication" to the "authenticity" of the art is obvious, even if those weaned on Domino's find these refined pizzas a bit "bland" and "not crunchy enough"; it's living up to predictions that it is "on its way to greatness" despite the need to "work out a few kinks"; N.B. its outdoor patio is a neighborhood blessing.

219 S | 19 | 21 | 19 | $37 |
219 King St. (Fairfax St.), Alexandria, VA, 703-549-1141
■ Evoking the "atmospheric" "French Quarter", this "charming" Old Town fixture sets the stage for a "tasty"

Washington, DC

F | D | S | C

New Orleans experience with its cozy downstairs bar, "great" "upstairs jazz" lounge, "lovely" drawing rooms and "romantic" all-weather terrace; most say it's a "safe bet" for "acceptable" Cajun-Creole food, but purists proclaim it a Big Easy "knockoff."

Two Quail S
21 | 23 | 21 | $39

320 Massachusetts Ave., NE (bet. 3rd & 4th Sts.), 202-543-8030

◪ Nearly everyone "succumbs" to this "romantic" Capitol Hill "darling", which manages to endear with "eccentric", "cluttered" parlors (a cross "between Laura Ashley and a Paris bordello"), favored for "private conversations" and "proposals" of all sorts, and an English garden–style patio; "starry-eyed lovers" who have enjoyed "many happy returns" here cherish it as a "one-of-a-kind" "favorite" with "fine" American vittles (the "signature dish is quite good", natch), but lonely hearts are unmoved by it all.

Udupi Palace S
23 | 11 | 18 | $18

1329 University Blvd. E. (New Hampshire Ave.), Langley Park, MD, 301-434-1531

◪ "Authentic and delicious, not to mention cheap", a meal at this "sweet" Langley Park Indian is a "singularly satisfying" vegetarian experience; the decidedly unpalatial site "isn't much to look at" (though a recent paint job might help), but the kitchen knows what it's doing with a "stunning blend of exotic spices", with special praise reserved for its "fabulous dosas", "delicious" curries and "beautiful" desserts.

Uni S
21 | 17 | 17 | $28

2122 P St., NW (bet. 21st & 22nd Sts.), 202-833-8038

◪ "Modern sushi in a mod setting" is the calling card of this new wave "adult" Japanese off Dupont Circle, where "fresh fish" can be matched with "imaginative" small plates and trendy saketinis; though a few sense that it's "trying too hard to be hip", groupies retort that what it "lacks in quality it makes up for in originality."

Union St. Public House S
17 | 18 | 17 | $25

121 S. Union St. (bet. King & Prince Sts.), Alexandria, VA, 703-548-1785

◪ Downstairs at this all-purpose Old Town tavern near the waterfront, a young local crowd meets over microbrews and "upscale" bar food for a "boisterous" "good" time; upstairs, the "broad" Southern-accented American menu and "English pub" rusticity appeal to families and "tourists", who begin a meal with oysters from the "reliable" raw bar and follow with ribs or chicken smoked over "real wood."

U-topia ●S
18 | 19 | 17 | $25

1418 U St., NW (bet. 14th & 15th Sts.), 202-483-7669

◪ "Creativity" flows freely at this "funky", "late-night" New U social center where there's "cool rotating art" on

Washington, DC F | D | S | C

the walls, "groovy" live jazz in the air and International food on the plates; the fare is "pleasant, if unmemorable", and the staff "friendly" though "s-l-o-w", but fans "return often just for the music" and "eclectic people-watching."

Vegetable Garden S 20 | 13 | 18 | $18
11618 Rockville Pike (bet. Nicholson Ln. & Old Georgetown Rd.), Rockville, MD, 301-468-9301

■ Those who "go meatless" salute this Rockville alchemist's ability to turn soy and such into "good" approximations of their favorite Asian chicken and meat dishes; its "organic and macrobiotic" Vegetarian options make it an "'in' spot among the granola crowd", but critics who conclude that the menu pictures make the food "look more appetizing" than it tastes advise "BYOS (bring your own seasonings)."

Vida S – | – | – | M
1120 20th St., NW (bet. L & M Sts.), 202-293-5433

High ceilings, bold colors and a handsome tequila-lined bar welcome suits at lunchtime and hipsters in the evening to this festive Nuevo Latino addition in the Golden Triangle; the spacious courtyard patio is an inviting happy-hour hangout and there's a dance club upstairs, but the kitchen is serious; top toque Raynold Mendizabal Betancourt prepares Cuban-influenced dishes of roast pork, lobster and grilled fish.

VIDALIA S 26 | 23 | 24 | $51
1990 M St., NW (bet. 19th & 20th Sts.), 202-659-1990

■ Look forward to "a little love on every plate" and an "explosion of tastes" at this "stylish" Dixie-influenced New American in the Golden Triangle; despite its basement setting (being glamorized as we go to press by a new wine bar and subdued lighting), it delivers a "top-notch" "culinary adventure when you want something both delicious and a little different", although service can be "slow"; P.S. turn "luxury dining" into a "deal" with the prix fixe lunch.

Vignola 19 | 12 | 16 | $24
113A N. Washington St. (bet. Beall Ave. & Middle Ln.), Rockville, MD, 301-340-2350

■ This "family-run" Rockville Italian deli offers "great" lunchtime subs and "homemade" pastas that are ordered at the counter for carryout or a casual "eat-in" meal; it morphs into a full-service venue at night, while on weekends, "live music adds charm" to the "simple" space; Italophiles, however, are "lukewarm" about the results, citing merely "passable" food and "seriously lacking" service.

Village Bistro S 21 | 15 | 19 | $31
Colonial Village, 1723 Wilson Blvd. (Quinn St.), Arlington, VA, 703-522-0284

■ "Tucked" away in an "unassuming" Arlington strip mall, this Continental bistro establishes its own "neighborhood

Washington, DC   F | D | S | C

atmosphere" with a "quirky" touch and "rough"-edged quarters that somehow make people feel at home (as does the "personable owner"); the "extensive" seafood-slanted menu is "satisfying and well priced" and the service "accommodating", leading regulars who "go weekly" to "only hope" this "quiet" "hidden treasure" "stays a secret."

Visions S   14 | 20 | 14 | $16

1927 Florida Ave., NW (bet. Connecticut Ave. & 19th St.), 202-667-0090

◪ Featuring a "winning" script for "one-stop dating", this Eclectic cafe "conveniently" set in the Visions cinema house above Dupont Circle offers a diverse menu of "modestly priced" Mediterranean and Middle Eastern tapas, snacks and beverages (alcoholic and otherwise) along with showings of independent flicks; even if the mostly pre-made eats are "only so-so" and the service is "disorganized", it's still a "great alternative to movie concession stands"; a full bar is a recent addition.

Vivo! S   20 | 17 | 19 | $33

1509 17th St., NW (bet. P & Q Sts.), 202-986-2627

◪ Just "like a trattoria in Northern Italy", only it's in Dupont Circle East, applaud admirers of this "charming" eatery that turns out "delicious" pastas (notably the homemade agnolotti) and specialties from the wood-burning oven; something of a "sleeper", it's one of Roberto Donna's (of Galileo fame) projects and said to be a "training ground" for his up-and-coming chefs, but despite its credentials "disappointed" detractors demand to know "is mediocrity contagious on 17th Street?"

Warehouse Bar & Grill S   19 | 17 | 19 | $31

214 King St. (bet. Fairfax & Lee Sts.), Alexandria, VA, 703-683-6868

◪ Caricatures of local movers and shakers decorate the walls of this two-story Cajun-Creole seafood pub near Old Town's waterfront, where the drill is to sit upstairs at a "window table", order the "awesome she-crab soup" and "reliably good" crawfish étouffée, and save room for the "absolute best chocolate crème brûlée"; though some feel it has grown "indifferent" over the years, loyalists still find it a "comfortable" respite.

Washington Cafe   ∇ 24 | 20 | 24 | $21

1025 Vermont Ave., NW (K St.), 202-347-7700

■ Sarajevo's loss is Downtown's gain, as Bianca and Dxevad Topic bring their native Bosnian recipes to this "wonderful" brick-walled enclave; *chivapichichi* (seasoned sausages), the specialty of the house, along with some wines from Montenegro, draw expats from Southern Europe for home cooking, live music and fellowship (on weekends, it's their unofficial community center).

Wazuri [S] – – – M

1836 18th St., NW (bet. Swann & T Sts.), 202-797-4930
Providing a culinary adventure inspired by the African diaspora, this warm-toned, art-filled venue is a one-of-a-kind experience in Adams Morgan; the far-reaching menu touches upon the regional cooking of Africa, Brazil, the Caribbean, Indonesia and beyond, and it's offered on two townhouse levels, out on the sidewalk patio and (best of all) up on the tree-shaded rooftop deck; overseeing all is Kojo Davis, who knows how to make everyone feel at home.

WILLARD ROOM 24 27 25 $59

Willard InterContinental Washington,
1401 Pennsylvania Ave., NW (14th St.), 202-637-7440
◪ A place to "spoil" someone with "timeless" "elegance, fine dining and history", this "magnificent" "Edwardian" hotel dining room Downtown is a "culinary wonderland" that makes you "feel like you've arrived"; amid "stunning" surroundings with "ornate" appointments, an "impeccable" service team brings to table "marvelous" New American–New French fare, leading legions to avow that it's "*the*" place to "celebrate", despite the "stuffy" ambiance.

Willow Grove Inn [S] ▽ 24 25 22 $51

14079 Plantation Way (Rte. 15), Orange, VA, 540-672-5982
■ Nestled in the rolling foothills of the Blue Ridge Mountains in Virginia's plantation country (not far from Montpelier or Monticello), this "antebellum" "charmer" "beautifully" reflects innkeeper Angela Mulloy's "personal touch"; amid "period" furnishings like heirloom quilts and handwoven rugs, a "friendly" staff serves an "excellent" seasonal menu of updated regional Southern fare; brunch-only on Sundays.

Wok & Roll [S] – – – I

604 H St., NW (bet. 6th & 7th Sts.), 202-347-4656
In ever-changing Chinatown, this au courant Asian near the MCI Center offers "good food at a good price" in simple, smart surroundings; not only does it serve traditional Chinese and Japanese crowd-pleasers (including roast duck and sushi), but it makes the "best bubble tea in DC" and it's open till 3 AM on weekends.

Wolfgang Puck Express [S] – – – I

Pentagon Row, 1301 S. Joyce St. (Army Navy Dr.),
Pentagon City, VA, 703-412-3550
Wolfgang Puck's signature Cal-Ital pizzas, pastas, salads, sandwiches and rotisserie chicken give fast food a gourmet spin at this national chain outpost debuting on Arlington's Pentagon Row; its bright melon colors, clean lines and eye-catching open kitchen (with a hearth and fresh ingredients on display) have a California feel, while its counter service is enhanced by touches like buzzers that signal when an order is ready and videos of Wolf cooking menu items.

Washington, DC | F | D | S | C |

Woo Lae Oak Ⓢ | 23 | 17 | 19 | $29 |
River House, 1500 S. Joyce St. (15th St.), Arlington, VA, 703-521-3706
◪ Reputedly, every Korean president to visit DC has dined at this "authentic" Seoul stalwart in Arlington, a veritable "HQ for Korean VIPs on expense accounts" and "homesick" expats; the wide-ranging menu features many "serious" specialties, though novices tend to stick to easy choices such as the "BBQ grilled tableside" (a "must-have"), the "best bulgoki" and a "great seafood pancake"; be warned, though, of "slow", "curt" service and language barriers.

Wurzburg Haus Ⓢ | 20 | 15 | 19 | $25 |
Red Mill Shopping Ctr., 7236 Muncaster Mill Rd. (Shady Grove Rd.), Rockville, MD, 301-330-0402
◪ "Lovers of German food" make frequent "pilgrimages" to this "old-world" Bavarian in Rockville for a "tempting" "taste" of bratwurst, boar (in season) and Wiener schnitzel "done properly" (plus seafood and vegetarian options) and washed down with "great imported beers"; a Saturday-night accordion player adds to the "lively" atmosphere.

Yama Ⓢ | – | – | – | M |
328 Maple Ave. W. (Nutley St.), Vienna, VA, 703-242-7703
"They do everything right" say ardent admirers about this "always busy" traditional Japanese in Vienna, which many insist prepares the "best sushi in Northern Virginia"; aside from its "interesting selection" of "super-fresh" raw fish, it also features a broad, affordably priced menu of "very good" cooked dishes.

Yanÿu Ⓢ | 24 | 24 | 21 | $47 |
3433 Connecticut Ave., NW (bet. Connecticut & Ordway Sts.), 202-686-6968
◪ For an "exotic adventure to Asia" visit this "refreshingly different", "ultra-modern" "sophisticate" in Cleveland Park, where the "refined", "highly delectable" plates (inspired by the cuisines of China, Malaysia, Vietnam, Thailand and beyond) are simply a "revelation" (the "Peking duck is unparalleled"); as "beautiful" as the presentations is the "serene" room, and though some complain that the prices are as "pretentious" as the ambiance, devotees promise that the "divine tasting menu is worth" it all.

Yee Hwa Ⓢ | – | – | – | M |
1009 21st St., NW (bet. K & L Sts.), 202-833-1244
This Golden Triangle Asian has a comprehensive Korean menu (something largely missing from the Downtown dining scene) as well as plenty of Japanese offerings; the subdued palette, ample booths and other dignified appointments work well for a business meeting with both Seoul-food novices and experts, while raw-fish soloists can gravitate to the serious sushi bar.

vote at zagat.com

Yoko [S] ▽ 23 | 16 | 22 | $27

Hunter Mill Plaza, 2946J Chain Bridge Rd. (Hunter Mill Rd.), Oakton, VA, 703-255-6644

Yoko II [S]

Herndon Center V, 332 Elden St. (Herndon Pkwy.), Herndon, VA, 703-464-7000

■ Situated in "unassuming" "shopping centers" in Northern Virginia, these separately owned "family-friendly" Japanese eateries earn a "key spot in the rotation" of appreciative locals due to their "consistently good" raw fish and special rolls, as well as extensive sake selections, all at equally "good" prices; N.B. the Oakton location has recently revamped and added a full sushi bar.

Yosaku [S] 22 | 14 | 20 | $30

4712 Wisconsin Ave., NW (Chesapeake St.), 202-363-4453

■ Some recognizable faces salute this modest Upper NW "pleaser" as "one of the best unknown Japanese" in town thanks to "always fresh" (if not cutting-edge) sushi, "authentic shabu-shabu" and "solid" udon noodles; the digs have lately been spruced up, helping to maintain its status as a "favorite no-special-occasion" "neighborhood" place.

Zaytinya ◐ [S] – | – | – | M

701 Ninth St., NW (G St.), 202-638-0800

This elegant, soaring Penn Quarter newcomer celebrates the foods and wines of Greece, Lebanon and Turkey; its innovative meze choices (many vegetarian) demonstrate how well those countries' culinary heritages are adapted to the small-plate concept popularized by its Spanish sister, Jaleo; the multi-faceted setting offers convivial backdrops for anything from a casual bar snack to sophisticated group dining as conceived by chef/co-owner Jose Andres.

Zed's [S] 20 | 17 | 19 | $25

1201 28th St., NW (M St.), 202-333-4710

◪ Set in an "inviting" townhouse in Georgetown, this "white-tablecloth" Ethiopian decorated with fresh flowers and carved artifacts has a certain "class" about it; it's an "enduring presence due to its tasty", vegetarian-friendly cooking and "respectful" service, but a handful of critics blast the "beginner" seasoning and gripe that the "dressy" digs don't suit the "eating-with-your-hands" experience.

Zola [S] – | – | – | E

International Spy Museum, 800 F St., NW (8th St.), 202-654-0999

Rich colors and sleek lines define this New American in the Penn Quarter Spy Museum, where peepholes let diners keep tabs on the kitchen as it turns out market-driven dishes designed to appeal to your Kansas cousins, their Congressman and his cool clerk; savor the sight lines from a barstool perch or indulge your inner spy in a private dining room stocked with state-of-the-art audiovisual gadgets.

Washington, DC Indexes

CUISINES
LOCATIONS
SPECIAL FEATURES

Indexes list the best of many within each category

Washington, DC – Cuisine Index

CUISINES

Afghan
Afghan
Faryab
Panjshir

African
Tropics
Wazuri

American (New)
Addie's
Arbor
Ardeo
Ashby Inn
Bardeo Wine Bar
Bistro Bistro
Blackie's
Black's Bar
Blue Iguana
Boulevard Woodgrill
Brasserie at Watergate
Butterfield 9
Cafe Bethesda
Carlyle
Cashion's Eat Pl.
Caucus Room
Chef Geoff's
Circle Bistro
Coeur de Lion
Colorado Kitchen
Colvin Run Tavern
Corduroy
David Greggory
DC Coast
Dean & DeLuca
DuPont Grille
eCiti
Elysium
Equinox
Evening Star
Fahrenheit & Degrees
Fairfax Room
Felix
15 ria
Firefly
Four/Twenty Blackbirds
Grapeseed
Greenwood
Grille 88
Inn/Little Washington
Jefferson
jordans
Kinkead's
Lafayette
Landmark
Library Lounge
Lightfoot
Local 16
Majestic Cafe
Market St. Bar
Matchbox
Melrose
Mendocino Grille/Wine
Mie N Yu
Mimi's American
Morrison-Clark Inn
Nectar
New Heights
Nora
Nouveau East
Occidental
Old Angler's Inn
Oval Room
Palena
Peacock Cafe
Persimmon
Portabellos
Poste
Red Sage
Restaurant 7
Restaurant 2941
Rhodeside Grill
Ritz-Carlton (DC)
Ritz-Carlton (Pentagon)
Robert's
Roof Terrace
Seasons
701
1789
Signatures
Smith Point
Starland Cafe
Tabard Inn
Thyme Square
Topaz Bar
Vidalia
Willard Room
Zola

American (Traditional)
Artie's
Bailiwick Inn
Ben's Chili Bowl
Bob & Edith's
Boulevard Woodgrill
Broad St. Grill
Cafe Deluxe

Washington, DC – Cuisine Index

Cheesecake Factory
Chef Geoff's
Clyde's
Colorado Kitchen
Daily Grill
Diner, The
Dish
District ChopHse./Brew
Firehook Bakery
Franklin's
Hard Times Cafe
Helix Lounge
Kramerbooks
Luna Grill
M & S Grill
Mark's Kitchen
Monocle
Nathans
Oceanaire Seafood
Old Ebbitt Grill
Rail Stop
Ray's The Steaks
R.F.D. Washington
Sequoia
Tower Oaks Lodge
Tuscarora Mill
Two Quail
Union St.

Asian
Bambu
Big Bowl
Ching Ching Cha
Nouveau East
Oodles Noodles
Raku
Saigon Asia
Saki
Seven Seas
Teaism
Toka Cafe
Vegetable Garden
Wok & Roll

Asian Fusion
Asia Nora
Cafe Japoné
Kaz Sushi
Nouveau East
Perry's
Raku
Saigon Asia
Saki
Spices
TenPenh
Toka Cafe
Yanÿu

Bakeries
Bread Line
Firehook Bakery
La Madeleine Bakery

Barbecue
Ben's Whole Hog
Green Field Chur.
Hee Been
Old Glory BBQ
Red Hot & Blue
Rocklands
Tony Cheng's
Woo Lae Oak

Belgian
Bistrot Belgique
Mannequin Pis
Marcel's

Bolivian
Pike's

Bosnian
Washington Cafe

Brazilian
Green Field Chur.
Grill from Ipanema

Burmese
Burma
Myanmar

Cajun/Creole
Black's Bar
B. Smith's
Cantina Marina
Louisiana Express
RT's
219
Warehouse B&G

Californian
California Tortilla
Paolo's
Saveur
Wolfgang Puck Exp.

Caribbean/Cuban
Banana Café/Piano
Café Salsa
Caribbean Feast
Cubano's
Havana Breeze
Islander Caribbean
Lauriol Plaza
Negril

Washington, DC – Cuisine Index

Ortanique
South Beach
Tropics

Chinese
A&J
China Star
City Lights of China
Dragon
Eat First
Fortune
Full Kee
Full Key
Good Fortune
Hollywood East
Hope Key
Hunan Lion
Hunan Palace
Joe's Noodle
Mark's Duck
Meiwah
Mr. K's
New Fortune
Oriental East
Peking Gourmet
P.F. Chang's
Seven Seas
Wok & Roll

Coffeehouses/Dessert
Bread Line
Cheesecake Factory
Kramerbooks
Mirage Kabob/Sweets
Tryst

Coffee Shops/Diners
Ben's Chili Bowl
Bob & Edith's
Diner, The
Firehook Bakery

Continental
Fairfax Room
Ritz-Carlton (Pentagon)
Tivoli
Village Bistro

Delis/Sandwich Shops
Chutzpah
Krupin's
Parkway Deli
Vignola

Dim Sum
A&J
Dragon
Fortune
Good Fortune
Mark's Duck
New Fortune
Oriental East
Rabieng

Eclectic/International
Acropolis
Bar Rouge
Bread Line
C.F. Folks
Cities
Fireflies
International
Local 16
Noodles & Co.
Rico y Rico
Signatures
Toka Cafe
U-topia
Visions

English
Siné

Ethiopian
Dukem
Meskerem
Zed's

French
Chez Marc
Jean-Michel
Jeffrey's at Watergate
La Bergerie
La Chaumiere
La Colline
La Côte d'Or
La Ferme
La Miche
L'Auberge Chez Fr.
L'Auberge Prov.
Le Gaulois
Le Refuge
Le Relais
Les Halles
Le Tire Bouchon
Mediterranee
Prince Michel

French (Bistro)
Bistro Bis
Bistro D'Oc
Bistro Français
Bistro Lafayette
Bistro 123
Bistrot du Coin
Bistrot Lepic/Wine
La Brasserie
La Chaumiere

Washington, DC – Cuisine Index

La Fourchette
La Madeleine Bakery
Lavandou
Le Gaulois
Le Petit Mistral
Mon Ami Gabi
Montmartre
Petits Plats

French (New)
Brasserie Monte Carlo
Café 15
Citronelle
El Manantial
Gerard's Place
Le Relais
Marcel's
Matisse
Restaurant 2941
Saveur
Willard Room

German
Wurzburg Haus

Greek
Acropolis
Mykonos Grill
Zaytinya

Hamburgers
Addie's
Carlyle
Clyde's
Five Guys
Morton's
Nathans
Occidental
Ray's The Steaks
R.F.D. Washington
Siné
Union St.

Indian/Pakistani
Amma Vegetarian
Bombay Bistro
Bombay Club
Bombay Palace
Bombay Tandoor
Cafe Taj
Connaught Place
Delhi Dhaba
Haandi
Heritage India
Indique
Jaipur
Kabob Palace
Tandoori Nights
Udupi Palace

Irish
Fadó Irish Pub
Siné

Italian
(N=Northern; S=Southern)
Al Tiramisu
Amada Amante
Argia's
Arucola
Barolo (N)
BeDuCi
Buca di Beppo
Cafe Milano
Café Mileto (S)
Capri
Centro (N)
Cesco (N)
Coppi's
Da Domenico (N)
da Vinci
Dolce Vita
El Manantial
Etrusco (N)
Faccia Luna
Filomena
Finemondo
Fontina Grille
Galileo
Generous George's
Geranio
Il Cigno
Il Pizzico
Il Radicchio
i Ricchi (N)
Kuna
Landini Brothers (N)
Luigino
Maestro
Maggiano's (S)
Mamma Lucia
Obelisk (N)
Olazzo (S)
Panino (N)
Paolo's
Pasta Mia
Pasta Plus
Pesto
Primi Piatti
Renato
Ristorante La Perla
Ristorante Murali
Savino's Cafe
Sesto Senso (N)
Skewers/Cafe Luna
Spezie

vote at zagat.com

Washington, DC – Cuisine Index

Teatro Goldoni
Tempo
Terrazza (N)
That's Amore (S)
Timpano Chophse.
Tivoli (N)
Tosca (N)
Tragara (N)
Trattoria Liliana (N)
2 Amys
Vignola
Vivo! (N)
Wolfgang Puck Exp.

Jamaican
Negril

Japanese
Acropolis
Cafe Japoné
Chopsticks
Hakuba
Hama Sushi
Hinode
Kanpai
Kaz Sushi
Konami
Makoto
Matuba
Mondo Sushi
Murasaki
Niwano Hana
Perry's
Sakana
Sushi-Ko
Sushi Taro
Tachibana
Tako Grill
Tono Sushi
Uni
Wok & Roll
Yama
Yee Hwa
Yoko
Yosaku

Korean
Cho's Garden
Hee Been
Mark's Kitchen
Sorak Garden
Woo Lae Oak
Yee Hwa

Latin American/ Nuevo Latino
Agua Ardiente
Andale
Banana Café/Piano
Cafe Atlantico
Café Salsa
Chi-Cha Lounge
Crisp & Juicy
El Golfo
El Mariachi
El Pollo Rico
Gabriel
Green Field Chur.
Grill from Ipanema
Gua-Rapo
Lauriol Plaza
Ortanique
Pike's
Red Sage
Vida

Malaysian
Malaysia Kopitiam
Penang

Mediterranean
Amada Amante
BeDuCi
Bistro Bistro
Café Olé
Cafe Promenade
Circle Bistro
El Manantial
Kazan
Le Tarbouche
Levante's
Matisse
Mediterranee
Mezza9
Mimi's American
Olives

Mexican/Tex-Mex
Andale
Austin Grill
Burrito Brothers
Burro
Cactus Cantina
California Tortilla
Cantina Marina
El Mariachi
Guajillo
Lauriol Plaza
Mi Rancho
Rio Grande Cafe
Taqueria Poblano
Vida

Middle Eastern
Bacchus
Cafe Divan
Faryab

Washington, DC – Cuisine Index

Kabob Palace
Kazan
Kuzine
Lebanese Taverna
Le Tarbouche
Local 16
Meze
Mirage Kabob/Sweets
Moby Dick
Neyla
Nizam's
Skewers/Cafe Luna
Temel
Zaytinya

Moroccan
Taste of Morocco

Pan-Asian
Asia Nora
Cafe Asia
Joe's Noodle
Malaysia Kopitiam
Spices
TenPenh
Yanÿu

Persian
Moby Dick

Peruvian
Crisp & Juicy
El Pollo Rico

Pizza
Arucola
Café Mileto
Coppi's
Dolce Vita
Ella's Pizza
Faccia Luna
Fontina Grille
Generous George's
Il Radicchio
Levante's
Mamma Lucia
Matchbox
Pasta Plus
Pike's
Pizzeria Paradiso
2 Amys

Russian
Maxim

Seafood
Black's Bar
Blue Point Grill
DC Coast
El Golfo
Fin
Finn & Porter
Grillfish
Harry's Tap Rm.
Jerry's Seafood
Johnny's Half Shell
Kinkead's
Legal Sea Foods
McCormick/Schmick's
Oceanaire Seafood
Palm
Pesce
Prime Rib
Ray's The Steaks
RT's
Sea Catch
Seven Seas
Simply Fish
Starfish Cafe
Tony/Joe's Seafood
Warehouse B&G

Southern/Soul
B. Smith's
Florida Ave. Grill
Georgia Brown's
Majestic Cafe
Vidalia
Willow Grove Inn

Southwestern
Gabriel
Jeffrey's at Watergate
Red Sage
Sweetwater Tavern

Spanish
Andalucia
Anzu
El Manantial
El Sol de Andalusia
Gabriel
Jaleo
Lauriol Plaza
Mar de Plata
Taberna del Alab.

Steakhouses
Angelo & Maxie's
Bobby Van's Steak
Capital Grille
Caucus Room
Charlie Palmer Steak
District ChopHse./Brew
Finn & Porter
Fleming's
Harry's Tap Rm.
Les Halles
Maggiano's

Washington, DC – Cuisine Index

Morton's
Nick & Stef's Steak
Nick's Chophse.
Palm
Prime Rib
Ray's The Steaks
Ruth's Chris
Sam & Harry's
Shula's Steak
Smith & Wollensky
Timpano Chophse.

Tapas/Bar Dining

Acropolis
Agua Ardiente
Bardeo Wine Bar
Bar Rouge
Bistrot Lepic/Wine
Cafe Asia
Cafe Atlantico
Cafe Japoné
Café Olé
Chi-Cha Lounge
Citronelle
eCiti
Felix
Gabriel
Grapeseed
Gua-Rapo
Helix Lounge
Indique
International
Jaleo
Johnny's Half Shell
Mar de Plata
McCormick/Schmick's
Meze
Mezza9
Mondo Sushi
Nathans
Neyla
Perry's
Rico y Rico
Saki
Savino's Cafe
701
Signatures
Taberna del Alab.
TenPenh
Toka Cafe
Topaz Bar
Vida
Visions
Zaytinya

Tearooms

Ching Ching Cha
Teaism

Thai

Bambu
Bangkok Blues
Benjarong
Big Bowl
Busara
Crystal Thai
Duangrat's
Haad Thai
Napa Thai
Neisha Thai
Rabieng
Sakoontra
Sala Thai
Singh Thai
Sweet Basil
Tara Thai
T.H.A.I.
Thai Basil
Thai Farm
Thaiphoon
Thai Tanic

Turkish

Cafe Divan
Kazan
Meze
Nizam's
Temel
Zaytinya

Vegetarian

Amma Vegetarian
Mark's Kitchen
Minh
Thyme Square
Udupi Palace
Vegetable Garden
Zaytinya

Vietnamese

Green Papaya
Huong Que
Little Saigon
Little Viet Garden
Minh
Nam's of Bethesda
Nam Viet
Pho 75
Queen Bee
Saigon Asia
Saigonnais
Saigon Saigon
Taste of Saigon
Thanh Thanh

Washington, DC – Location Index

LOCATIONS

WASHINGTON, DC

Capitol Hill
Banana Café/Piano
Barolo
Bistro Bis
B. Smith's
Burrito Brothers
Charlie Palmer Steak
Firehook Bakery
Il Radicchio
La Brasserie
La Colline
Monocle
Montmartre
Starfish Cafe
Two Quail

Chinatown/Penn Quarter/ MCI Center
Andale
Angelo & Maxie's
Austin Grill
Burma
Cafe Atlantico
Capital Grille
Caucus Room
District ChopHse./Brew
Eat First
Ella's Pizza
Fadó Irish Pub
Firehook Bakery
Full Kee
Haad Thai
Jaleo
Luigino
Matchbox
Nick & Stef's Steak
Poste
R.F.D. Washington
Ristorante Murali
Ruth's Chris
701
Signatures
Teaism
Tony Cheng's
Wok & Roll
Zaytinya
Zola

Downtown
Bar Rouge
Bistro D'Oc
Bobby Van's Steak
Bread Line
Butterfield 9
Café 15
Chef Geoff's
Coeur de Lion
Corduroy
DC Coast
Dean & DeLuca
15 ria
Finemondo
Firehook Bakery
Georgia Brown's
Gerard's Place
Havana Breeze
International
Jefferson
jordans
Les Halles
Library Lounge
M & S Grill
Maxim
Morrison-Clark Inn
Occidental
Oceanaire Seafood
Old Ebbitt Grill
Ortanique
Red Sage
Shula's Steak
Teaism
TenPenh
Tosca
Washington Cafe
Willard Room

Dupont Circle
Acropolis
Al Tiramisu
BeDuCi
Bistrot du Coin
Buca di Beppo
Burrito Brothers
Cafe Japoné
City Lights of China
DuPont Grille
Etrusco
Fairfax Room
Firefly
Firehook Bakery
Gabriel
Johnny's Half Shell
Kramerbooks
Levante's

vote at zagat.com

Washington, DC – Location Index

Luna Grill
Mimi's American
Moby Dick
Nora
Obelisk
Pesce
Pizzeria Paradiso
Raku
Ruth's Chris
Sakana
Sala Thai
Savino's Cafe
Tabard Inn
Teaism
Thaiphoon
Topaz Bar
Uni
Visions

Dupont Circle East/Adams Morgan

Anzu
Arbor
Burrito Brothers
Cashion's Eat Pl.
Cities
Diner, The
Felix
Grille 88
Grill from Ipanema
La Fourchette
Lauriol Plaza
Meskerem
Meze
Pasta Mia
Perry's
Saigonnais
Saki
Skewers/Cafe Luna
Sushi Taro
Tryst
Vivo!
Wazuri

Foggy Bottom/K Street

Bombay Palace
Brasserie at Watergate
Dish
Jeffrey's at Watergate
Kinkead's
Legal Sea Foods
Mr. K's
Nectar
Prime Rib
Primi Piatti
Roof Terrace

Georgetown/Glover Park

Amma Vegetarian
Austin Grill
Bistro Français
Bistrot Lepic/Wine
Busara
Cafe Divan
Cafe Milano
Ching Ching Cha
Chopsticks
Citronelle
Clyde's
Daily Grill
Dean & DeLuca
Faccia Luna
Fahrenheit & Degrees
Filomena
Firehook Bakery
Heritage India
La Chaumiere
La Madeleine Bakery
Mendocino Grille/Wine
Mie N Yu
Moby Dick
Morton's
Nathans
Neyla
Old Glory BBQ
Paolo's
Peacock Cafe
Pizzeria Paradiso
Rocklands
Saveur
Sea Catch
Seasons
Sequoia
1789
Smith Point
Sushi-Ko
Tony/Joe's Seafood
Zed's

Golden Triangle

Bacchus
Bombay Club
Burrito Brothers
Burro
Cafe Promenade
C.F. Folks
Daily Grill
Equinox
Fin
Firehook Bakery
Galileo
Grillfish
i Ricchi
Kaz Sushi

Washington, DC – Location Index

Lafayette
Le Tarbouche
Malaysia Kopitiam
McCormick/Schmick's
Morton's
Olives
Oodles Noodles
Oval Room
Palm
Penang
Sam & Harry's
Sesto Senso
Smith & Wollensky
Spezie
Taberna del Alab.
Teatro Goldoni
Toka Cafe
Vida
Vidalia
Yee Hwa

Maine Avenue/ SW Waterfront
Cantina Marina

New U/Logan Circle
Ben's Chili Bowl
Chi-Cha Lounge
Coppi's
Dukem
Florida Ave. Grill
Helix Lounge
Islander Caribbean
Kuna
Local 16
Mar de Plata
Thai Tanic
U-topia

Northeast
Colorado Kitchen

Upper NW
Arucola
Bambu
Cafe Deluxe
Café Olé
Cheesecake Factory

Chef Geoff's
Delhi Dhaba
Greenwood
Krupin's
Maggiano's
Makoto
Matisse
Murasaki
Negril
Pesto
Starland Cafe
Trattoria Liliana
2 Amys
Yosaku

West End
Agua Ardiente
Asia Nora
Blackie's
Circle Bistro
David Greggory
Landmark
Marcel's
Meiwah
Melrose
Ristorante La Perla
Ritz-Carlton (DC)

Woodley Park/ Cleveland Park
Ardeo
Bardeo Wine Bar
Cactus Cantina
Firehook Bakery
Indique
Lavandou
Lebanese Taverna
Nam Viet
New Heights
Palena
Petits Plats
Robert's
Sala Thai
Spices
Tono Sushi
Yanÿu

NEARBY MARYLAND

Bethesda/Chevy Chase
Austin Grill
Bacchus
Black's Bar
Brasserie Monte Carlo
Cafe Bethesda

Cafe Deluxe
California Tortilla
Centro
Cesco
Clyde's
Delhi Dhaba

vote at zagat.com

Washington, DC – Location Index

Faryab
Grapeseed
Green Papaya
Haandi
Hard Times Cafe
Heritage India
Hinode
Jaleo
Jean-Michel
La Ferme
La Madeleine Bakery
La Miche
Legal Sea Foods
Levante's
Louisiana Express
Mamma Lucia
Matuba
McCormick/Schmick's
Moby Dick
Mon Ami Gabi
Nam's of Bethesda
Napa Thai
Olazzo
Oodles Noodles
Persimmon
Raku
Rio Grande Cafe
Ruth's Chris
Sala Thai
South Beach
Sweet Basil
Tako Grill
Tara Thai
Terrazza
Thyme Square
Tragara

Gaithersburg/Shady Grove/Olney

Buca di Beppo
Café Mileto
China Star
Dragon
Hakuba
Hunan Palace
Mamma Lucia
Mannequin Pis
Mi Rancho
Moby Dick
Negril
New Fortune
Noodles & Co.
Red Hot & Blue
Rico y Rico
Rio Grande Cafe
Tandoori Nights
Tara Thai
Tropics

Hyattsville/College Park/Lanham/Laurel

Franklin's
Hard Times Cafe
Jerry's Seafood
Negril
Noodles & Co.
Pasta Plus
Pho 75
Red Hot & Blue
Udupi Palace

Potomac/Glen Echo

California Tortilla
Old Angler's Inn
Renato

Rockville/White Flint

A&J
Addie's
Amada Amante
Andalucia
Benjarong
Bombay Bistro
Caribbean Feast
Cheesecake Factory
Crisp & Juicy
El Mariachi
El Sol de Andalusia
Fontina Grille
Green Field Chur.
Hard Times Cafe
Hinode
Il Pizzico
Joe's Noodle
Kuzine
La Madeleine Bakery
Lebanese Taverna
Mamma Lucia
Mykonos Grill
Nick's Chophse.
Niwano Hana
P.F. Chang's
Pho 75
Seven Seas
Tara Thai
Taste of Saigon
Thai Farm
That's Amore
Timpano Chophse.
Tower Oaks Lodge
Vegetable Garden
Vignola
Wurzburg Haus

Washington, DC – Location Index

Silver Spring/Wheaton
Crisp & Juicy
Cubano's
El Golfo
El Pollo Rico
Full Key
Good Fortune
Hollywood East
Mark's Kitchen
Mi Rancho
Negril
Oriental East
Parkway Deli
Thanh Thanh

NEARBY VIRGINIA

Alexandria
Afghan
Austin Grill
Bistro Lafayette
Blue Point Grill
Café Salsa
Clyde's
Elysium
Evening Star
Faccia Luna
Finn & Porter
Fireflies
Firehook Bakery
Five Guys
Generous George's
Geranio
Haad Thai
Hard Times Cafe
La Bergerie
La Madeleine Bakery
Landini Brothers
Le Gaulois
Le Refuge
Majestic Cafe
Red Hot & Blue
RT's
Simply Fish
Taqueria Poblano
Tempo
219
Union St.
Warehouse B&G

Arlington
Big Bowl
Bob & Edith's
Boulevard Woodgrill
Cafe Asia
Crisp & Juicy
Crystal Thai
Delhi Dhaba
El Pollo Rico
Faccia Luna
Hard Times Cafe
Harry's Tap Rm.
Hope Key
Il Radicchio
Kabob Palace
La Côte d'Or
Lebanese Taverna
Legal Sea Foods
Little Viet Garden
Luna Grill
Matuba
Mediterranee
Minh
Mondo Sushi
Morton's
Nam Viet
Noodles & Co.
Nouveau East
Pike's
Portabellos
Queen Bee
Rio Grande Cafe
Ristorante Murali
Ritz-Carlton (Pentagon)
Rocklands
Ruth's Chris
Saigon Asia
Saigon Saigon
Sala Thai
Siné
Singh Thai
Taqueria Poblano
Tara Thai
Taste of Morocco
Thaiphoon
Wolfgang Puck Exp.
Woo Lae Oak

Fairfax/Springfield/Annandale
A&J
Artie's
Austin Grill
Bailiwick Inn
Blue Iguana
Bombay Bistro
Cho's Garden
Chutzpah
Connaught Place

vote at zagat.com

Washington, DC – Location Index

da Vinci
Dolce Vita
Five Guys
Hard Times Cafe
Hee Been
Jaipur
Le Tire Bouchon
Mark's Duck
Moby Dick
Noodles & Co.
Red Hot & Blue
Sakoontra
Sorak Garden
Temel
Yoko

Falls Church/Baileys Crossroads

Argia's
Bangkok Blues
Broad St. Grill
Crisp & Juicy
Duangrat's
Fortune
Full Kee
Haandi
Huong Que
La Madeleine Bakery
Little Saigon
Mirage Kabob/Sweets
Myanmar
Neisha Thai
Panjshir
Peking Gourmet
Pho 75
Rabieng
Restaurant 2941
Tara Thai

Great Falls

L'Auberge Chez Fr.
Le Relais

Leesburg/Middleburg/The Plains

Lightfoot
Rail Stop
Red Hot & Blue
Tuscarora Mill

Manassas/Centreville/Prince William County

Ben's Whole Hog
Bistrot Belgique
Chez Marc
Hard Times Cafe
Old Glory BBQ
Panino
Red Hot & Blue
Sweetwater Tavern

McLean

Cafe Taj
Capri
Kazan
Le Petit Mistral
Tachibana

Reston/Herndon/Chantilly

Angelo & Maxie's
Big Bowl
Clyde's
El Manantial
Fortune
Hama Sushi
Hard Times Cafe
Il Cigno
La Madeleine Bakery
Market St. Bar
McCormick/Schmick's
Morton's
Paolo's
Pho 75
Rio Grande Cafe
Sweetwater Tavern
Thai Basil
That's Amore
Yoko

Rosslyn/Courthouse

Guajillo
Gua-Rapo
Kanpai
Mezza9
Pho 75
Ray's The Steaks
Red Hot & Blue
Rhodeside Grill
Tivoli
Village Bistro

Shirlington

Bistro Bistro
Carlyle
T.H.A.I.

Tysons Corner/Vienna

Amma Vegetarian
Bistro 123
Bombay Tandoor
Burrito Brothers
Busara
Cafe Deluxe
Capital Grille
Clyde's

Washington, DC – Location Index

Colvin Run Tavern
Da Domenico
Daily Grill
eCiti
Fleming's
Hunan Lion
Konami
La Madeleine Bakery
Legal Sea Foods
Maestro
Maggiano's
McCormick/Schmick's
Moby Dick
Morton's
Neisha Thai
Nizam's
Palm
Panjshir
P.F. Chang's
Restaurant 7
Sam & Harry's
Shula's Steak
Sweetwater Tavern
Tara Thai
Taste of Saigon
That's Amore
Yama

VIRGINIA COUNTRYSIDE

Ashby Inn
Four/Twenty Blackbirds
Inn/Little Washington
L'Auberge Prov.
Prince Michel
Willow Grove Inn

Washington, DC – Special Feature Index

SPECIAL FEATURES

(Restaurants followed by a † may not offer that feature at every location.)

Additions
Agua Ardiente
Amada Amante
Anzu
Bambu
Bistro D'Oc
Bistro Lafayette
Café Salsa
Cantina Marina
Charlie Palmer Steak
Chopsticks
Cho's Garden
Circle Bistro
David Greggory
da Vinci
Dish
Dragon
DuPont Grille
El Golfo
Ella's Pizza
El Manantial
El Sol de Andalusia
Fahrenheit & Degrees
15 ria
Fin
Finn & Porter
Fireflies
Firefly
Harry's Tap Rm.
Helix Lounge
Indique
International
Kanpai
Kuzine
Landmark
Le Tire Bouchon
Local 16
Maggiano's
Matchbox
Mie N Yu
Mirage Kabob/Sweets
Mondo Sushi
Nectar
Noodles & Co.
Nouveau East
Olazzo
Pesto
Poste
Restaurant 2941
R.F.D. Washington
Ristorante La Perla
Ristorante Murali
Saigon Asia
Saki
Simply Fish
Singh Thai
Smith Point
Thai Farm
Thai Tanic
Tower Oaks Lodge
Trattoria Liliana
Tropics
Wolfgang Puck Exp.
Yee Hwa
Zaytinya
Zola

Breakfast
(See also Hotel Dining)
Ben's Chili Bowl
Bob & Edith's†
Bread Line
Daily Grill†
Diner, The
Florida Ave. Grill
La Colline
Louisiana Express
Old Ebbitt Grill
Signatures
Teaism

Brunch
A&J
Addie's
Arbor
Artie's
Ashby Inn
Austin Grill
Banana Café/Piano
Bistro Bis
Bombay Club
B. Smith's
Cafe Atlantico
Cafe Promenade
Carlyle
Cashion's Eat Pl.
Clyde's
Coeur de Lion
Colorado Kitchen
David Greggory

Washington, DC – Special Feature Index

Dragon
Evening Star
Felix
Four/Twenty Blackbirds
Gabriel
Georgia Brown's
Grille 88
Harry's Tap Rm.
Kramerbooks
L'Auberge Prov.
Le Relais
Maestro
Majestic Cafe
Market St. Bar
Mark's Duck
Melrose
Morrison-Clark Inn
New Heights
Old Ebbitt Grill
Oriental East
Paolo's
Parkway Deli
Peacock Cafe
Perry's
Portabellos
Rabieng
Rail Stop
Restaurant 7
Rhodeside Grill
Ritz-Carlton (DC)
Ritz-Carlton (Pentagon)
Seasons
Sequoia
Seven Seas
Tabard Inn
Thyme Square
Tony/Joe's Seafood
219
Willow Grove Inn

Business Dining

Addie's
Amada Amante
Angelo & Maxie's†
Argia's
Artie's
Bacchus
Barolo
Bistro Bis
Bobby Van's Steak
Bombay Club
Bombay Tandoor
Butterfield 9
Café 15
Cafe Promenade
Capital Grille
Capri
Caucus Room
Charlie Palmer Steak
Circle Bistro
Citronelle
Colvin Run Tavern
da Vinci
DC Coast
DuPont Grille
El Manantial
El Sol de Andalusia
Equinox
Fahrenheit & Degrees
Fairfax Room
Finemondo
Finn & Porter
Fleming's
Fontina Grille
Gabriel
Galileo†
Georgia Brown's
Gerard's Place
Haad Thai†
Hakuba
Harry's Tap Rm.
i Ricchi
Jaipur
Jeffrey's at Watergate
jordans
Kaz Sushi
Kinkead's
Konami
Lafayette
Landmark
Legal Sea Foods†
Le Relais
Le Tire Bouchon
Library Lounge
Maestro
Maggiano's
M & S Grill
Marcel's
Market St. Bar
McCormick/Schmick's
Melrose
Mezza9
Monocle
Morton's†
Nouveau East
Occidental
Oceanaire Seafood
Old Ebbitt Grill
Olives
Oval Room
Palm
Poste

Washington, DC – Special Feature Index

Prime Rib
Primi Piatti
Red Sage
Restaurant 7
Restaurant 2941
Ristorante La Perla
Ristorante Muralit
Ritz-Carlton (DC)
Ritz-Carlton (Pentagon)
Ruth's Christ†
Sam & Harry's
Seasons
701
Signatures
Smith & Wollensky
Spezie
Taberna del Alab.
Tandoori Nights
Taste of Saigon
Teatro Goldoni
Thai Farm
Tivoli
Tosca
Tower Oaks Lodge
Tuscarora Mill
Vidalia
Willard Room
Yee Hwa
Zola

Catering

Al Tiramisu
Amma Vegetarian†
Andale
Bacchus
Ben's Whole Hog
Bread Line
Burrito Brothers†
Cafe Milano
California Tortilla
Cantina Marina
Caribbean Feast
C.F. Folks
Chef Geoff's†
Cho's Garden
Chutzpah
Citronelle
Clyde's†
da Vinci
Dean & DeLuca
Dragon
El Golfo
El Sol de Andalusia
Fin
Firehook Bakery
Hard Times Cafe†
Helix Lounge
Il Radicchio
Islander Caribbean
Jeffrey's at Watergate
Kanpai
Kazan
Krupin's
Kuzine
Lafayette
La Madeleine Bakery†
Lebanese Taverna
Library Lounge
Louisiana Express
Maggiano's†
Malaysia Kopitiam
Market St. Bar
Mark's Kitchen
Mie N Yu
Mondo Sushi
Noodles & Co.†
Nouveau East
Olazzo
Old Ebbitt Grill
Old Glory BBQ
Pesto
Red Hot & Blue†
Red Sage
Rocklands
Sala Thai†
Simply Fish
Thai Farm
Thaiphoon†
Tivoli
Washington Cafe
Wurzburg Haus
Yanyu
Zed's

Chef's Table in Kitchen

Citronelle
Galileo
Marcel's
Matisse
Tosca

Child-Friendly

(Besides the normal fast-food places; * children's menu available)
Arucola
Austin Grill†
Big Bowl†
Cactus Cantina
Clyde's†
Ella's Pizza
Filomena

Washington, DC – Special Feature Index

Franklin's
Generous George's*
Hard Times Cafe†
Lebanese Taverna†
Legal Sea Foods†
Mamma Lucia†
Mark's Kitchen
Matuba
Noodles & Co.†
Red Hot & Blue†
Rio Grande Cafe*
Rocklands†
Tara Thai†
2 Amys
Wolfgang Puck Exp.

Delivery/Takeout
(D=delivery, T=takeout)

Addie's (T)
Al Tiramisu (T)
Andale (T)
Andalucia (T)
Angelo & Maxie's (T)
Arbor (T)
Ardeo (T)
Argia's (T)
Arucola (D,T)
Austin Grill (T)
BeDuCi (T)
Ben's Whole Hog (T)
Big Bowl†
Bistro Bistro (T)
Black's Bar (T)
Blue Iguana (T)
Bobby Van's Steak (T)
Bombay Club (T)
Boulevard Woodgrill (T)
Brasserie at Watergate (T)
Bread Line (T)
Cafe Deluxe (T)
Cafe Milano (T)
Café Mileto (D,T)
Café Olé (T)
Capital Grille (T)
Caucus Room (T)
Centro (T)
Cesco (T)
Cheesecake Factory†
Cho's Garden (T)
Cities (T)
Clyde's (T)
eCiti (T)
Finemondo (T)
Fontina Grille (T)
Gabriel (T)
Galileo†
Georgia Brown's (T)
Heritage India†
Jaleo (T)
Jeffrey's at Watergate (T)
Jerry's Seafood (T)
Johnny's Half Shell (T)
Kaz Sushi (T)
Konami (T)
La Brasserie (D,T)
Lavandou (T)
Lebanese Taverna (T)
Legal Sea Foods†
Le Relais (T)
Le Tarbouche (T)
Lightfoot (T)
Luigino (T)
M & S Grill (T)
McCormick/Schmick's (T)
Melrose (T)
Mendocino Grille/Wine (D,T)
Mon Ami Gabi (T)
Montmartre (T)
Nick's Chophse. (T)
Oceanaire Seafood (T)
Old Ebbitt Grill (T)
Oval Room (T)
Palm (T)
Pesce (T)
Pizzeria Paradiso†
Red Sage (D,T)
Renato (T)
Restaurant 7 (T)
Rocklands†
Sam & Harry's†
Seasons (T)
Sesto Senso (D,T)
701 (T)
Smith & Wollensky (T)
Teatro Goldoni (T)
TenPenh (T)
Tivoli (T)
2 Amys (T)
Vidalia (T)

Dessert

Bread Line
Carlyle
Cashion's Eat Pl.
Chef Geoff's†
Citronelle
David Greggory
DC Coast
Dean & DeLuca†
Firehook Bakery†
Galileo†
Inn/Little Washington

Washington, DC – Special Feature Index

Johnny's Half Shell
jordans
Kinkead's
Kramerbooks
Majestic Cafe
Melrose
Nectar
Obelisk
Palena
Red Sage
Restaurant 2941
1789
TenPenh
Thyme Square
Tivoli
Tragara
2 Amys

Dining Alone
(Other than hotels and places with counter service)
Al Tiramisu
Bread Line
Cafe Divan
C.F. Folks
Clyde's†
DC Coast
Dean & DeLuca†
Diner, The
Dish
Ella's Pizza
15 ria
Finemondo
Firefly
Grapeseed
Harry's Tap Rm.
Helix Lounge
Indique
International
Johnny's Half Shell
Kanpai
Kaz Sushi
Kinkead's
Mamma Lucia†
Marcel's
Matchbox
Mondo Sushi
Old Ebbitt Grill
Olives
Pizzeria Paradiso†
Raku
Rocklands†
Spezie
Teaism
Toka Cafe
Uni
Visions
Zaytinya

Entertainment
(Call for days and times of performances)
Acropolis (jazz)
Agua Ardiente (DJ)
Andalucia (flamenco)
Banana Café/Piano (piano)
Bangkok Blues (varies)
Bar Rouge (DJ)
Bistro Bistro (bands/guitar)
Blackie's (DJ)
Blue Iguana (DJ)
Bombay Club (piano)
B. Smith's (jazz)
Cafe Milano (DJ)
Café Olé (guitar)
Cafe Promenade (jazz brunch)
Café Salsa (band)
Cantina Marina (varies)
Chef Geoff's†
Chi-Cha Lounge (bands)
Cho's Garden (karaoke)
Cities (DJ)
Clyde's†
Coeur de Lion (jazz/piano)
Connaught Place (sitar)
David Greggory (piano)
da Vinci (band/karaoke/magic)
Dean & DeLuca†
Dolce Vita (guitar/piano)
Duangrat's (Thai dance)
Dukem (Ethiopian)
eCiti (DJ)
Elysium (piano)
Evening Star (jazz)
Fadó Irish Pub (modern Irish)
Fahrenheit & Degrees (piano)
Felix (DJ/jazz/piano)
Four/Twenty Blackbirds (harp)
Georgia Brown's (jazz brunch)
Grille 88 (piano bar)
Hakuba (bands)
Helix Lounge
Il Cigno (guitar/vocals)
Islander Caribbean (jazz/piano)
Jaleo†
Jefferson (piano)
Kinkead's (jazz)
Kramerbooks (varies)
Lafayette (piano)
Le Tarbouche (belly dancer/DJ)
Local 16 (DJ/jazz)
Marcel's (piano)
Market St. Bar (jazz)

Washington, DC – Special Feature Index

Maxim (dancing/vocals)
Melrose (ballroom/jazz)
Meze (Turkish)
Mie N Yu (DJ)
Mimi's (singing waiters)
Mondo Sushi (DJ)
Ortanique (dancing)
Penang (DJ)
Perry's (drag brunch)
Pike's (Latino)
Prime Rib (bass/piano)
Rhodeside Grill (rock)
Rico y Rico (harp)
Ritz-Carlton (DC) (jazz/piano)
Ruth's Chris†
Saki (DJ)
Sala Thai†
Sesto Senso (DJ/dancing)
701 (jazz/piano)
Signatures (jazz)
South Beach (DJ)
Starland Cafe (varies)
Taste of Morocco (belly dancer)
Teatro Goldoni (jazz)
Timpano (bands/swing)
Tony/Joe's Seafood (vocals)
Tropics (bands)
219 (jazz)
U-topia (blues/jazz)
Vida (DJ)
Vignola (piano)
Washington Cafe (varies)
Willard Room (piano)
Willow Grove Inn (piano)
Wurzburg Haus (accordion)
Zaytinya (belly dancer)

Family-Style

Arucola
Buca di Beppo
Cho's Garden
Green Field Chur.
Maggiano's
Mamma Lucia†
That's Amore
Tony Cheng's

Fireplaces

Al Tiramisu
Ashby Inn
Bistro Bis
Cities
Clyde's†
Coeur de Lion
Dish
Dukem
Fadó Irish Pub
Fairfax Room
15 ria
Jefferson
La Chaumiere
La Ferme
La Madeleine Bakery†
L'Auberge Prov.
Le Gaulois
Lightfoot
Matisse
Old Angler's Inn
Petits Plats
Pizzeria Paradiso†
Sea Catch
1789
Siné
Tabard Inn
Timpano Chophse.
Vivo!

Historic Places

(Year opened; *building)
1753 L'Auberge Prov.*
1778 Willow Grove Inn*
1800s Bailiwick Inn*
late 1800s Lightfoot*
1851 Willard Room*
1860 Old Angler's Inn*
1860 Poste
1860 1789*
1865 Morrison-Clark Inn*
1887 Tabard Inn*
1890 Nora*
1904 Two Quail*
1908 B. Smith's*
1910 Four/Twenty Blackbirds*
1930 Fahrenheit & Degrees
1940s Majestic Cafe*

Hotel Dining

Ashby Inn
  Ashby Inn
Bailiwick Inn
  Bailiwick Inn
Four Seasons
  Seasons
Georgetown Inn
  Daily Grill†
Henley Park
  Coeur de Lion
Hotel George
  Bistro Bis
Hotel Helix
  Helix Lounge
Hotel Monaco
  Poste
Hotel Rouge

vote at zagat.com

Washington, DC – Special Feature Index

Bar Rouge
Hotel Tabard Inn
  Tabard Inn
Hyatt Arlington
  Mezza9
Hyatt Regency Reston
  Market St. Bar
Inn at Little Washington
  Inn/Little Washington
Jefferson, The
  Jefferson
Jurys Washington
  DuPont Grille
Latham Hotel
  Citronelle
Melrose Hotel
  Landmark
Morrison House
  Elysium
Morrison-Clark Inn
  Morrison-Clark Inn
Omni Shoreham
  Robert's
One Washington Circle
  Circle Bistro
Park Hyatt Washington
  Melrose
Radisson Barcelo
  Gabriel
Renaissance Mayflower
  Cafe Promenade
Ritz-Carlton Georgetown
  Fahrenheit & Degrees
Ritz-Carlton Pentagon City
  Ritz-Carlton
Ritz-Carlton Tysons Corner
  Maestro
Ritz-Carlton Washington, D.C.
  Ritz-Carlton
Rive Inn
  Dish
Sheraton Four Points
  Corduroy
Sofitel Lafayette Square
  Café 15
St. Regis
  Library Lounge
Swissôtel-The Watergate
  Jeffrey's at Watergate
Topaz Hotel
  Topaz Bar
Washington Terrace
  15 ria
Westin Embassy Row
  Fairfax Room
Willard Inter-Continental
  Willard Room
Willow Grove Inn
  Willow Grove Inn
Wyndham City Center
  Shula's Steak†

Late Dining

(Weekday closing hour)
Acropolis (12 AM)
Ben's Chili Bowl (2 AM)
Bistro Français (3 AM)
Cafe Japoné (1:30 AM)
Dukem (1 AM)
Eat First (2 AM)
Full Kee†
Full Key (1:30 AM)
Good Fortune (1 AM)
Hard Times Cafe†
Hollywood East (1 AM)
Hope Key (1 AM)
Kramerbooks (1:30 AM)
Meze (2 AM)
New Fortune (1 AM)
Old Ebbitt Grill (1 AM)
Old Glory BBQ†
Smith & Wollensky (1:30 AM)
Tryst (2 AM)
Vivo! (2:30 AM)

Meet for a Drink

(Most top hotels and the following standouts)
Acropolis
Agua Ardiente
Artie's
Banana Café/Piano
Bardeo Wine Bar
Bar Rouge
Bistro Bis
Black's Bar
Cantina Marina
Caucus Room
Chef Geoff's†
Circle Bistro
Cities
Clyde's†
David Greggory
eCiti
El Golfo
Fahrenheit & Degrees
Fairfax Room
15 ria
Gabriel
Harry's Tap Rm.
Helix Lounge
Indique
International
Jaleo

Washington, DC – Special Feature Index

jordans
Landini Brothers
Landmark
Les Halles
Le Tarbouche
Library Lounge
Local 16
Marcel's
Market St. Bar
Matchbox
McCormick/Schmick's
Melrose
Mezza9
Mimi's American
Nathans
Nectar
Old Ebbitt Grill
Olives
Ortanique
Penang
Poste
Red Sage
Restaurant 7
R.F.D. Washington
Saki
Sequoia
701
Siné
South Beach
Spezie
Tandoori Nights
Teaism
TenPenh
Toka Cafe
Topaz Bar
Tryst
Visions
Zaytinya
Zola

Offbeat

Agua Ardiente
Ben's Chili Bowl
Bob & Edith's†
Cantina Marina
Ching Ching Cha
Dukem
Florida Ave. Grill
Franklin's
Greenwood
Johnny's Half Shell
Malaysia Kopitiam
Mark's Kitchen
Matuba†
Maxim
Meskerem
Mie N Yu
Mimi's American
Perry's
Pike's
R.F.D. Washington
Smith Point
Tabard Inn
Teaism
Toka Cafe
Tropics
Washington Cafe
Wazuri
Zola

Outdoor Dining

(G=garden; P=patio;
S=sidewalk; T=terrace;
W=waterside)
Addie's (P)
Agua Ardiente (P)
Arbor (P)
Argia's (P)
Arucola (P)
Ashby Inn (P)
Bacchus (P)
Banana Café/Piano (S)
BeDuCi (T)
Big Bowl†
Bistro Bis (S)
Bistro 123 (T)
Bistrot Belgique (P)
Black's Bar (P)
Blue Point Grill (P)
Bobby Van's Steak (P)
Bombay Club (S)
Brasserie at Watergate (T)
Bread Line (S)
Broad St. Grill (S)
Busara†
Cactus Cantina (S)
Cafe Atlantico (S)
Cafe Bethesda (P)
Cafe Deluxe†
Café 15 (T)
Cafe Japoné (S)
Cafe Milano (P)
Café Mileto (P)
Café Olé (P)
Cantina Marina (P)
Carlyle (P)
Cashion's Eat Pl. (S)
Centro (P)
Cesco (P)
C.F. Folks (P)
Charlie Palmer Steak (T)
Chef Geoff's†
Circle Bistro (P)
David Greggory (P)

vote at zagat.com

Washington, DC – Special Feature Index

Dean & DeLuca (P)
DuPont Grille (P)
El Golfo (P)
Equinox (S)
Etrusco (S)
Evening Star (P)
Faccia Luna†
15 ria (T)
Fin (P)
Finn & Porter (P)
Fireflies (P)
Firehook Bakery†
Fontina Grille (P,S)
Galileo†
Gerard's Place (S)
Green Papaya (S)
Grille 88 (S)
Grill from Ipanema (P)
Hakuba (P)
Harry's Tap Rm. (P)
Il Cigno (T,W)
Inn/Little Washington (G,P)
Jaipur (T)
Jaleo†
jordans (P)
Kanpai (P)
Konami (G)
Kramerbooks (P,S)
Kuzine (P)
La Brasserie (P)
La Ferme (T)
La Fourchette (T)
La Miche (S)
L'Auberge Chez Fr. (G)
L'Auberge Prov. (T)
Lauriol Plaza (P,T)
Lebanese Taverna†
Le Gaulois (G)
Les Halles (P)
Levante's (P)
Little Viet Garden (P)
Local 16 (T)
Luna Grill (P)
Maggiano's†
Mamma Lucia†
Marcel's (P)
Melrose (P)
Meze (P)
Mimi's American (S)
Minh (P)
Mi Rancho (P)
Mon Ami Gabi (P)
Mondo Sushi (P)
Montmartre (P)
Napa Thai (S)
New Heights (S)
Neyla (P)
Occidental (P,S)
Old Angler's Inn (T)
Old Glory BBQ†
Oval Room (S)
Palena (S)
Paolo's (P)
Peacock Cafe (P,S)
Penang (P)
Perry's (T)
Petits Plats (P)
Poste (P)
Primi Piatti (S)
Prince Michel (P)
Rail Stop (T)
Raku†
Renato (S)
Restaurant 2941 (T)
R.F.D. Washington (P)
Rhodeside Grill (S)
Rico y Rico (P)
Rio Grande Cafe†
Ristorante Murali (P)
Robert's (T)
Roof Terrace (T)
Savino's Cafe (S)
Sea Catch (P,T,W)
Sequoia (T)
701 (P)
Siné (P)
Singh Thai (P)
Skewers/Cafe Luna (P)
Smith & Wollensky (S)
Starland Cafe (P)
Sweetwater Tavern†
Tabard Inn (G)
Tandoori Nights (S)
Tara Thai†
Taste of Saigon (P)
Teaism†
TenPenh (P)
Terrazza (T)
T.H.A.I. (P)
Thaiphoon†
Thyme Square (P)
Toka Cafe (P)
Tony/Joe's Seafood (P,W)
Tropics (P)
Tuscarora Mill (P)
2 Amys (P)
219 (T)
Two Quail (P)
Vida (P)
Visions (P)
Wazuri (T)
Willow Grove Inn (P,T)
Wolfgang Puck Exp. (P)
Yosaku (P)

Washington, DC – Special Feature Index

Zaytinya (P)
Zed's (P)

Parking
(L=lot, V=valet, *=validated)
Addie's (L)
Al Tiramisu (V)
Andale (V)
Ardeo (V)
Arucola (L)
Asia Nora (V)
Bacchus (V)
Bailiwick Inn (L)
Bardeo Wine Bar (V)
BeDuCi (V)
Bistro Bis (V)
Blackie's (V)
Black's Bar*
Blue Point Grill (L)
Bobby Van's Steak (V)
Bombay Club (V)
Bombay Palace (V)
Boulevard Woodgrill (L)
Brasserie at Watergate (V)
Broad St. Grill (L)
B. Smith's*
Butterfield 9 (V)
Cafe Atlantico (V)
Cafe Bethesda (V)
Cafe Milano (L)
Café Olé*
Cafe Promenade (V)
Capital Grille (V)*
Carlyle (L)
Cashion's Eat Pl. (V)
Caucus Room (V)
Centro (L,V)
Cesco (V)
Chef Geoff's†
Cities (V)
Citronelle (V)
Clyde's†
Coeur de Lion (L,V)
Colvin Run Tavern (V)*
Corduroy (V)*
Da Domenico (L)
DC Coast (V)
Dean & DeLuca†
eCiti (V)
Elysium (L,V)
Equinox*
Fairfax Room*
Faryab (L)
Felix (L)
Finemondo (V)
Full Kee†
Full Key (L)
Gabriel (V)
Galileo (V)
Georgia Brown's (V)
Gerard's Place (V)
Grapeseed (V)
Greenwood (L)
Heritage India (V)
Hunan Lion (L)
i Ricchi (V)
Jaleo†
Jean-Michel (L)
Jefferson (L,V)
Jeffrey's at Watergate (V)
jordans (V)
Kinkead's (V)
La Bergerie (L)
La Chaumiere*
La Colline*
La Miche (V)
Landini Brothers*
L'Auberge Chez Fr. (L)
Lauriol Plaza*
Les Halles (L,V)
Le Tarbouche (L)
Lightfoot (L)
Maestro (L,V)
M & S Grill (V)
Marcel's (V)
Melrose (V)
Mezza9*
Mon Ami Gabi (V)
Mondo Sushi*
Monocle (L,V)
Morrison-Clark Inn*
Mr. K's (V)
New Heights (V)
Neyla (V)
Nick & Stef's Steak (V)
Nora (V)
Nouveau East*
Obelisk (L)
Occidental (V)
Oceanaire Seafood (V)
Old Ebbitt Grill (V)
Olives (V)
Oval Room*
Palena (L)
Penang (V)
Persimmon (L)
Pesce (V)
Prime Rib (V)
Primi Piatti (L,V)
Red Sage (V)*
Restaurant 7 (L,V)
Ritz-Carlton (DC) (V)
Ritz-Carlton (Pentagon) (V)
Robert's (V)

Washington, DC – Special Feature Index

Rocklands†
Ruth's Chris†
Sam & Harry's (L,V)
Sea Catch (L,V)
Seasons (L,V)
Sequoia (L)
Sesto Senso (L,V)
701 (V)
1789 (V)
Smith & Wollensky (V)
Spezie (V)
Sushi-Ko (V)
Sushi Taro (L)
Tabard Inn (L,V)
Taberna del Alab. (L)
Teatro Goldoni (V)
TenPenh (V)
Terrazza*
Thyme Square (L)
Tivoli (L)
Tosca (V)
Vidalia (V)
Village Bistro (L)
Yanÿu (V)

People-Watching

Acropolis
Anzu
Arbor
Ardeo
Bar Rouge
Bistro Bis
Bistro Français
Black's Bar
Bob & Edith's†
Bread Line
Cafe Deluxe
Café 15
Cafe Japoné
Cafe Milano
Cafe Promenade
Carlyle
Cashion's Eat Pl.
Caucus Room
Charlie Palmer Steak
Cities
David Greggory
DC Coast
Dean & DeLuca†
Diner, The
DuPont Grille
eCiti
Equinox
15 ria
Fin
Firefly
Galileo†
Georgia Brown's
Helix Lounge
Inn/Little Washington
International
Jaleo
Johnny's Half Shell
jordans
Kinkead's
Kramerbooks
La Brasserie
La Colline
Landmark
Lauriol Plaza
Levante's
Local 16
Meze
Mon Ami Gabi
Monocle
Neyla
Nora
Old Ebbitt Grill
Olives
Ortanique
Oval Room
Palm†
Penang
Poste
Primi Piatti
Red Sage
Restaurant 7
Restaurant 2941
Rhodeside Grill
Ristorante Murali†
Sam & Harry's†
Savino's Cafe
Seasons
Sequoia
701
Skewers/Cafe Luna
TenPenh
Thaiphoon†
Tower Oaks Lodge
Tryst
Vida
Vidalia
Yanÿu
Zaytinya
Zola

Power Scenes

Ardeo
Bistro Bis
Bobby Van's Steak
Bombay Club
Capital Grille
Caucus Room
Charlie Palmer Steak

Washington, DC – Special Feature Index

Citronelle
Colvin Run Tavern
DC Coast
Equinox
Etrusco
Fahrenheit & Degrees
Galileo
Inn/Little Washington
Jeffrey's at Watergate
Kinkead's
La Colline
Le Relais
Maestro
Marcel's
Monocle
Morton's†
Nick & Stef's Steak
Nora
Occidental
Old Ebbitt Grill
Olives
Oval Room
Palena
Palm
Prime Rib
Restaurant 7
Restaurant 2941
Sam & Harry's
Seasons
701
Signatures
Taberna del Alab.
Teatro Goldoni
Tosca
Tower Oaks Lodge
Tuscarora Mill
Vidalia
Willard Room
Zaytinya
Zola

Pre-Theater Menus
(Call for prices and times)
Bistro Français
Bistro 123
Brasserie at Watergate
Cafe Atlantico
Carlyle
Circle Bistro
Clyde's
Gabriel
Jeffrey's at Watergate
La Côte d'Or
Lavandou
Marcel's
Oval Room
Petits Plats
Portabellos
Roof Terrace
701
Tivoli

Private Rooms
(Call for capacity)
Agua Ardiente
Amada Amante
Anzu
Ardeo
Asia Nora
Barolo
BeDuCi
Big Bowl†
Bistro Bis
Bistro D'Oc
Bistrot Lepic/Wine
Blackie's
B. Smith's
Buca di Beppo†
Cafe Milano
Caucus Room
Charlie Palmer Steak
Chef Geoff's
China Star
Circle Bistro
Citronelle
Colvin Run Tavern
David Greggory
da Vinci
Dish
Duangrat's
DuPont Grille
El Sol de Andalusia
Equinox
Etrusco
Evening Star
Fahrenheit & Degrees
Fin
Finemondo
Finn & Porter
Firefly
Firehook Bakery†
Galileo
Greenwood
Gua-Rapo
Havana Breeze
Hee Been
Helix Lounge
Heritage India†
Hinode
i Ricchi
Kinkead's
La Bergerie
La Brasserie
Lafayette

Washington, DC – Special Feature Index

La Ferme
L'Auberge Prov.
Lebanese Taverna†
Lightfoot
Local 16
Maestro
Marcel's
Maxim
Melrose
Mie N Yu
Morton's†
Mr. K's
New Heights
Nick & Stef's Steak
Nora
Old Ebbitt Grill
Olives
Ortanique
Oval Room
Pesto
Poste
Red Sage
Restaurant 2941
R.F.D. Washington
Rico y Rico
Ristorante Murali†
Ruth's Chris
Sala Thai†
Sam & Harry's
Seasons
701
Signatures
Simply Fish
Sorak Garden
Sushi-Ko
Taberna del Alab.
Teatro Goldoni
Tivoli
Tono Sushi
Tosca
Tragara
Tuscarora Mill
219
Vida
Vidalia
Yanÿu

Prix Fixe Menus
(Call for prices and times)
Bailiwick Inn
BeDuCi
Bistro Français
Bistro 123
Blue Iguana
Bombay Club
Bombay Palace
Brasserie at Watergate
Cafe Atlantico

Cafe Promenade
Caucus Room
Chez Marc
Ching Ching Cha
Citronelle
City Lights of China
Coeur de Lion
Colvin Run Tavern
Elysium
Evening Star
Finemondo
Geranio
Greenwood
Inn/Little Washington
Jefferson
Jeffrey's at Watergate
La Côte d'Or
La Fourchette
L'Auberge Chez Fr.
L'Auberge Prov.
Le Petit Mistral
Les Halles
Le Tarbouche
Maestro
Marcel's
Melrose
Morrison-Clark Inn
Obelisk
Oval Room
Palena
Persimmon
Petits Plats
Red Sage
Ritz-Carlton (DC)
Saveur
Seasons
701
1789
Sushi-Ko
Tivoli
Tosca
Vidalia
Willard Room

Quiet Conversation
Asia Nora
Bailiwick Inn
Bombay Club
Butterfield 9
Cafe Bethesda
Caucus Room
Ching Ching Cha
Circle Bistro
Citronelle
Coeur de Lion
Elysium
Fahrenheit & Degrees

Washington, DC – Special Feature Index

15 ria
Gerard's Place
Heritage India†
Indique
Inn/Little Washington
La Ferme
Maestro
Majestic Cafe
Makoto
Melrose
Morrison-Clark Inn
New Heights
Obelisk
Oceanaire Seafood
Palena
Ritz-Carlton (Pentagon)
Robert's
Sea Catch
Seasons
1789
Taberna del Alab.
Temel
Terrazza
Tosca
Willard Room

Raw Bars
Bambu
Black's Bar
Blue Point Grill
Clyde's†
eCiti
Fin
Finn & Porter
Johnny's Half Shell
Kinkead's
Legal Sea Foods†
McCormick/Schmick's†
Old Ebbitt Grill
Sea Catch
701
Tony/Joe's Seafood

Romantic Places
Al Tiramisu
Asia Nora
Bombay Club
Circle Bistro
Citronelle
Coeur de Lion
Green Papaya
Inn/Little Washington
International
La Bergerie
L'Auberge Chez Fr.
Le Refuge
Le Tarbouche
Majestic Cafe
Melrose
Nectar
New Heights
Nora
Obelisk
Old Angler's Inn
Ortanique
Palena
Seasons
701
1789
Tabard Inn
Taberna del Alab.
Two Quail
Yanyu

Senior Appeal
Blackie's
Brasserie Monte Carlo
Capri
Chef Geoff's†
Colvin Run Tavern
Crystal Thai
El Sol de Andalusia
Fireflies
Jean-Michel
Jeffrey's at Watergate
Krupin's
La Bergerie
La Chaumiere
La Ferme
La Miche
L'Auberge Chez Fr.
Le Gaulois
Le Petit Mistral
Le Tire Bouchon
Matisse
Morton's†
Nizam's
Oceanaire Seafood
Parkway Deli
Peking Gourmet
Pesto
Prime Rib
Prince Michel
Renato
Ristorante La Perla
Ritz-Carlton (DC)
Roof Terrace
Ruth's Chris†
Simply Fish
Tako Grill
Thai Farm
That's Amore†
Tivoli
Tower Oaks Lodge
Tragara

Washington, DC – Special Feature Index

Trattoria Liliana
Willard Room
Wurzburg Haus

Singles Scenes
Acropolis
Agua Ardiente
Angelo & Maxie's†
Arbor
Artie's
Austin Grill
Bardeo Wine Bar
Bar Rouge
Boulevard Woodgrill
Cafe Asia
Cafe Atlantico
Cafe Deluxe
Cafe Japoné
Cafe Milano
Chi-Cha Lounge
eCiti
Felix
Grille 88
Gua-Rapo
Helix Lounge
Kramerbooks
Le Tarbouche
Local 16
McCormick/Schmick's
Meze
Mie N Yu
Mondo Sushi
Nathans
Neyla
Old Ebbitt Grill
Old Glory BBQ†
Paolo's†
Peacock Cafe
Perry's
Red Sage
R.F.D. Washington
Rocklands†
Saki
Savino's Cafe
Sequoia
Sesto Senso
Siné
Smith Point
South Beach
Sweetwater Tavern†
TenPenh
Thai Tanic
Timpano Chophse.
Toka Cafe
Tony/Joe's Seafood
Topaz Bar
Tryst
Uni
Union St.
U-topia
Vida
Zaytinya

Tea Service
Bailiwick Inn
Ching Ching Cha
Jefferson
Ritz-Carlton (DC)
Ritz-Carlton (Pentagon)
Teaism†
Willard Room

Theme Restaurants
Agua Ardiente
Buca di Beppo
Cities
Green Field Chur.
Mie N Yu
Mimi's American
Red Sage
Zola

Transporting Experiences
(Like traveling to another place and time)
Bar Rouge
Bombay Club
Caucus Room
Ching Ching Cha
Green Papaya
Heritage India†
Inn/Little Washington
L'Auberge Chez Fr.
Makoto
Maxim
Neyla
Red Sage
Tara Thai†
Topaz Bar
Tower Oaks Lodge
Zaytinya
Zola

Views
Cantina Marina
Charlie Palmer Steak
Finn & Porter
Gerard's Place
Il Cigno
Lafayette
L'Auberge Chez Fr.
Local 16

Washington, DC – Special Feature Index

New Heights
Perry's
Restaurant 2941
Rico y Rico
Ristorante La Perla
Roof Terrace
Ruth's Chris†
Sea Catch
Sequoia
701
Tower Oaks Lodge

Visitors on Expense Account

Amada Amante
Bailiwick Inn
Barolo
Butterfield 9
Café 15
Capital Grille
Capri
Caucus Room
Charlie Palmer Steak
Citronelle
Colvin Run Tavern
Elysium
Etrusco
Fahrenheit & Degrees
Galileo
Gerard's Place
Inn/Little Washington
i Ricchi
Jeffrey's at Watergate
jordans
Kinkead's
Lafayette
Maestro
Marcel's
Morton's†
Mr. K's
Nick & Stef's Steak
Oceanaire Seafood
Olives
Palena
Palm
Prime Rib
Restaurant 2941
Ristorante La Perla
Ritz-Carlton (DC)
Ritz-Carlton (Pentagon)
Ruth's Chris†
Sam & Harry's†
1789
Signatures
Tosca
Vidalia

Willard Room
Yanÿu

Winning Wine Lists

Amada Amante
Ashby Inn
Barolo
Bistro Bis
Bistro Français
Cafe Atlantico
Café 15
Capital Grille
Carlyle
Cashion's Eat Pl.
Caucus Room
Cesco
Charlie Palmer Steak
Citronelle
Colvin Run Tavern
Elysium
Etrusco
Evening Star
Fahrenheit & Degrees
Gabriel
Galileo
Gerard's Place
Grapeseed
Inn/Little Washington
Jaleo
Johnny's Half Shell
jordans
Kinkead's
La Chaumiere
La Colline
Le Relais
Maestro
M & S Grill
Marcel's
Melrose
Mendocino Grille/Wine
Mezza9
Mon Ami Gabi
Nathans
New Heights
Nick & Stef's Steak
Nora
Obelisk
Occidental
Old Ebbitt Grill
Oval Room
Palena
Palm
Prime Rib
Prince Michel
Restaurant 7
Restaurant 2941

Washington, DC – Special Feature Index

Rico y Rico
Sam & Harry's
Seasons
Smith & Wollensky
Sushi-Ko
Taberna del Alab.
Tivoli
Tosca
Vidalia
Washington Cafe
Willard Room
Zaytinya
Zola

Worth a Trip
Boyce, VA
  L'Auberge Prov.
Flint Hill, VA
  Four/Twenty Blackbirds
Leon, VA
  Prince Michel
Orange, VA
  Willow Grove Inn
Paris, VA
  Ashby Inn
The Plains, VA
  Rail Stop
Washington, VA
  Inn/Little Washington

Baltimore, Annapolis and the Eastern Shore

Baltimore's Most Popular

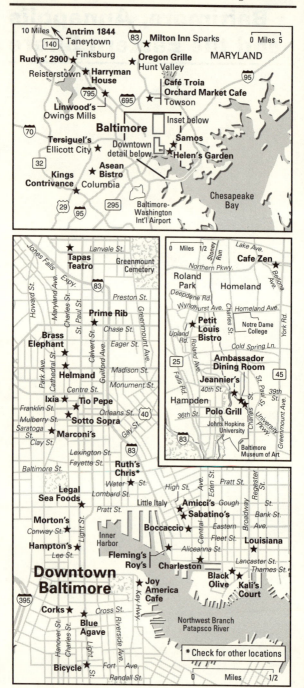

Baltimore's Top Ratings

Excluding places with low voting. An asterisked restaurant is tied with the one directly above it. All restaurants are in the Baltimore area unless otherwise noted (A=Annapolis and E=Eastern Shore).

Most Popular

1. Charleston
2. Prime Rib
3. Tio Pepe
4. Helmand
5. Ruth's Chris
6. Morton's
7. Linwood's
8. Petit Louis Bistro
9. Ambassador Din. Rm.
10. Boccaccio
11. Tersiguel's
12. Bicycle
13. Brass Elephant
14. Oregon Grille
15. Black Olive
16. Legal Sea Foods*
17. Hampton's
18. Milton Inn
19. Kali's Court
20. Sotto Sopra
21. Helen's Garden
22. Orchard Market Cafe
23. Antrim 1844
24. Kings Contrivance
25. Blue Agave
26. Louisiana
27. Ixia
28. Samos
29. Corks
30. Fleming's
31. Cafe Zen
32. Amicci's
33. Marconi's*
34. Rudys' 2900*
35. Jeannier's
36. Joy America Cafe*
37. Asean Bistro
38. Harryman House*
39. Café Troia
40. Sabatino's*
41. Tapas Teatro*
42. Roy's

It's obvious that many of the restaurants on the above list are among the Baltimore area's most expensive, but if popularity were calibrated to price, we suspect that a number of other restaurants would join the above ranks. Given the fact that both our surveyors and readers love to discover dining bargains, we have added a list of 40 Best Buys on page 162. These are restaurants that give real quality at extremely reasonable prices.

vote at zagat.com

Top Food

Top 20 Food

- **28** Prime Rib
- **27** Samos
  - Charleston
  - Hampton's
  - Stone Manor
  - 208 Talbot/E
  - Joss Cafe & Sushi/A
  - Trattoria Alberto
- **26** Milton Inn
  - Lewnes' Steakhse./A
  - Helmand
  - Linwood's
  - Bistro St. Michaels/E
  - Antrim 1844
  - Boccaccio
  - Tio Pepe
  - Rudys' 2900
- **25** Les Folies/A
  - Oregon Grille
  - Tersiguel's

By Cuisine

American (New)
- **27** Charleston
  - Hampton's
  - Stone Manor
- **26** Linwood's
  - Antrim 1844

American (Traditional)
- **26** Milton Inn
- **25** Oregon Grille
- **24** Brass Elephant
- **21** Harryman House
- **20** SoBo Cafe

Asian Fusion/Pan-Asian
- **24** Purple Orchid
- **23** Asean Bistro
  - Ixia
  - Yin Yankee Cafe/A
  - Eurasian Harbor

Chesapeake Bay
- **25** Brighton's
  - Narrows/E
- **24** Pierpoint
- **23** Harry Browne's/A
- **21** Gertrude's

Chinese
- **24** Szechuan Best
- **23** Szechuan House
- **21** Cafe Zen
- **20** P.F. Chang's

Continental
- **27** 208 Talbot/E
- **26** Rudys' 2900
- **24** Northwoods/A
- **22** Josef's Country Inn
  - Marconi's

Crab Houses
- **25** Costas Crab
- **23** Cantler's Riverside/A
- **21** Obrycki's Crab
  - Harris Crab/E
- **20** Crab Claw/E

French
- **25** Tersiguel's
- **23** Jeannier's
- **22** Martick's
- **20** Crêpe du Jour

French (Bistro)
- **26** Bistro St. Michaels/E
- **25** Les Folies/A
- **24** Petit Louis Bistro
- **20** Cafe Normandie/A
  - Crêpe du Jour

Greek
- **27** Samos
- **24** Kali's Court
- **21** Ikaros
  - Zorba's

Top Food

Italian
- 27 Trattoria Alberto
- 26 Boccaccio
- 24 Sotto Sopra
- 23 Café Troia
- 22 La Scala

Seafood
- 25 O'Learys Seafood/A
  Black Olive
- 23 Faidley's Seafood
  Pisces
- 22 Sam's Waterfront/A

Steakhouses
- 28 Prime Rib
- 26 Lewnes' Steakhse./A
- 25 Oregon Grille
- 24 Ruth's Chris
  Morton's

Sushi
- 27 Joss Cafe & Sushi/A
- 25 Matsuri
- 24 Edo Sushi
  Sushi Hana
  Tsunami/A

By Special Feature

Boat-Accessible
- 25 Narrows/E
- 23 Cantler's Riverside/A
- 22 Sam's Waterfront/A
- 21 Harris Crab/E
- 20 Crab Claw/E

Breakfast†
- 25 Brighton's
- 23 Blue Moon Cafe
- 19 City Cafe
- 17 Baugher's
- 16 Cafe Hon

Brunch
- 24 Ambassador Din. Rm.
- 23 Blue Moon Cafe
  Pisces
- 21 Carrol's Creek/A
- 19 City Cafe

Business Dining
- 27 Charleston
  Hampton's
- 26 Linwood's
  Boccaccio
- 23 Harry Browne's/A

Historic Places
- 26 Milton Inn
- 22 Elkridge Furnace Inn
- 21 Baldwin's Station
- 20 Treaty of Paris/A
- 18 Woman's Industrial Ex.

Hotel Dining
- 27 Hampton's
  Harbor Court Hotel
- 25 Brighton's
  Harbor Court Hotel
- 24 Morton's
  Sheraton Inner Harbor
- 23 Pisces
  Hyatt Regency
- 20 Windows
  Renaissance Harborplace

Newcomers
- b
- 4 West
- La Mona Lisa/A
- Reynolds Tavern/A
- Tiburzi's

Worth a Trip
- 27 Stone Manor
  Middletown
  208 Talbot/E
  St. Michaels
- 26 Antrim 1844
  Taneytown
- 25 Narrows/E
  Grasonville
- 23 Cantler's Riverside/A
  Annapolis

† Other than hotels

vote at zagat.com

Top Food

By Location

Annapolis
- **27** Joss Cafe & Sushi
- **26** Lewnes' Steakhse.
- **25** Les Folies
  O'Learys Seafood
- **24** Northwoods

Downtown North/Charles St./Mt. Vernon
- **28** Prime Rib
- **26** Helmand
- **24** Brass Elephant
  Sotto Sopra
- **23** Tapas Teatro

Eastern Shore
- **27** 208 Talbot
- **26** Bistro St. Michaels
- **25** Narrows
- **21** Harris Crab
- **20** Michael Rork's

Fells Point
- **25** Louisiana
  Black Olive
- **24** Pierpoint
  Kali's Court
  Peter's Inn

Inner Harbor
- **27** Hampton's
- **25** Brighton's
- **24** Purple Orchid
- **23** Pisces
- **22** Joy America Cafe

Inner Harbor East/Little Italy
- **27** Charleston
- **26** Boccaccio
- **22** La Scala
- **21** Amicci's
- **20** Sabatino's

Outer Baltimore
- **27** Trattoria Alberto
- **26** Milton Inn
  Linwood's
  Rudys' 2900
- **25** Tersiguel's

South Baltimore
- **25** Bicycle
  Matsuri
- **24** Corks
- **21** Vespa
  Blue Agave

Top 20 Decor

28 Hampton's
 Antrim 1844
27 Stone Manor
 Milton Inn
 Brighton's
26 Ixia
 Brass Elephant
 Oregon Grille
 Charleston
 Prime Rib
 Louisiana
 Eurasian Harbor
25 Linwood's
 Aldo's
 Ambassador Din. Rm.
 Elkridge Furnace Inn
 Sotto Sopra
24 Pisces
 Roy's
 Joy America Cafe

Outdoors

Ambassador Din. Rm.
Cantler's Riverside/A
Carrol's Creek/A
Crêpe du Jour
Harris Crab/E
Helen's Garden
Joy America Cafe
L.P. Steamers
Narrows/E
Reynolds Tavern/A
River Watch
Tapas Teatro

Romance

Ambassador Din. Rm.
Cafe de Paris
Charleston
Columbia/E
Hampton's
Healing Heart
Helen's Garden
La Mona Lisa/A
Milton Inn
208 Talbot/E
Woman's Industrial Ex.
Ze Mean Bean

Rooms

Ambassador Din. Rm.
Brass Elephant
Cafe de Paris
Columbia/E
Eurasian Harbor
Hampton's
Inn at Perry Cabin/E
Milton Inn
Sascha's 527
Woman's Industrial Ex.

Views

Brighton's
Gertrude's
Hampton's
Inn at Perry Cabin/E
Joy America Cafe
L.P. Steamers
Phillips
Pisces
River Watch
Windows

Top 20 Service

27 Prime Rib
 Hampton's
26 Charleston
 208 Talbot/E
 Antrim 1844
25 Milton Inn
 Boccaccio
 Linwood's
 Brighton's
 Stone Manor*
24 Northwoods/A
 Lewnes' Steakhse./A
 Tersiguel's
 Marconi's
 Les Folies/A
 Ambassador Din. Rm.
 Brass Elephant
 Helmand
 Aldo's
 Oregon Grille

vote at zagat.com

Best Buys

Top 20 Bangs for the Buck

1. Woman's Industrial Ex.
2. Samos
3. Attman's Deli
4. Chick & Ruth's/A
5. Holy Frijoles
6. Blue Moon Cafe
7. Faidley's Seafood
8. Jimmy's
9. Baugher's
10. Szechuan Best
11. Szechuan House
12. SoBo Cafe
13. Cafe Zen
14. Cafe Hon
15. Crêpe du Jour
16. Suzie's Soba
17. Holly's/E
18. Banjara
19. Helmand
20. Thai

Other Good Values

Barn
Bill's Terrace Inn
Chameleon Café
City Cafe
Costas Crab
Fuji
Helen's Garden
Ikaros
Jalapeño/A
Kelly's
L.P. Steamers
Martick's
McNasby's/A
Peppermill
River Watch
Sabatino's
Szechuan
Thai Arroy
Timbuktu
Zorba's

Baltimore, Annapolis and the Eastern Shore Restaurant Directory

Baltimore

F | D | S | C

Abacrombie [S] – | – | – | E
Badger Inn, 58 W. Biddle St. (Cathedral St.), 410-837-3630
Melanie and Sonny Sweetman, new owners of the B&B upstairs from this Contemporary American, have freshened up the former La Tesso Tana to provide a pretty, tranquil and intimate alternative before the Meyerhoff Symphony Hall across the street or the Lyric, a block away; the limited bill of fare may be expanded later, but for now, it's enough that they get everyone calmly out by curtain time.

Acacia [S] – | – | – | E
129 N. Market St. (Patrick St.), Frederick, 301-694-3015
Constrained by its brewpub formula but aspiring to be more, Brewer's Alley has spawned a civilized, pretty cousin across the street, with a California-inspired, Asian-tinged New American menu that chef Frank Tyerer hopes will raise the bar for fine dining on Downtown Frederick's restaurant row, sans DC prices; an appreciative audience agrees, necessitating reservations for weekends.

AIDA Bistro – | – | – | E
7185A Gateway Dr. (Rte. 175), Columbia, 410-953-0500
Happy regulars at the bar in this mustard-colored, high-ceilinged room forget they're in a Columbia strip mall, especially with jazz on Wednesdays, while they chow down on chef de cuisine Eric Sollohub's Italian-accented New American offerings like lime juice–braised pork loin on saffron pappardelle or asparagus risotto with tarragon; now that the word's out, weekend reservations are a good idea.

Aldo's [S] 24 | 25 | 24 | $45
306 S. High St. (Fawn St.), 410-727-0700
◪ "Expensive but worth it" say surveyors smitten by this "posh", "family-run" Southern Italian in Little Italy, which delivers "beautiful food in a beautiful setting" by a staff that pampers "like royalty"; those who "love it go back" often for a "truly gourmet", "elegant evening" out that "gets better" with the years, but detractors think "they take themselves too seriously" and object to their "dog and pony show."

AMBASSADOR DINING ROOM [S] 24 | 25 | 24 | $28
3811 Canterbury Rd. (bet. 39th St. & University Pkwy.), 410-366-1484
■ Known for "distinctive, complex" Indian food "at its best", this "regal" "gem" in Homewood near the Hopkins campus "appeals even to people who think they don't like

Indian"; "cushy and intimate inside", with "magical" garden dining outside, it provides "a return to the days of the Raj", replete with "marvelously" "gracious" service that helps make it a "romantic" "special-occasion kind of place."

Amicci's [S] 21 | 15 | 19 | $24

231 S. High St. (bet. Fawn & Stiles Sts.), 410-528-1096

◪ "Solid pastas at prices that are hard to beat" ensure "long lines" at this "simple", "laid-back" Italian "find" with "no pretensions"; supporters swear it's "just as good as many other places in Little Italy, only with college-student decor", but they gladly overlook the "minimalist" digs because "you can't go wrong" with the "super" food; added seating should ease the "cramped" quarters.

Angelina's [S] 18 | 11 | 16 | $27

7135 Harford Rd. (Rosalie Ave.), 410-444-5545

◪ "Long considered to make the best crab cakes in the city", this "homey" "neighborhood" Italian quartered in an "ancient row house" in Northeast Baltimore has been feeding generations for half a century; "disappointed" diners, however, who lament that the once "highly touted" "baseball-size" signature item is now "no big deal" and caution that the rest of the menu is "hit-or-miss" yet "overpriced", conclude that it's "living on its reputation."

ANTRIM 1844 [S] 26 | 28 | 26 | $60

30 Trevanion Rd. (Rte. 140), Taneytown, 410-756-6812

■ "Romantics" "swoon" over this "historic" country inn "wonderfully" "secluded" in the Catoctin Mountains near Gettysburg; it takes visitors back "to a more genteel era" with its "elegant" interior, "gorgeous" gardens, veranda dining and "impeccably courteous" service; admirers predict that chef Michael Gettier's "superb" French-accented New American menu "will make it one of the top destinations in Maryland"; though "you may need a bank loan and three hours" for dinner, it's "worth" it.

Asean Bistro [S] 23 | 22 | 21 | $27

8775 Centre Park Dr. (Rte. 108), Columbia, 410-772-5300

◪ Far "less stereotypical" than what you'd expect of a "strip-mall" establishment, "consummate restaurateur" Jesse Wong's "fancy" Pan-Asian bistro in Columbia appeals with a "great variety of dishes presented with artistic flair" in "spiffy" surroundings; a few frugal types who deem it "a little pricey", though, quip "a piano player shouldn't make Chinese food cost this much."

Atlantic [S] 21 | 23 | 19 | $36

American Can Company Bldg., 2400 Boston St. (Hudson St.), 410-675-4565

◪ Luring a "hip crowd" to Canton, this "chic" seafood-centric New American with "big city" decor is a "visual pleasure" with tiered seating overlooking a central dance floor/sushi bar; at peak times there's a "terrific din (be ready to yell)", especially when there's live entertainment.

Attman's Delicatessen [S] 23 9 15 $12

1019 E. Lombard St. (bet. Central Ave. & Fallsway), 410-563-2666

◪ "If you get a yen for a hot corned beef sandwich or a fat hot dog", head to this "classic Jewish-style deli" in East Baltimore, "give your order" to the "colorful countermen" and carry your meal to the "tacky" dining room that "hasn't changed in years"; it may be located in a "bleak" area east of Downtown, but it's "worth the drive from Washington" to "hit that certain spot"; closes by 6:30 PM daily.

Austin Grill [S] 16 15 16 $21

American Can Company Bldg., 2400 Boston St. (Hudson St.), 410-534-0606

See review in Washington, DC Directory.

b [S] – – – M

1501 Bolton St. (Mosher St.), 410-383-8600

Helmand and Tapas Teatro's new sibling opened to enthusiastic acclaim from Bolton Hill neighbors parking their strollers by sidewalk tables and chatting in the comfortable high-ceilinged corner storefront over cutting-edge Eclectic–New American dishes that manage to feel homey, like grilled polenta and portabello with caramelized onion marmalade, designer pizzas and diet-breakers à la a transcendent bread pudding with vanilla sauce.

Babalu Grill [S] 20 21 18 $31

32 Market Pl. (Water St.), 410-234-9898

■ "Deliberately hip" and "always packed", this "Nuevo Latino" supper club near the Inner Harbor is a hot "place to see and be seen", attracting a "20s-to-30s" crowd with its throbbing music; fans think it's off to a "good start", even if skeptics feel it's "trying too hard to be trendy. "

Baldwin's Station and Pub [S] 21 22 21 $34

7618 Main St. (Rte. 32), Sykesville, 410-795-1041

◪ "Trains still go by" this "beautiful historic station" at the "rural" Carroll County crossroads of Sykesville, "worth a detour" for "imaginative" New American dining with "a bit of sophistication" (but "kids are welcome"), as well as for the "picturesque" view of the Patapsco River from the deck; the "folk musicians on Wednesday evenings" add a sweet touch, but disgruntled passengers report being derailed by "unpredictable quality" and service that can be "lacking."

Banjara [S] 23 18 21 $22

1017 S. Charles St. (Hamburg St.), 410-962-1554

■ "Blissful" Indian food "where you'd least expect it" – South Baltimore – awaits at this "cozy", "candlelit" (read:

Baltimore

F | D | S | C

"dark") nook, a "great date" place with "excellent" dishes served by a "hospitable", "accommodating" staff in a "traditionally" decorated room; regulars swear they've "never had a bad meal here."

Barn S
▽ 19 | 12 | 18 | $25

9527 Harford Rd. (Joppa Rd.), Parkville, 410-882-6182
■ Apparently, "the Baltimore Colts haven't departed" the building, because at this "raucous basement crab house" tucked under a Parkville bar north of the Beltway, photos of Johnny Unitas and other former players still reign; amid a "wall-to-wall warm community feeling", fans tackle piles of "big and delicious" steamed crabs served year-round on long tables covered with paper; it's a "great place to spend an evening" talking sports, politics and philosophy.

Baugher's S
17 | 12 | 18 | $15

289 W. Main St. (Rte. 31), Westminster, 410-848-7413
■ "Step back in time" at this American "tradition" in Westminster, embraced by loyalists for its "country" food and "what-a-bargain" prices; "genuinely nice" "farmers' daughters and sons serve plain meals" "just like mom used to cook", followed by "wholesomely decadent desserts" of "homemade ice creams and pies"; though skeptics sniff "nothing spectacular", at least "you won't leave hungry."

Bertha's S
17 | 16 | 16 | $24

734 S. Broadway (Lancaster St.), 410-327-5795
■ "Dark" and "funky", this "classic" "watering hole" pioneered the gentrification of now "tourist-filled" Fells Point, and it "still looks like a place where Captain Ahab's crew might walk in"; the seafood-slanted menu stars its "world-famous mussels", though schools of critics carp that the bivalves are as "gritty" as the "grungy" decor, adding that it's "totally" "resting on its laurels"; "love it or hate it, you have to at least try" it.

Bicycle
25 | 20 | 22 | $35

1444 Light St. (Fort Ave.), 410-234-1900
■ Addicts "would pedal 100 miles" to this "very hip" South Baltimore "storefront" for the chance to savor chef-owner Barry Rumsey's "playful perfection", exemplified by his Thai-style rockfish baked in banana leaves and teamed with chutney, red curry sauce and black sticky rice; the other dishes on the Eclectic menu are equally "complex and interesting", making this "tiny" "husband-and-wife"-run bistro a true "foodie haven", but better "reserve weeks in advance" and perhaps "bring earplugs."

Bill's Terrace Inn S
▽ 23 | 12 | 18 | $28

200 Eastern Blvd. (Mace Ave.), Essex, 410-687-5996
■ "There's no Bill, no terrace and no inn", but there is "great food worth waiting for" at this "straightforward"

Baltimore

F | D | S | C

crab house in old Essex; catering to a "true Bawlmer crowd", it serves "terrific steamed crabs" in the proper manner – dumped on paper-covered tables, accompanied by mallets and pitchers of beer; there are "no tourists" and "no atmosphere" either ("decor? – ha!"), just "real serious" eating "year-round."

Black Olive S   25 | 18 | 22 | $44
814 S. Bond St. (Shakespeare St.), 410-276-7141

◪ Be "transported to the Mediterranean" at this pair of "charming" renovated row houses in Fells Point, "heaven for serious seafood lovers"; "meet your treat before you eat" by taking the "fish tour" given by the "friendly owners", then have the "amazingly fresh" fare (including "exotic types that'll wow even aficionados") "simply prepared"; some wallet-watchers carp "sooo good but sooo pricey", but those who are hooked "always leave happy."

Blue Agave S   21 | 20 | 19 | $29
1032 Light St. (Cross St.), 410-576-3938

◪ At this "festive" hot spot in "revitalized" South Baltimore, the kitchen prepares "solidly good" "real" Mexican ("not American Mexican") dishes with a "nouveau twist", though the cocktails at the "superb" bar (stocked with a "wide variety of tequilas", it makes "amazing margaritas" that'll "make you smile") can eclipse the food; as a result, it often gets "too loud for conversation", you may feel a "bit rushed" and the service is "hit-or-miss."

Blue Moon Cafe S   23 | 16 | 17 | $15
1621 Aliceanna St. (bet. Bond St. & Broadway), 410-522-3940

■ "Go early or wait long", especially during Sunday brunch, at this "tiny" "hippie" cafe set in an old Fells Point house, but it's "worth" it because it "raises breakfast to real-meal" status; it's "hard to decide" between the "best cinnamon buns in the world", "excellent crab omelets", "phenomenal" eggs Benedict and other "superior" American fare, served by "down-to-earth" folks; the "portions are huge" and the prices "low", but note its "odd hours" (Friday and Saturday, it's open overnight).

BOCCACCIO S   26 | 23 | 25 | $46
925 Eastern Ave. (bet. Exeter & High Sts.), 410-234-1322

■ "Memories of the meal linger for days" rhapsodize admirers of this "extraordinary" Northern Italian "paradise", a "longtime favorite" of many; the "delicate", "delicious and different" dishes ("not the standard" suspects) are served amid "beautiful", "inviting" quarters by an "impeccable" team, so even though "it'll cost you" big ("thank God for expense accounts"), it's "first-class in every way" and it fully "deserves its reputation as one of Little Italy's best."

Baltimore | F | D | S | C |

Brass Elephant ⑤ | 24 | 26 | 24 | $41 |
924 N. Charles St. (bet. Eager & Read Sts.), 410-547-8480
■ Dating from Charles Street's grand era, this "beautiful 1850 merchant's townhouse" "elegantly" appointed with Italian white-marble fireplaces, "hand-carved" wood accents and Waterford crystal chandeliers may be an "old warhorse, but it still runs like a winner"; the daily bill of fare showcases "reinvented" Continental-American "classics" brought to table by an "attentive" staff, making it a "classy" destination for any "special occasion."

Brewer's Alley ⑤ | 20 | 18 | 19 | $23 |
124 N. Market St. (bet. Church & 2nd Sts.), Frederick, 301-631-0089
◪ Set in Frederick's onetime town hall and opera house, this "lively" hangout is a "casual spot" with an American menu that's "a step up from regular pub food", as well as a "variety" of "tasty" "beers brewed on-premise"; insiders advise come with "moderate expectations and you'll be all right", so best "stick to the basics."

Brighton's ⑤ | 25 | 27 | 25 | $44 |
Harbor Court Hotel, 550 Light St. (bet. Conway & Lee Sts.), 410-347-9750
■ A "perfect" "take-your-mother-to-lunch" kind of place, this "bright" and "gorgeous" (it always "feels like a spring day" here) hotel dining room boasts a view of the Inner Harbor that's "too good to be true"; it's located down the hall from well-regarded sibling Hampton's at the Harbor Court, and the link shows – from the "fancy" Chesapeake-inspired breakfast and lunch menus to the "delightful afternoon tea" and "excellent" dinner choices.

Cafe de Paris ⑤ | – | – | – | E |
8808 Centre Park Dr. (Rte. 108), Columbia, 410-997-3560
Erik Rochard's warm Country French bistro has found solid footing in Howard County, offering fans prix fixe or à la carte choices, a serious wine focus and occasional piano performances by Erik himself in a pretty office-building space lined with red banquettes; his wife, Patricia, serves simple lunches from her deli next door.

Cafe Hon ⑤ | 16 | 16 | 17 | $17 |
1002 W. 36th St. (bet. Falls Rd. & Roland Ave.), 410-243-1230
◪ Take a "trip back to the '50s" at this tribute to the blue-collar past of Hampden, a "Norman Rockwell painting come to life", where "real Bawlmer hons" sling "mom's kitchen" dishes (think American eats like meatloaf with mashed potatoes and homemade pies) in a "kitschy" "hodgepodge" of a setting; fans who love it "for what it is" beg "please don't change", but foes who think its "camp value" has worn thin lament that it has become "a victim of its own success."

vote at zagat.com

Café Troia [S] 23 20 22 $37

28 W. Allegheny Ave. (Washington Ave.), Towson, 410-337-0133

☐ In a suburban office building, this "unassuming" yet "sophisticated" family-run cafe is where a "veritable who's who of Towson" congregates for "refined" Tuscan-style specialties prepared "like they are in Italy"; the cooking seems more "seductive" than ever ("better than most in Little Italy"), but "parking is still always a problem."

Cafe Zen [S] 21 14 19 $18

438 E. Belvedere Ave. (York Rd.), 410-532-0022

☐ "Fast and efficient", this "neighborhood old faithful" near the Senator Theatre is ideal for a bite before or after a movie; in a small, "spare room" with "fluorescent lighting" and "a hint of Berkeley" in the air, sample a "tasty" variety of Chinese dishes that are "fresh and healthy" (including sushi and "lots of veggie choices").

Cangialosi's – – – M

336 N. Charles St. (bet. Pleasant & Saratoga Sts.), 410-547-7122

At night David Cangialosi's deli dining room emerges as a suave, serious supper spot with blond wood and an unhurried pace, serving after-work and pre-theater audiences Italian classics like chicken cacciatore and piles of pasta – kind of like Little Italy, where the chef toiled, but without the tourists; Charles Street parking's a bit tricky, as it's just above the Downtown business district, but prices are moderate.

Captain Harvey's [S] 19 15 17 $31

11510 Reisterstown Rd. (Delight Rd.), Owings Mills, 410-356-7550

☐ Over three generations, this Owings Mills seafood house has cultivated a "longtime following" with its "generous portions" of "good all-around" Chesapeake-style dishes, delivered with "motherly service" in a clubby, "comfortable" room with a "nautical" motif; those looking for a more "laid-back" meal repair to the adjacent "down-home crab shack" for "steamed-to-order" crustaceans; critics, however, carp "ordinary" and choose to "fish elsewhere."

Carlyle Club [S] – – – E

Carlyle Club, 500 W. University Pkwy. (41st St.), 410-243-5454

It's complicated: Lebanese cuisine interpreted by Indians trying to please both blue-hairs and long-hairs in an apartment-hotel dining room on the razor's edge between staid Roland Park and young Charles Village; loyalists like its exoticness, eagerness to please and live music, which help offset the area's parking challenges.

Center City Restaurant [S] – – – E

8 E. Preston St. (N. Charles St.), 410-986-0331

Arts district businesspeople, UB faculty and theatergoers are all hoping this brave new entry will succeed on a less-

Baltimore

| F | D | S | C |

than-tony block off N. Charles Street, below the train station; a busy cellar bar with banquettes, aquariums and plasma screens contrasts with a minimalist, windowless upstairs dining room where the focus is on chef David Gutman's New American dishes; plans call for light post-theater/night-owl fare till 4 AM Fridays and Saturdays.

Chameleon Café ∇ 26 | 19 | 23 | $27

4341 Harford Rd. (3 blocks south of Cold Spring Ln.), 410-254-2376

■ Appropriately named, this "absolute gem" "looks like a neighborhood coffee joint" but is a serious food-lover's haunt with a "creative" French–New American menu that has quickly made Harford Road an "unlikely" "new culinary destination"; it may be "out of the way", but these "world-class" dishes justifiably "draw patrons from all over town", and "once you discover it, you'll be back" too; dinner only.

CHARLESTON 27 | 26 | 26 | $53

1000 Lancaster St. (Exeter St.), 410-332-7373

■ Surveyors swoon over chef Cindy Wolf's "sublime" "see-and-be-seen" scene at Inner Harbor East, voted the Most Popular restaurant in Baltimore; it's an "impressive" "special-occasion" treat that's just about "perfect" – from her "inventive" New American menu influenced by the Low Country and the wine cellar overseen by husband Tony Foreman to the "elegant" environs and "impeccable" service, this is a "top-notch" experience "to be relished and lingered over."

Cheesecake Factory ●S 19 | 17 | 17 | $23

Harborplace Pratt Street Pavilion, 201 E. Pratt St. (South St.), 410-234-3990

See review in Washington, DC Directory.

Cibo S – | – | – | M

100 Painters Mill Rd. (Dolfield Rd.), Owings Mills, 410-902-2426

The Vitale family, of Little Italy's Aldo's, saw their Northwest customers less than they liked, so they built an outpost in Owings Mills with fancified New American dishes like lacquered salmon to accompany Italian offerings like dressed-up pastas and pizzas; the jury is still out on the dark, angular office-building space and pulsing techno music designed to raise voices, but the food and moderate prices have found early approval.

City Cafe S 19 | 17 | 17 | $20

1001 Cathedral St. (Eager St.), 410-539-4252

■ Once merely a "delightful place for coffee and dessert", this Mt. Vernon "hangout" has grown up to become a "crucial urban-energy center" that's "warm and alive", attracting a "hip, diverse Downtown crowd"; whether you're meeting friends to chat or you come alone to "sit and read", you'll be served "solid" American-Eclectic food by

Baltimore

| F | D | S | C |

a "friendly" crew, making it a "relaxing" "oasis in the city" and "a must on the weekend-brunch circuit."

City Crab & Seafood Company S — | — | — | M
Green Spring Station, 2360 W. Joppa Rd. (Falls Rd.), Brooklandville, 410-339-6300
Baltimore native Andy Silverman brings home a branch of his NYC good-times seafood pub and has been drawing a crowd at lunch with big burgers, fresh-cut fries, rich soups and some ambitious seafood entrees; the bar can get noisy, especially with Thursday's live music, but outside, the Greenspring Station office building's courtyard garden is a peaceful spot to chat while you chew.

Clyde's S 18 | 20 | 19 | $27
10221 Wincopin Circle (Little Patuxent Pkwy.), Columbia, 410-730-2829
See review in Washington, DC Directory.

Combalou Cafe S — | — | — | M
818 N. Calvert St. (Read St.), 410-528-1117
A shrine to artisanal cheeses, with a dining room furnished whimsically with "cheesy cow-print couches", this casual spot showcases the glory of dairy in every dish, from the International sampler plates to the "really unusual" salads, soups, sandwiches, quiches and seasonal specials; it's a good choice before Center Stage events or for a "light lunch" east of the Charles Street corridor.

Corks S 24 | 20 | 22 | $42
1026 S. Charles St. (bet. Cross & Hamburg Sts.), 410-752-3810
■ With a name like this, the fruit of the vine is the focus at this oenophile's dream set in an 1849 row house in Federal Hill; the "well-versed" servers "know their stuff", and they happily "guide" novices through the "heavenly", "fairly priced" compendium, which highlights boutique American labels ("some you'll never see anywhere else"); in the same user-friendly spirit, each item on the "arty", "seasonal" New American menu is paired with a suggested glass of wine.

Costas Crab House ●S 25 | 12 | 19 | $34
4100 N. Point Blvd. (Wise Ave.), Dundalk, 410-477-1975
■ "Super", "huge steamed crabs" (the "best") served in a "no-nonsense" manner in a "plain" atmosphere makes this seafood "joint" "worth the trip to Dundalk, hon"; if you "want to show guests the real B-more", bring them to this "blue-collar fantasy" of good grub (like a solid crab cake) at moderate prices, located not far from the steel mill.

Crêpe du Jour S 20 | 15 | 14 | $17
1609 Sulgrave Ave. (Kelly Ave.), 410-542-9000
☑ Bringing a "little bit of Paris" to Mt. Washington, this "cute little place" provides a "nice change of pace" with

Baltimore | F | D | S | C |

its "delicious" crêpes, both savory and sweet ("don't miss" the Nutella-banana version for dessert), and other serious bistro items; good news: the "cramped" digs are now less so after the addition of an expansive deck out back.

Da Mimmo ●S | 23 | 20 | 22 | $47 |
217 S. High St. (Stiles St.), 410-727-6876
◪ "Frequented by Baltimore's big names", the "nouveau riche and conventioneers on expense accounts" ("less so by natives"), this "swanky" Italian ristorante in Little Italy with "lovely old-world" decor is famed for its "to-die-for veal chop"; scores of "extremely disappointed" diners, however, complain about the "pretentious", "starstruck" staff and warn about the "astronomical" tabs, particularly the "specials without [announced] prices" (some "wish they could say it's worth the money, but it's not").

Della Notte S | 20 | 21 | 21 | $32 |
801 Eastern Ave. (President St.), 410-837-5500
◪ "Crazy neo-Roman" decor, with a "tree right in the middle" of the "open" room ("we're not ashamed to admit that we like sitting under the big branches"), sets the stage at this "busy" Italian; the "surprisingly" "solid" fare (traditional and "creative") "goes beyond marinara", even if it's "a little overpriced", but rare for Little Italy is the fact that it actually has parking; critics, though, pan the "generic" food, "overdone" appointments and "variable" service.

Due S | 23 | 23 | 22 | $37 |
McDonogh Crossroads, 25 Crossroads Dr. (McDonogh & Reisterstown Rds.), Owings Mills, 410-356-4147
◪ Owings Mills' "'in' crowd" patronizes this "more informal", "more affordable" "sister restaurant of Linwood's" next door when it "doesn't feel like getting as dressed up"; it's a "pretty place for a fine-dining experience", featuring "wonderful" Northern Italian dishes prepared in the shared kitchen, but even fans admit it's still "expensive" (though it remains "one of our favorite overpriced restaurants").

Dutch's Daughter S | – | – | – | M |
581 Himes Ave. (Rte. 40), Frederick, 301-668-9500
"Relocated to the edge of Frederick", this "old-style" American seafooder is housed in a stadium-size building and prepares some of the "best crab cakes and crab imperial around"; the rest of the menu is pretty "terrific" too, "very fresh" and reasonably priced.

Edo Sushi S | 24 | 17 | 22 | $25 |
Padonia Mall, 53 E. Padonia Rd. (York Rd.), Timonium, 410-667-9200
Garrison Forest Shopping Ctr., 10347 Reisterstown Rd. (Rosewood Ln.), Owings Mills, 410-363-7720
◪ Though the York Road corridor is home to a number of sushi houses, this small BYO Japanese "hidden in a strip

Baltimore

| F | D | S | C |

mall" in Timonium (and its new Owings Mills sibling) is worth seeking out; the "friendly owner" and "entertaining", "chatty" chefs "remember everything and everyone", which explains why it has become a "nice neighborhood place" with "a large following of regular customers"; the only drawbacks: minimal decor and the "lack of a liquor license."

Elkridge Furnace Inn S | 22 | 25 | 23 | $41 |
5745 Furnace Ave. (bet. Main St. & Race Rd.), Elkridge, 410-379-9336
◪ Set on tree-dotted grounds a stone's throw from the Patapsco River, this "beautiful" 18th-century inn in Elkridge may be the "most romantic restaurant in the Baltimore" area; the frequently changing French menu is "generally very good", but the consensus is that the food and the "erratic" service are "no match" for the "appealing" setting.

Ethel & Ramone's S | – | – | – | M |
1615 Sulgrave Ave. (Kelly Ave.), 410-664-2971
"If you like New Orleans gumbo, this is the place" to go in Mt. Washington say boosters of "talented" chef-owner Edward Bloom's "funky" Creole-accented Eclectic set in a patchwork of tiny spaces in an old house; his "innovative" menu "changes seasonally", but those in-the-know urge "get any of the specials" and "don't miss the soup sampler"; the vibe is "so friendly you'll feel like a regular right away" and if you're "lucky", "you'll sit out on the porch."

Eurasian Harbor S | 23 | 26 | 21 | $38 |
Pier 5 Hotel, 711 Eastern Ave. (President St.), 410-230-9992
◪ Eliciting "wows" for its "chic" setting, this "great addition to the B-more dining" scene at the Inner Harbor "tries" to offer "something for everyone"; the Eurasian "fusion" repertoire presents "delicious combinations" that admirers say are "a treat", while the "hip bar" concocts "splashy drinks"; detractors counter that despite "fabulous menu descriptions", the "food doesn't live up to the fancy decor."

Faidley's Seafood | 23 | 11 | 15 | $15 |
Lexington Mkt., 203 N. Paca St. (Lexington St.), 410-727-4898
◪ "Full of lump meat", the "perfect crab cakes" prepared at this Lexington Market seafood stall have long been the "standard of comparison" in Charm City; not only are they the "freshest in town", but they're also blessed with chef/co-owner Nancy Devine's "secret seasoning", so even if you "must stand to eat" them in "very, um, rustic" digs, who cares when they're absolutely the "real thing"?

Fernando's Salsa Grill | – | – | – | I |
6644 Security Blvd. (bet. I-695 & Woodlawn Dr.), Woodlawn, 410-265-5552
A strip-mall storefront is home to a mix of traditional Central and South American countryside dishes, an expatriate

Baltimore

| F | D | S | C |

staff and friendly owner/ambassador Jay Angle, who introduces real Peruvian dishes like *escaveche de corvina* stuffed with crabmeat and *papa rellena* to lunchtime adventurers from nearby Social Security HQ and a nighttime date crowd that happily overlooks the spartan setting; there are Maryland crab cakes for less-adventurous types too.

Fleming's S
23 | 23 | 22 | $49
720 Aliceanna St. (President St.), 410-332-1666
See review in Washington, DC Directory.

4 West S
– | – | – | VE
The Inn at the Colonnade, 4 W. University Pkwy. (Charles St.), 410-235-8200
A new generation of chef (Jerome Dorsch) and owner (Rob Freeman) have updated the former Polo Grill, offering au courant New American tastes – and holdover favorites – in a revamped room with an enlarged cushy bar; hotel guests, professors from the Hopkins Homewood campus and the region's power players still happily speak in non-hushed tones, especially when the bar hops with live music; don't overlook the flashy starters, hand-cut fries or cheese course, all relative bargains.

Friendly Farm S
21 | 13 | 21 | $22
17434 Foreston Rd. (Mount Carmel Rd.), Upperco, 410-239-7400
◪ "Eat till you burst" at this "family-style" Traditional American set on a "scenic", "expansive" Upperco farm replete with ducks and geese in the ponds; "don't go when you're counting calories", as the long tables positively groan with "down-home" platters of "yummy fried chicken", "excellent crab cakes" and all the "country" fixings, and better prepare for lots of "children and grandchildren" running around, because this "informal" "throwback to the '50s" puts on "the ultimate family sit-down" supper.

Fuji S
∇ 24 | 16 | 22 | $24
10226 Baltimore Nat'l Pike (2 mi. west of Rte. 29), Ellicott City, 410-750-2455
■ "A jewel in an otherwise drab strip mall" in an "out-of-the-way area" west of Ellicott City, this "unassuming" "find" is a "nice family restaurant" that features "sushi like butter", as well as "hot dishes cooked with care" (notably the "superb tempura"); it's "small" yet it "doesn't feel too cramped", and the staff is "charming and friendly", leaving envious sorts "wishing it were in my neighborhood."

G&M S
21 | 8 | 15 | $23
804 N. Hammonds Ferry Rd. (Nursery Rd.), Linthicum, 410-636-1777
◪ "Locals are bemused" by the "never-ending lines" for the "softball-size" crab cakes prepared by this American

Baltimore   F | D | S | C

"dump" "near BWI Airport"; it may be "a one-trick pony", but addicts insist it's "well worth the trip" to Linthicum for this "lump meat", served up in a bare-bones setting; natives who dismiss it as "very overrated", however, sniff "only a tourist could love" these "disappointing" "boulders."

Gertrude's S   21 | 23 | 20 | $30
Baltimore Museum of Art, 10 Art Museum Dr. (Charles St.), 410-889-3399

▰ The "tranquility" of the "sculpture garden provides a lovely setting" for "Old Baltimore elements" to dine in "gracious" style at this "real restaurant" at the Baltimore Museum of Art; enthusiasts "love" what "TV chef" John Shields' (an avid advocate of Chesapeake Bay cookery) kitchen "does with Maryland seafood", but "disappointed" diners who deem it a "major letdown" lament "if only the food matched the surroundings" and add that the "service could be improved" too; N.B. closes by 9 PM.

HAMPTON'S S   27 | 28 | 27 | $59
Harbor Court Hotel, 550 Light St. (bet. Conway & Lee Sts.), 410-347-9744

■ Voted No. 1 for Decor in Baltimore, this "opulent" hotel dining room with an "unbeatable view" "overlooking the Inner Harbor" virtually guarantees a "stellar" experience, "spoiling" guests with "refined, delectable" New American dishes served by a staff that "treats you like royalty"; when you demand "first-class everything" for a "big-time special occasion", this "classy place" is a sure thing; needless to say, it's "very expensive."

Hard Times Cafe S   18 | 14 | 16 | $15
8865 Stanford Blvd. (Dobbin Rd.), Columbia, 410-312-0700
See review in Washington, DC Directory.

Harryman House S   21 | 21 | 21 | $33
340 Main St. (1¼ mi. north of Franklin Blvd.), Reisterstown, 410-833-8850

▰ "Between casual and fancy" describes the tone at this "historic log cabin" set on Reisterstown's old Main Street, which brims with quaint antique shops; folks meet here for "comforting" "country" American vittles served in "warm", "rustic" quarters made even "cozier" by its fireplaces; even if it's "maybe a little pricey for what you get", it seems just about "perfect on a crisp autumn evening."

Healing Heart Blues Bistro ◐S   – | – | – | M
1207 Liberty Rd. (MD Rte. 32), Eldersburg, 410-549-6000
An instantly popular tony club with an ambitious New American menu pops up nightly in a most unlikely spot: a farmland crossroads strip-mall slot that's a coffee shop by day; stylish tiered seating provides pleasantly surprised Carroll Countians good sightlines to blues and jazz vocalists,

Baltimore | F | D | S | C |

with distractions like sautéed lump crabmeat in vermouth cream sauce over pasta; kitchen tinkering is ironing out some opening kinks.

Helen's Garden S | 22 | 20 | 20 | $27 |
2908 O'Donnell St. (Linwood Ave.), 410-276-2233
■ First-time "customers are greeted as new friends" at this "relaxing oasis" in the "bar-infested Canton Square" area run by "exceptionally" "nice" owners who are "a trip"; it's a "genuine neighborhood cafe" with "colorful" paintings on display, providing an "arty" backdrop for "innovative" New American dishes with plenty of "pizzazz", along with a "super wine selection"; P.S. "the garden is a bargain on Wednesday nights", when $10 entrees are offered.

HELMAND S | 26 | 22 | 24 | $26 |
806 N. Charles St. (bet. Madison & Read Sts.), 410-752-0311
■ "Afghanistan's gift to Baltimore" has always maintained a "strong following for good reason", but now it is "enjoying renewed interest" due to world events; "no longer a hidden find in Mt. Vernon", it beckons with "exotic" dishes that "consistently" "hit the mark" (you "must try" the *kaddo* – "it'll forever change how you think about pumpkins" – and the *choppan*, "charcoaled rack of lamb at its absolute zenith"), "graciously" served by an "attentive" staff in an "elegant" room; to boot, it's an "incredible value."

Henninger's Tavern | 24 | 23 | 22 | $30 |
1812 Bank St. (bet. Ann & Wolfe Sts.), 410-342-2172
■ The "best-kept secret in Fells Point" is this "charming", "off-the-beaten-path" tavern, an "intimate", tin-ceilinged "treasure" set in a former candy store; it's a "wonderful blend of casual neighborhood bar and comfortable dining area with linen cloths and fresh flowers", but don't expect the usual pub grub because from the kitchen emerges "excellent", "imaginative" New American fare (including some of the "best mussels we've ever had").

Henry's, an American Bistro S | – | – | – | M |
Manor Shopping Ctr., 3493 Sweet Air Rd. (Jarrettsville Pike), Phoenix, 410-667-6600
In the horse country of Phoenix, north of Towson, this New American features a quiet sunroom up front, a granite-topped bar that buzzes with real estate and tack talk, and a simply appointed main room; wherever you sit, look for a menu that ranges from sandwiches like a grilled salmon BLT to pastas like 'Henry's almost famous' penne with blackened chicken.

Holy Frijoles S | 21 | 14 | 17 | $14 |
908 W. 36th St. (bet. Elm & Roland Aves.), 410-235-2326
☑ "Squeezing" into this "crammed" "hangout for Baltimore's alternative crowd" on Hampden's main drag is "like taking

Baltimore

| F | D | S | C |

a trip south of the border with a van full of art students"; that doesn't seem to bother the amigos who are "prepared to wait" for a "satisfying", "cheap" Mexican meal by passing the time "in the bar across the street" (a new liquor license means you can have a drink with your meal as well); critics who find the setup "awkward and uncomfortable", however, sniff "Tex-Mex by a bunch of gringos."

Ikaros S | 21 | 14 | 20 | $24 |
4805 Eastern Ave. (Ponca St.), 410-633-3750

■ "Just like being in Greece", this "pleasant" "family place" in Greektown is an "old-fashioned" "Baltimore tradition" for "delicious", "honest cooking" ("you can't go wrong with the grilled lamb or whole fish"); there's "nothing sophisticated" about this "time warp", but the people are "wonderfully friendly" and the portions so "enormous" (the "salad is a meal by itself") that stuffed surveyors quip "save time and ask for half of your order in a doggy bag."

Ironbridge Wine Co. ●S | - | - | - | M |
10435 MD Rte. 108 (Centennial Ln.), Columbia, 410-997-3456

Columbia residents fed up with chains find just what they want in this wine store that's also an intimate New American with dishes like seared scallops with saffron cream sauce; owners Steve and Rob Wecker, who honed their hosting skills at the original Elkridge Furnace Inn, oversee this comfortable space with its view of rolling farm fields; N.B. the bottles on the shelves can be bargain accompaniments for a small corkage fee.

Ixia | 23 | 26 | 21 | $41 |
518 N. Charles St. (Centre St.), 410-727-1800

◪ "Strange and interesting", this usually uncrowded Mt. Vernoner boasts a setting so "dramatically" "stunning" it's "like a stage set"; "almost as special as the fabulous space" is its "newfangled" Asian fusion cuisine, which "artfully" "mixes Eastern and Western flavors" to come up with dishes like pistachio-crusted black cod with a lobster relish and chocolate pavé with dulce du leche ice cream and chocolate rum sauce; skeptics, though, feel it's all "a little too contrived."

Jeannier's S | 23 | 18 | 22 | $35 |
Broadview Apts., 105 W. 39th St. (University Pkwy.), 410-889-3303

◪ "Not for the fast crowd", this "traditional" French grande dame set in a staid apartment building near Johns Hopkins is where "baby boomers take mom" on her special day; whether you opt for the "attractive" bar/cafe up front or the more "formal" dining room in the back, you'll be presented with "excellent" "standards", but those who aren't members of the "velvet-headband set" "would like to see a little creativity" on the menu.

Baltimore

	F	D	S	C

Jennings Cafe ◐ — 18 | 12 | 19 | $18
808 Frederick Rd. (Mellor Ave.), Catonsville, 410-744-3824
◪ Catonsville locals "couldn't do without" this "homey" American "institution", a "neighborhood bar" – "nothing more, nothing less" – staffed by genuine "Baltimore hons" who'll "scold you if you don't clean your plate", which is not hard to do, as "there are no better burgers in town" (the "crab cakes and oyster stew are fine" too); as for the "secondhand smoke", it's just "part of the ambiance."

Jimmy's Ⓢ — 17 | 12 | 17 | $14
801 S. Broadway (Lancaster St.), 410-327-3273
◪ "After you work the overnight shift", "stop in" at this "quintessential Bawlmer" version of "a corner diner" in Fells Point (it opens at 5 AM) and "say hello to Nick", the owner; "it looks like a dive, but breakfast is pretty good" and the "wide assortment of people" (including "celebrities, TV people and politicians") eating here lends it plenty of "local color"; though it's strictly "no frills", the "long lines" attest that it "must be doing something right."

JJ's Everyday Cafe Ⓢ — 19 | 11 | 18 | $21
2141 York Rd. (Timonium Rd.), Timonium, 410-308-2700
◪ Granted, "there's absolutely no atmosphere" at this "stark" little "local walk-in" stuck in a "drab" strip mall across from the Timonium fairgrounds, but "loyal" patrons return often for its "varied menu" of "surprisingly good" American chow ("try the crab cakes") at "good-value" prices; regulars regard it as a "real" BYO "find", but cynics carp "we went in with low expectations and they were met."

John Steven, Ltd. Ⓢ — 20 | 17 | 17 | $24
1800 Thames St. (Ann St.), 410-327-5561
◪ "You might just spot a pirate" at this "local joint" near the waterfront, a "diamond in the rough" with a "great Old Baltimore feel" that "epitomizes" Fells Point; it's a "fun place to hang out" (especially on the "pleasant" patio), down a few cold beers and take in the "people-watching"; the seafood-slanted menu is fairly extensive, but those in-the-know advise sticking with the basics by ordering the "awesome" mussels, clams or shrimp from the steamer bar.

Jordan's Steakhouse Ⓢ — – | – | – | E
8085 Main St. (Old Columbia Pike), Ellicott City, 410-461-9776
This fancy steakhouse on Ellicott City's Main Street is a highly comfortable temple of meat where the plush dining rooms are quiet and dark, with lots of space between tables, and most cuts of beef are available in choice or prime.

Josef's Country Inn Ⓢ — 22 | 21 | 21 | $37
2410 Pleasantville Rd. (Fallston Rd.), Fallston, 410-877-7800
◪ "Hearty", "old-fashioned" Continental-German fare "competently" turned out in "lovely" surroundings with a

Baltimore F | D | S | C

"quaint country feel" makes this stalwart "worth the drive" to Fallston; longtimers say the "dependable" "kitchen knows what it's doing" with the classics and also offers "a number of intriguing specials", but the unimpressed are left "lukewarm" by the experience.

Joy America Cafe S — 22 | 24 | 20 | $38
American Visionary Art Museum, 800 Key Hwy. (Covington St.), 410-244-6500
■ This "definitely different" dining room at the "zany" American Visionary Art Museum serves up "inventive" Latin American–Caribbean dishes like guacamole made tableside; even "cooler" than the culinary concoctions is the terrace with its "beautiful view" of the harbor as well as the adjacent three-story-tall whimsical whirligig; those who don't get it, though, proclaim it "strange."

Kali's Court S — 24 | 24 | 21 | $43
1606 Thames St. (bet. Bond St. & Broadway), 410-276-4700
■ "They know their fish" at this "attractive" "see-and-be-seen" Med seafood scene in Fells Point, and it's so "amazingly fresh" "it's worth the effort to try to find a parking place", especially if you can "hold court out on the lovely patio"; detractors note, though, that "reservations aren't honored on time", "it's noisy in the extreme" and the staff can be "rude"; the bottom line: the finny fare is "a treat, but expect to pay for it", in more ways than one.

Kelly's ●S — ▽ 21 | 12 | 18 | $20
2108 Eastern Ave. (bet. Chester St. & Collington Ave.), 410-327-2312
■ "Everyone's a regular" at this quintessential local spot, an "honest" workingman's bar in East Baltimore where first-timers become "instant friends" as they bond over a pile of steamed "crabs, crabs, crabs" and other Chesapeake-inspired seafood dishes ("without the touristy prices"); given the "old tunes" playing, as well as karaoke on the weekends, "warm, good times" are just about guaranteed.

Kings Contrivance, The S — 23 | 24 | 23 | $42
10150 Shaker Dr. (Rtes. 29 & 32), Columbia, 410-995-0500
■ Set in a "lovely", "historic" mansion, this "romantic" "special destination" has cultivated a loyal following with its "fancy" "old-world" setting (its "many little quaint rooms" foster a "quiet", "intimate dinner") and "consistently fine" New American menu; it's considered one of the "best that Columbia has to offer", but critics who don't think it's "worth a detour" find it "a little tired" and "haughty."

La Madeleine
French Bakery & Café S — 16 | 16 | 13 | $17
6211 Columbia Crossing Dr. (Dobbin Rd.), Columbia, 410-872-4900
See review in Washington, DC Directory.

La Scala [S] 22 19 23 $32

1012 Eastern Ave. (Central Ave.), 410-783-9209

◪ Three words you can't refuse: "grilled Caesar salad", the signature dish at this non-touristy Italian contender in Little Italy, where a meal is "like dining in [chef-owner] Nino Germano's home"; "truly one of Baltimore's best-kept secrets", it "comforts" fans with "thoughtfully prepared" dishes served in a "relaxing" ambiance, but "disappointed" detractors gripe "no surprises" here; P.S. "his mama's wonderful cannoli" is "not to be missed."

Legal Sea Foods [S] 19 16 18 $32

100 E. Pratt St. (Calvert St.), 410-332-7360

See review in Washington, DC Directory.

Liberatore's [S] 22 20 21 $33

Freedom Village Shopping Ctr., 6300 Georgetown Blvd. (Liberty Rd.), Eldersburg, 410-781-4114

New Town Village Ctr., 9712 Groffs Mill Dr. (Lakeside Blvd.), Owings Mills, 410-356-3100

Timonium Corporate Ctr., 9515 Deereco Rd. (Padonia Rd.), Timonium, 410-561-3300

140 Village Shopping Ctr., 521 Jermor Ln. (Rte. 97), Westminster, 410-876-2121

◪ "Always bustling", this growing family-operated mini-chain does "upscale suburban Italian" that admirers swear is "as good as Little Italy"; while set in places like "sterile office parks" and strip malls, the "exteriors belie the intimate interiors", which form "pleasant" backdrops for "solid", if "unremarkable", food; P.S. the Timonium branch boasts perhaps the "best adult bar scene in the county."

LINWOOD'S [S] 26 25 25 $45

McDonogh Crossroads, 25 Crossroads Dr. (McDonogh & Reisterstown Rds.), Owings Mills, 410-356-3030

■ "Cool elegance and seductive fare" combined with "smooth" service make this "sleek" New American "the place to be seen" in Owings Mills; it's "popular" for "power lunches, business dinners" and "long meals with friends", appealing with dishes that "sparkle" and a "Manhattan nightclub" feel; if the "softly lit" dining room is too formal for your taste, "you can go more casual and sit at the counter around the open kitchen" or out on the landscaped patio.

Louisiana [S] 25 26 23 $46

1708 Aliceanna St. (Broadway), 410-327-2610

■ Occupying a "beautifully redone" building in Fells Point, this "opulently" "over-the-top" "beauty" could provide the "setting for an Anne Rice novel"; nearly as "fabulous" as the surroundings are the New American dishes "inventively" spun with a Creole twist and brought to table by an "attentive" crew; the consensus: this is a "special-occasion" "keeper" that'll "impress anyone."

L.P. Steamers [S] ▽ 20 10 17 $20
1100 E. Fort Ave. (Woodall St.), 410-576-9294
◪ A "salty joint" filled with "neighborhood" characters who are definitely "part of its charm", this seafood bar set in a South Baltimore row house "just down the road from Ft. McHenry" is "worth going off-the-beaten-crab-path" (ask chef-owner Bud about his decadent deep-fried hard crabs); it can get smoky inside, but the rooftop deck is a fine place to take in the urban skyline.

Manor Tavern [S] 19 19 18 $32
15819 Old York Rd. (Manor Rd.), Monkton, 410-771-8155
◪ Trying to offer "something for everyone", this "pleasant horse-country tavern" in Monkton is a "favorite of the rural set" thanks to its "bucolic setting" amid rolling farmland; though its all-American bill of fare is "not exceptional" in any way, it's fine for a burger and a beer by the fire after a "beautiful ride through the Maryland" countryside.

Marconi's 22 18 24 $38
106 W. Saratoga St. (bet. Cathedral St. & Park Ave.), 410-727-9522
◪ "It hasn't changed since my grandfather ate here" marvel surveyors of this "man's restaurant" Downtown, and that's just swell by the stalwarts who feel that this "charming" relic of "Old Baltimore still stands up"; its Continental preparations are "frozen in tradition", so even if the "old-school" fare "isn't for gourmet diners", veterans "love it."

Martick's 22 17 17 $30
214 W. Mulberry St. (bet. Howard St. & Park Ave.), 410-752-5155
◪ "Eccentric owner-waiter-chef" Morris Martick, a "real character", "keeps hanging in there" at his highly "quirky" labor of love west of Downtown; though it's set in a sketchy neighborhood of the commercial district, intrepid types are rewarded with an "eclectic treat" of a "daily menu" that's "advertised as French" but brims with whimsical twists, which always results in an "exciting meal"; you'll either "love it or hate it", but there's "nothing quite like it."

Matsuri [S] 25 15 19 $25
1105 S. Charles St. (Cross St.), 410-752-8561
■ At the crossroads of South Baltimore's restaurant scene is this "casual", "popular" Japanese "hangout" that overflows quickly since it's "smaller than a bento box", but those in-the-know are adamant that it's "worth the wait" for some of "the best sushi in town", "terrific teriyaki" and a "good vegetarian selection"; though on "busy nights there's nowhere to queue up" except outside, the "friendly" service and "great prices" more than compensate.

Baltimore | F | D | S | C |

McCabe's S   20 | 13 | 18 | $23
3845 Falls Rd. (41st St.), 410-467-1000
▰ "The burger is worth putting up with the smoke" (as are the "remarkable" crab cakes) wafting through this "cute hole-in-the-wall" in Hampden, a "friendly neighborhood place where everyone knows your name"; the all-American eats "draw locals and folks from across the city", but the "too popular" "joint" is "tiny", so "be prepared for a wait."

McCormick & Schmick's S   21 | 21 | 20 | $37
Pier 5 Hotel, 711 Eastern Ave. (President St.), 410-234-1300
See review in Washington, DC Directory.

MILTON INN S   26 | 27 | 25 | $50
14833 York Rd. (3 mi. north of Shawan Rd.), Sparks, 410-771-4366
■ "Far away from the city" above Hunt Valley is this "quaint", "romantic country inn" that has "survived" for more than half a century; quartered in a 260-year-old fieldstone house, it serves "excellent" "traditional" American "standards" in a series of formal stone-and-wood rooms replete with fireplaces; "expensive but worth it", "it's a perfect place to take your rich uncle when he visits."

MORTON'S, THE STEAKHOUSE S   24 | 21 | 23 | $53
Sheraton Inner Harbor Hotel, 300 S. Charles St. (Conway St.), 410-547-8255
See review in Washington, DC Directory.

Obrycki's Crab House S   21 | 15 | 18 | $34
1727 E. Pratt St. (bet. Ann St. & Broadway), 410-732-6399
▰ "Crab in all forms" is the headliner at this sprawling brick fortress in East Baltimore; it's located near enough to the Downtown hotels that lots of "out-of-town visitors" cab over for a meal, but the natives are decidedly divided: while fans say it's "still the place" for seafood, foes carp that it's "too gentrified", "touristy" and "pricey"; P.S. it's best to "call ahead" to "order the big ones."

Orchard Market Cafe S   25 | 20 | 22 | $24
Orchard Plaza, 8815 Orchard Tree Ln. (Joppa Rd.), Towson, 410-339-7700
■ A gastronomic "oasis in the desert" east of Towson, this "small, simple", "family-run" place stuck "in a strip mall behind a strip mall" thrills those who "can find it" with "lovingly prepared" Persian food delivered in a "warm" atmosphere; its "exotic fare with a homey touch" makes it a "tasty" "change of pace" in the suburbs, while its BYO policy keeps the tabs even more "moderate."

Oregon Grille S   25 | 26 | 24 | $50
1201 Shawan Rd. (Beaver Dam Rd.), Hunt Valley, 410-771-0505
▰ "For an elegant night out" west of Hunt Valley, the "who's who" "straps on the money belt" and heads to this "clubby"

Baltimore   F | D | S | C

American steakhouse set in a "picturesque" 19th-century farmhouse; "dripping with horse-country richness", it showcases "superb" dry-aged sirloins in a "sleek" setting that "makes you want to sit up straight"; it's "definitely a player", but foes who gripe "way overpriced" wonder "why would anyone pay for so much attitude?"

Paolo's S   18 | 18 | 17 | $29
Harborplace Light Street Pavilion, 301 Light St. (Pratt St.), 410-539-7060
1 W. Pennsylvania Ave. (York Rd.), Towson, 410-321-7000
See review in Washington, DC Directory.

Papermoon Diner ●S   – | – | – | I
227 W. 29th St. (Remington Ave.), 410-889-4444
You'll either "love the atmosphere" or frown that it's "somewhat disturbing" say those who know this "bizarre" but entertaining 24/7 American diner in Remington, where "Barbies fly through the sky" and a "mannequin" poses in the "psychedelic bathroom"; once the haunt of milkmen and cops, it now feeds a mix of "yuppie" and "traditional" eats to bohemians and "Hopkins students"; the chow is "decent", though it's the decor that makes it a "must-see."

Pazza Luna   23 | 21 | 21 | $38
1401 E. Clement St. (Decatur St.), 410-727-1212
◪ "In Garlic We Trust" is stamped on the menu at this "intimate" homage to Italian-American life set in an old melting pot neighborhood near Ft. McHenry, so you should know what to expect from the celestial Northern Italian menu; it's a "warm and wonderful" refuge, and "they try hard to please", but "don't go if you don't like Frank Sinatra."

Peppermill S   19 | 16 | 20 | $25
Heaver Bldg., 1301 York Rd. (bet. I-695 & Seminary Ave.), Lutherville, 410-583-1107
◪ "Not only the senior set" enjoys the "good" American "home cooking" offered at this "pleasant" fallback tucked away in a Lutherville office tower; "youngsters" ("if you're under 60, you'll feel like a kid") come too for a "something for everyone" menu of "reliable, if unexciting", dishes priced "moderately" and served by "charming" folks.

Peter's Inn   24 | 17 | 20 | $23
504 S. Ann St. (Eastern Ave.), 410-675-7313
◪ "Where else can you eat scallops with caviar while only three feet from a biker drinking beer from a can?" ask regulars of this "tiny" row house in Fells Point, which looks like a "total dive bar" but actually turns out "gourmet" "comfort food"; though "there aren't many choices" on the Eclectic menu, the lineup changes weekly and most everything that emerges from the kitchen is "delicious"; "if you don't like smoke", however, keep moving.

PETIT LOUIS BISTRO [S] 24 22 22 $35
4800 Roland Ave. (Upland Rd.), 410-366-9393
◪ Like "a trip to Paris for $50, and they like Americans too" marvel devotees of this "perfect re-creation of a French bistro" "in the middle of Roland Park"; the "charming" brainchild of chef Cindy Wolf and wine director (and husband) Tony Foreman (the owners of Charleston), it's an "energetic" gathering place suitable for both "drop-in or special-occasion" dining, pleasing with "hearty" fare prepared with "panache" and paired with an "exciting" wine program; the "tables are close" and "the din makes conversation difficult", but it "deserves its popularity."

P.F. Chang's China Bistro [S] 20 20 18 $26
Mall in Columbia, 10300 Little Patuxent Pkwy. (Wincopin Circle), Columbia, 410-730-5344
See review in Washington, DC Directory.

Phillips [S] 15 15 14 $28
Harborplace Light Street Pavilion, 301 Light St. (Pratt St.), 410-685-6600
◪ Though "not a local favorite", this sprawling "tourist trap" "centrally located" in the Inner Harbor pulls in plenty of "visitors" with its "wonderful" outdoor tables ("great view" of the waterfront) and "abundant" seafood buffet ("be ready to strap on the feedbag"); it's "not too expensive" ("nothing to write home about" either), but the natives are "embarrassed" by the "mass-produced" grub (made with "foreign crabmeat") and warn there are "tons of better places in the area"; N.B. there's an outpost in Annapolis with a harbor view.

Pierpoint [S] 24 16 21 $38
1822 Aliceanna St. (bet. Ann & Wolfe Sts.), 410-675-2080
◪ "Old Maryland recipes get a contemporary makeover" (think "must-order smoked crab cakes") at this "small", "festive" (in a low-key way) eatery on the eastern edge of Fells Point; the consensus is that it can be "a little hit-or-miss", but when the kitchen's "clicking", the results are "superb" (it's at its "best when [chef-owner] Nancy Longo's cooking"), though be warned that the tables are "uncomfortably" tight.

Pisces [S] 23 24 23 $42
Hyatt Regency, 300 Light St. (bet. Conway & Pratt Sts.), 410-605-2835
■ "Don't let the hotel setting stop you" from trying this "beautiful" fish house atop the Hyatt Regency, which boasts a "spectacular harbor view"; it's an "impressive" destination for "creative", "surprisingly good seafood", as well as an extravagant Sunday champagne brunch buffet, tended to by a "skilled staff" in a "great" atmosphere; the "adequate wine list is a plus."

Baltimore

| F | D | S | C |

PRIME RIB 🆂 | 28 | 26 | 27 | $53 |
Horizon House, 1101 N. Calvert St. (Chase St.), 410-539-1804

■ "Old-time dress-up dining" distinguishes this "opulent" "'40s Manhattan–style supper club" set in a Downtown apartment house; voted No. 1 for both Food and Service in Baltimore, it promises a "special evening out", proffering "sublime prime rib" and other cuts in "luxurious" environs by "professional", tuxedoed waiters, with live music playing softly in the background; of course the "dollars add up", but this "venerable" "institution" elicits "wows on all fronts"; N.B. jacket required.

Purple Orchid 🆂 | 24 | 20 | 21 | $38 |
729 E. Pratt St. (President St.), 410-837-0080

◪ Easily overlooked at a busy intersection between the Inner Harbor and Little Italy, this "yummy" "find" is "still undeservedly undiscovered" after its move from Charles Street; that's a shame because its "amazing fusion of fine French and Pan-Asian" cuisines is "original" and "exquisitely presented" (there's a sushi bar too); "among the best of its genre", it's worth checking out.

Red Coral | – | – | – | M |
614 Water St. (Market Pl.), 410-528-1925

The Asian small-plate concept goes big-time commercial amid the party bars near the harbor, catering to business folks at lunch and the young and fashionable at night, who graze on sushi and Pan-Asian dishes that look trendy but include enough familiar tastes (like crab cakes) to satisfy all; dancing commences as the night wears on.

Red Maple ●🆂 | – | – | – | E |
930 N. Charles St. (Eager St.), 410-547-0149

"Perhaps more of a club" than a restaurant, this "chichi" Charles Streeter aspires to be "the hippest scene in Baltimore"; "gorgeous" in a "minimalist" way, it's a "cool" haunt with "exotic drinks", "tasty", "creative" Asian tapas (the "portions are very small", so "don't come hungry") and a DJ who ratchets up the music till late at night; it merits a visit if you're looking to be "transported", but better "wear black" (and don't expect comfortable seating).

River Watch 🆂 | 18 | 19 | 17 | $29 |
207 Nanticoke Rd. (Middleborough Rd.), Essex, 410-687-1422

◪ Moored on the workingman's "Riviera" in Essex, this colorful, boisterous summertime pleasure affords a "view that's alone worth the trip"; the seafood-slanted menu is only "acceptable", but if you "sit on the deck" "overlooking the marina" and order some steamed crabs and a pitcher of beer while listening to live music, you'll swear that this is the "best place in the world to eat in warm weather."

Baltimore   F D S C

Roy's ⓢ   24 | 24 | 23 | $45
720B Aliceanna St. (President St.), 410-659-0099

◪ "Way different for Bawlmer", this "glitzy" outpost of Roy Yamaguchi's Hawaiian fusion empire holds its own in Inner Harbor East, bringing his trademark "exotica" to Maryland (such as iron-seared mahi mahi with macadamia-lobster sauce, along with an "excellent variety of fish not usually found on the East Coast"); groupies cheer that it's "as pleasing to the eye as it is to the taste buds", but detractors who feel it's "too slick" for this town want to know "what's the big deal?"

Rudys' 2900 ⓢ   26 | 20 | 23 | $42
2900 Baltimore Blvd./Rte. 140 (Rte. 91), Finksburg, 410-833-5777

■ "Co-owners Rudy and Rudi", the "gracious proprietors", make it "worth the trip to Finksburg", because a "real pro is at work in the kitchen" (that would be "talented" German-born chef Rudy Speckamp), while the "best maitre d'" (Rudi Paul) tends to all details in the front of the house; expect Continental "classics" so "well prepared" that enthusiasts who have "always" enjoyed a "perfect meal" here swear that you "can't go wrong with whatever you order", though perhaps the decor could use "updating."

RUTH'S CHRIS STEAK HOUSE ⓢ   24 | 23 | 23 | $49
600 Water St. (bet. Gay St. & Market Pl.), 410-783-0033
1777 Reisterstown Rd. (Hooks Ln.), Pikesville, 410-837-0033
See review in Washington, DC Directory.

Sabatino's ◐ⓢ   20 | 16 | 19 | $29
901 Fawn St. (High St.), 410-727-9414

◪ No, this "unpretentious" Little Italy "landmark" is "not a hotbed of chic cuisine", but sometimes at "3 AM" its "old-world" "red-sauce cooking" is just what you need; at any time, expect a crowd of "genuine characters" (some with "really interesting hairdos") chowing down on its famous "Bookmaker salad" ("worth it for the dressing alone") and "dependable pastas" served by "career waitresses."

Saigon Remembered ⓢ   – | – | – | M
5857 York Rd. (Belvedere Ave.), 410-435-1300

The former Saigon has brought its solicitous service and extensive traditional Viet menu to new digs directly across from the Senator Theater in the blooming Belvedere Square environs, where there are plenty of seats for pho or flan fans before or after a flick.

SAMOS ⌀   27 | 16 | 23 | $16
600 S. Oldham St. (Fleet St.), 410-675-5292

■ "Where Baltimore's Greeks eat", this "bustling" little "neighborhood community center" in Greektown is "nothing fancy", but it exudes "true warmth", with a "welcoming

Baltimore | F | D | S | C |

staff that makes even sporadic visitors feel like regulars"; from his open kitchen, hardworking chef-owner Nick Georgalas satisfies his "big following" with "down-to-earth" dishes that are both Hellenic and "heavenly", and ridiculously "cheap" to boot.

San Sushi S | 22 | 14 | 18 | $25 |

9832 York Rd. (Padonia Rd.), Timonium, 410-453-0140
10 W. Pennsylvania Ave. (York Rd.), Towson, 410-825-0908

◼ Though "not much to look at", these Siamese siblings more than compensate with "terrific" food and "friendly" service; both feature "excellent sushi", but the Timonium branch also specializes in "great whole fish", while the Towson venue offers "wonderful", traditional tastes and Thai fusion cuisine; fence-sitters, however, shrug "above average", but "not worth going out of your way"; N.B. the York Road location is BYOB.

Sascha's 527 | 20 | 23 | 18 | $26 |

527 N. Charles St. (Centre St.), 410-539-8880

◼ "At the foot of Baltimore's Washington Monument", this "fancy yet funky" "hangout" housed in a former hair salon has won a following with its "over-the-top" decor and an "inventive" New American roster replete with a "mix-and-match sauce system"; admirers appreciate that the menu "includes both light fare and heavier dishes, to suit whatever appetite you may have", but conservative types counter that its "reach outstrips its grasp", resulting in a "disorganized" effort that "needs more work."

Shula's Steak House S | 20 | 18 | 18 | $46 |

Wyndham Baltimore, 101 W. Fayette St. (bet. Charles & Liberty Sts.), 410-385-6601
See review in Washington, DC Directory.

SoBo Cafe S | 20 | 15 | 17 | $18 |

6 W. Cross St. (Charles St.), 410-752-1518

◼ "Comfort food at a comfortable price in a comforting atmosphere" sums up this "small, friendly" "neighborhood dive" in South Baltimore; catering to "Generation X", it's an "unpretentiously" "hip scene" with "good art on the walls" and a frequently "changing menu that offers exciting options and old standbys" (including the "best mac 'n' cheese" and chicken pot pie) at "can't-beat prices."

Soigné | – | – | – | E |

554 E. Fort Ave. (Jackson St.), 410-659-9898

"Everyone's talking about" this "hot spot" near Ft. McHenry, and justifying the "great buzz" is Edward Kim's (the "accomplished" founding chef of Ixia) Pacific Rim "fusion" menu, which showcases "unbelievable combinations" of ingredients that result in "delicious" "innovations"; "a real plus for Baltimore", it's already "right at the top" of the town's restaurant pyramid according to fans who "would eat here every night if we could afford it."

Sotto Sopra [S] 24 25 23 $40

405 N. Charles St. (Mulberry St.), 410-625-0534

■ "Subdued fun" awaits at this "trendy" "date restaurant" on Charles Street that "lives up to the hype" by turning out "classics" so "outstanding" (the "homemade pastas are unusually good") they'll make "discriminating palates" "forget all about Little Italy"; the "eye-catching" decor forms a "lovely" backdrop for the "chichi crowd", which embraces it as a "tasteful" "place to see and be seen" that's "sure to impress your companion."

Spike & Charlie's [S] 21 18 18 $38

1225 Cathedral St. (Preston St.), 410-752-8144

◪ Since it's "across from the Meyerhoff Symphony Hall" and near the Lyric, this New American dining hall packs them in before events and focuses on getting them out by curtain; you can find "something unusual" on the menu, but clock-watchers who know the score opt for the well-rehearsed designer pizzas.

STONE MANOR [S] 27 27 25 $57

5820 Carroll Boyer Rd. (Sumantown Rd.), Middletown, 301-473-5454

■ Promising a "great getaway", this "gorgeous stone manor house" set on 114 acres of formal gardens and working farmland in the Middletown countryside is an "intimate, relaxing" "destination" for "memorable" New American cooking that amounts to "high art"; it's "beautifully presented" in "romantic", "understated" environs furnished with antiques and tended to by a "superb" staff, making it a near-"perfect" "experience" that the enchanted insist should "not be missed."

Strawberry's Bistro [S] – – – E

Bowie Town Ctr., 3851 Town Center Blvd. (Collington Rd.), Bowie, 301-262-7300

Almost hidden in the rear of Bowie's major shopping mall, ex BET executive Rosalyn Doaks' small, smart Southern-accented New American attracts a sophisticated audience glad to overlook the location to have a non-chain spot in restaurant-sparse Prince George's County; weekend music and a Sunday jazz brunch make it an entertainment destination as well.

Sushi Hana [S] 24 18 21 $23

6 E. Pennsylvania Ave. (York Rd.), Towson, 410-823-0372

◪ "Better than most of the other" Japanese options in town, this "reliable sushi" den in Towson pleases the cognoscenti with "consistently fresh and delicious" raw fish, "the most imaginative rolls around" and "excellent, personal" service; though it's often "filled with university students", it manages to pull off a "soothing" atmosphere that's only enhanced by the "pleasant" koi pond.

Suzie's Soba [S] 21 18 19 $21

1009 W. 36th St. (Roland Ave.), 410-243-0051

◪ Importing some international spice to old Hampden's restaurant row, this "cozy" Asian alternative offers "tasty" Korean dishes from owner Suzie Hong's native land, along with an "excellent" Japanese "noodle feast" ("packed with flavor") and sushi; boosters regard it as a "delightful" "little" "gem", but those who feel the "mediocre" food is "overpriced for what it is" ask "why bother?"

Szechuan ▽ 21 9 20 $18

1125 S. Charles St. (Cross St.), 410-752-8409

◪ Amid the Cross Street market hustle and bustle, this tiny "hole-in-the-wall" in South Baltimore is "often overlooked", but it "never fails to please" regulars with its "consistently" "wonderful" Chinese cooking; though it could use "serious redecorating", it's "family-friendly", the "pleasant" staff is "welcoming" and the prices are "cheap"; besides, "if the waitress likes you, you might get a naughty fortune."

Szechuan Best [S] 24 13 19 $18

8625 Liberty Rd. (Old Court Rd.), Randallstown, 410-521-0020

◪ "The Chinese community eats here, so you know it's good" say fans of this "neighborhood" "gem" that's "worth traveling" to Randallstown; "going way beyond the typical Chinese menu", it thrills connoisseurs with "authentic" fare ("great Peking duck"); who cares that "it's not much to look at"?

Szechuan House [S] 23 14 22 $19

1427 York Rd. (Seminary Ave.), Lutherville, 410-825-8181

◪ Lutherville's "nice little strip-mall find" is not so little anymore after doubling in size and adding a sushi bar; it's still "not fancy", but the Chinese food is as "tasty" as before, the service just as "friendly" and the "value" equally "great"; any surprise that partisans "dine here at least once a month"?; delivery is a perk rare in the area.

Tapas Teatro [S] 23 21 19 $25

1711 N. Charles St. (Lanvale St.), 410-332-0110

■ "How did we ever live without this place?" wonder regulars of this "frenetic" appendage to the Charles Theatre just above the train station; it delivers an "adventure" for the taste buds with its "array" of "wonderfully surprising" "little Mediterranean plates", presented in a room that's "upscale" in a "casual" way; "plan on waiting for a table", but it's "worth it" because this is a "great concept."

Baltimore | F | D | S | C |

Tasting Room | - | - | - | E |
101 N. Market St. (Church St.), Frederick, 240-379-7772
Decidedly cutting-edge, this addition to restaurant row in Frederick, set in a grand old merchant's corner store with big windows, is cultivating a tony following with its popular wine bar and creative, up-to-the-minute New American–Eclectic menu (think hoisin grilled pork loin with lobster whipped potatoes); N.B. closed on Sundays, except for its monthly wine tasting dinners.

Tersiguel's S | 25 | 24 | 24 | $46 |
8293 Main St. (Old Columbia Pike), Ellicott City, 410-465-4004
■ Savor "a small slice of the French countryside" at this "charming old house" in Ellicott City, a "sentimental favorite" for "robust", "remarkable" fare "beautifully plated"; devotees laud it as "all-around fabulous", with a series of "warm, comfortable" rooms and "attentive" service, adding up to a "special" "treat" that's "worth a trip" to the "outskirts"; the "underwhelmed", who find it "always good but unexciting", feel it's "living off its past."

Thai S | 23 | 14 | 20 | $21 |
3316-18 Greenmount Ave. (33rd St.), 410-889-6002
■ "Don't let the neighborhood turn you off" urge boosters of this "tacky" eatery located in a "questionable" part of Waverly, because the "real" Thai food prepared here is the "best in Baltimore" ("love the spring rolls"); not only are the dishes served "quickly", but they're "decently priced" too and there's a "parking lot in the back."

Thai Arroy S | - | - | - | M |
1019 Light St. (Cross St.), 410-385-8587
In bustling South Baltimore, couples on dates have long conversations in a peaceful storefront where émigré Thai ambassadors eagerly introduce their menu (duck dishes and many vegetarian choices) to newcomers; cognoscenti laud the authenticity, low prices and BYOB policy of this unassuming new favorite.

Thai Landing | 22 | 15 | 21 | $22 |
1207 N. Charles St. (Biddle St.), 410-727-1234
■ "Worth the parking trouble" in Mt. Vernon, this "small", "minimalist" Thai "near the opera and symphony" is a "so friendly" place to enjoy "flavorful", "lovingly prepared" dishes served by a "great" staff at "reasonable prices"; beware, though: "when they say spicy, they mean it."

That's Amore S | 16 | 15 | 17 | $27 |
Mall in Columbia, 10400 Little Patuxent Pkwy. (Broken Land Pkwy.), Columbia, 410-772-5900
10400 Little Patuxent Pkwy. (S. Entrance Rd.), Columbia, 410-772-5900
See review in Washington, DC Directory.

Tiburzi's — | – | – | M

900 S. Kenwood Ave. (Hudson St.), 410-327-8100
Canton neighbors and crosstown crowds have quickly taken to this handsome new corner row house bar with a friendly buzz, built and staffed as a family project by the extended eastside Tiburzi clan, for non-touristy Southern Italian fare and a few American selections like fat, flavorful crab cakes; an expansion next door is planned featuring a rooftop deck with panoramic harbor skyline views.

Timbuktu [S] 19 | 11 | 16 | $25

1726 Dorsey Rd. (Rte. 100), Hanover, 410-796-0733
◪ A "perfect meeting point" near BWI Airport (though "somewhat hard to find the first time"), this "nothing fancy" (a "dive", truth be told) "roadhouse" is "worth" seeking out for Chesapeake Bay fare including "big, real crab cakes" that are "highly superior to others nearby"; they're so "terrific" that they "defy description" and have become such a "cult phenomenon" that "addicts" have to "make a regular trek" here; "don't even bother" with anything else on the otherwise "ordinary" menu.

TIO PEPE [S] 26 | 22 | 23 | $44

10 E. Franklin St. (bet. Charles & St. Paul Sts.), 410-539-4675
◪ "We love it" shout aficionados of this "wonderful" Downtown "institution" that's renowned for preparing Spanish food "at its best"; it's a "Baltimore favorite for all celebrations" given its "amazing" fare served by a "well-seasoned" team in a "feel-good" atmosphere; for a "special night out", it's an "enduring tradition", but dissenters feel it's "overrated", citing dishes "adapted for the American palate", a "loud, cramped" setting and a "snobby" staff; P.S. "be prepared to wait, reservation" or not.

Trattoria Alberto 27 | 20 | 23 | $49

1660 Crain Hwy. S. (Rte. 100 underpass), Glen Burnie, 410-761-0922
◪ Lurking in an "unlikely", out-of-the-way stretch of Glen Burnie, this "expensive" (for the neighborhood) "strip-center" Northern Italian is "not well frequented", but those who've discovered it rhapsodize about "extraordinary" cooking; it's definitely "not your typical suburban spot", so be "prepared to spend big bucks before you ask Alberto to take care of you."

Union Hotel [S] ▽ 24 | 25 | 23 | $36

1282 Susquehanna River Rd. (south of Rte. 1), Port Deposit, 410-378-3503
■ Set in a "historic" former hotel tucked away in the woods of Port Deposit by the Susquehanna River, this "unique" country destination feels like an old log cabin, soothing with a "lovely" ambiance and crackling fireplaces; in a dining room filled with cozy nooks, waitresses in "period

Baltimore | F | D | S | C |

costumes" haul out "Fred Flintstone–size prime rib", "huge steaks" and other traditional American vittles; it's a "must-try at least once"; P.S. the "adjacent barn, converted into a bar", is a favorite among bikers.

Vespa | 21 | 20 | 19 | $31 |
1117-21 S. Charles St. (Cross St.), 410-385-0355
☒ "All the beautiful people" who "scoot" in attired "only in black" make this "spirited" South Baltimore Italian one "hip" hangout; featuring a "chic" "industrial look" (though the "noise level is a serious problem") and a "good-looking" staff, it's a "cool" place to dine on "excellent" fare (the starters are so "tasty" you could "make a meal out of them"), but expect to eat "elbow-to-elbow with strangers."

Viccino Bistro S | 22 | 18 | 21 | $36 |
1317 N. Charles St. (Mt. Royal Ave.), 410-347-0349
■ Just south of the train station by the UB campus, this onetime college-central pizzeria/deli has grown up to become a "pleasant" bistro featuring "artful presentations" of "creative", "consistently good" New American dishes; it's "convenient" to the "theater district" (it even offers a free "shuttle"), but it "deserves a visit even when you're not going to a show."

Windows S | 20 | 24 | 21 | $38 |
Renaissance Harborplace Hotel, 202 E. Pratt St. (bet. Calvert & South Sts.), 410-685-8439
☒ Boasting a "spectacular view of the Inner Harbor" from its fifth-floor perch at the Renaissance, this "lovely" New American dining room pulls in a "Baltimore power crowd" at lunchtime, while live jazz attracts a hotel audience at dinner; proponents say the food is a "pleasant surprise", but the "unimpressed" proclaim it "only ok" and advise "stick with the crab cakes."

Woman's Industrial Exchange | 18 | 18 | 22 | $13 |
333 N. Charles St. (Pleasant St.), 410-685-4388
■ Quite possibly the "last of the crafts and food shops for gentlewomen's" products around, this "landmark" Downtown is a "relic" of "kinder times"; like a cherished "snapshot", it keeps "memories alive" with its "ancient recipes and ancient waitresses"; this is "wholesome", "down-home" American cooking "like your grandma" used to make, served at prices so "inexpensive" it was voted the No. 1 Bang for the Buck in Baltimore; N.B. closed at press time for renovations but expected to reopen in late summer 2003.

Woodfire S | 19 | 18 | 19 | $26 |
580P Ritchie Hwy. (McKinsey Rd.), Severna Park, 410-315-8100
☒ "Wonderful wood-burning aromas" waft through this "neighborhood" American in Severna Park, which "doesn't

Baltimore

F | D | S | C

disappoint" fans with its "good food for the money" (it "doesn't hurt you with high wine prices" either); doubters, however, who judge it "so-so" think that the "inconsistent" menu and service "need to improve."

Ze Mean Bean Cafe S | 20 | 20 | 20 | $24
1739 Fleet St. (Ann St.), 410-675-5999
■ "Eat your dumplings" and other "stick-to-your-ribs" Eastern European fare at this "cozy spot" set "away from the intensity of Fells Point"; over the years, it has grown to be "more than the coffeehouse that its name implies", becoming a real restaurant with "honest" food, "attractive (if a bit cramped)" digs and "live [jazz and folk] music that lends a bohemian feel."

Zodiac S | - | - | - | M
1724 N. Charles St. (Lanvale St.), 410-727-8815
"A good choice before a show" at the Charles or Everyman Theatres across the street, this funky "scene" with '40s-style banquettes attracts a most interesting clientele, from pierced to political; Christina Miller's (who trained with Emeril) "varied" Eclectic menu is "frequently changing", so there's "always something new and different to try", and it's "vegan-friendly."

Zorba's Bar & Grill ●S | 21 | 13 | 17 | $22
4710 Eastern Ave. (Oldham St.), 410-276-4484
■ "If you make the trip down the gauntlet", past all the "men drinking at the bar", you'll be rewarded with "flavorful" Greek food at this late-night "gem of Greektown"; followers would gladly "move in" (even if they "need to work on the decor") to feast every day on the "best lamb chops in the world" and "charcoal-grilled" fish; it may be "intimidating at first", but bets are it'll fast become an oft-"visited favorite."

Annapolis

F	D	S	C

Aqua Terra 🆂   23 | 20 | 21 | $36
164 Main St. (Conduit St.), 410-263-1985
◪ "Remarkably adventurous for Annapolis", this "stylish" New American storefront introduces an "innovative" menu (seared tuna with lemongrass risotto, anyone?) and a "sophisticated" edge to the Main Street scene; "trendy" types "love" the "interesting formula", but conservative sorts deem the "cutting-edge" dishes "too experimental" (if not downright "weird").

Cafe Normandie 🆂   20 | 19 | 18 | $32
185 Main St. (Church Circle), 410-263-3382
◪ "Crêpes ahoy!" cheer devotees of this "cozy" version of a "French countryside bistro" located up Main Street from Annapolis' City Dock; though the area is tourist central, "most diners here seem like repeat customers" appreciating dishes prepared with "flair", but foes cite "inconsistent" food and service and warn about the too-"small" tables.

Cantler's Riverside Inn 🆂   23 | 16 | 18 | $28
458 Forest Beach Rd. (Browns Woods Rd.), 410-757-1311
◪ Boasting "atmosphere to the max", this "ultimate crab house" outside Annapolis is "nothing fancy", but if you "sit out on the deck" overlooking the creek and order a pile of steamed hard crabs and a frosty pitcher of beer, you'll have the "perfect afternoon"; that's enough to make "lines form in the street just to get into the lot", so consider "playing some summertime hooky" to "go during the week"; note, though, that "getting here is an adventure", so it's essential to "get good directions" or, "better yet, arrive by boat."

Carrol's Creek Cafe 🆂   21 | 21 | 19 | $34
410 Severn Ave. (4th St.), Eastport, 410-263-8102
◪ "Absolutely, the view of Annapolis'" harbor from the "seriously nice" waterside deck is the prime attraction of this Eastport New American cafe; the seafood-slanted menu is "good but not that different", though if you "go on Wednesday nights around 7, you can watch the sailboat races finish" while you sup; granted, it's "expensive for what you get", but someone has to "pay for that view."

Chick & Ruth's Delly 🆂   18 | 14 | 18 | $13
165 Main St. (Conduit St.), 410-269-6737
◪ "Where the locals go for breakfast" (when "they're not dieting"), this Annapolis "fixture" is a "real kick"; it's a "dowdy-chic" diner near the State House, where you can

Annapolis

F | D | S | C

"hobnob with the power people" and "find refuge from the shopping insanity" outside while being greeted with a "bowl of pickles on arrival"; the "pictures on the walls" hasten the "journey into nostalgia", as do the old-fashioned "milkshakes that are nothing short of heaven."

Davis' Pub S 18 | 13 | 15 | $18
400 Chester Ave. (4th St.), Eastport, 410-268-7432
■ Whether "fresh off the water" or direct from a B&B, "locals and visitors" jam themselves into this "very small", "hard-to-find" (though apparently not hard enough) "neighborhood dive", a "true Annapolis pub" in maritime Eastport, for "good grub" ("can't say enough about those crab cakes"), a couple of beers and "friendly" conversation.

Galway Bay S 22 | 19 | 20 | $24
61-63 Maryland Ave. (State Circle), 410-263-8333
■ "If you can't visit the Old Sod", this State House–vicinity watering hole may be the "next best thing"; it makes a gallant "effort at being a real Irish pub" (there's a "separate restaurant" area too), featuring "satisfying" "standards" like fish 'n' chips and corned beef 'n' cabbage in a setting so "warm and welcoming" that regulars "practically live here."

Harry Browne's S 23 | 22 | 22 | $38
66 State Circle (bet. East St. & Maryland Ave.), 410-269-5124
■ "Hang out with politicians" and other "movers and shakers" at this "clubby" Annapolis "institution" with a "smashing view of the grand old State House" across the street; supporters say it "keeps doing it right" with "dependably excellent" Continental and Chesapeake Bay dishes turned out in a "classy" room by a "smooth" service team; some like the "people-watching" when the "legislature is in session", but others say it's more "wonderful without the lobbyists."

Jalapeño S 24 | 17 | 22 | $27
Forest Plaza, 85 Forest Plaza (Riva Rd.), 410-266-7580
■ "Andalusia meets the Chesapeake" at this "pleasant surprise in a strip mall" west of Annapolis; it's a "terrific little place" – "a bit eccentric, a bit exotic" – for "flavorful" Spanish and Mexican dishes (including "excellent tapas" and the "best paella") and "killer margaritas" delivered by a staff that "tries hard", and it's all "reasonably priced", which explains why it's "popular" and thus "crowded."

Joss Cafe & Sushi Bar S 27 | 18 | 21 | $28
195 Main St. (Church Circle), 410-263-4688
■ "Hearty greetings" welcome sushi connoisseurs of "all ages and types" at this "little nook" near the State House, "one of the top places" of its kind "in the U.S." (for cooked Japanese fare as well); the "memorable" raw fish is so "fresh" "you'd think they caught it themselves", and the

staff is "well informed" and "entertaining", "impressing even native guests"; it may be "tight on space, but it's worth every bit of overcrowding."

La Mona Lisa [S] – | – | – | VE

Woodbridge Shopping Ctr., 2444 Solomons Island Rd. (Forest Dr.), 410-266-7595

Soon after its late spring 2003 opening, well-heeled locals were happily descending on this strip-mall slot on the western edge of Annapolis designed just for them with lush appointments; tuxedoed veterans serve elaborate Italian dishes like saffron-fennel lobster ravioli in Sambuca cream sauce, accompanied by interesting Italian wines.

Lebanese Taverna [S] 23 | 18 | 20 | $26

Annapolis Harbour Ctr., 2478 Solomons Island Rd. (Allen Blvd.), 410-897-1111

See review in Washington, DC Directory.

Les Folies Brasserie [S] 25 | 22 | 24 | $39

2552 Riva Rd. (Aris Allen Blvd.), 410-573-0970

■ Much "more promising than it looks from the outside", this "terrific" "surprise" is really a "bit of France not far from the bay" in Parole; it's the domain of veteran "French owners who know" how to run a "professional" operation and how to turn out "superb" brasserie "classics" served by a "knowledgeable" staff.

Lewnes' Steakhouse [S] 26 | 21 | 24 | $48

401 Fourth St. (Severn Ave.), Eastport, 410-263-1617

◩ "Local in every way", "Annapolis' own" steakhouse is a "manly kind of place" to celebrate a "special occasion"; it offers a "hard-to-beat" combination of "perfectly prepared prime beef" and a "fabulous wine list", along with "private booths" and "attentive" service; a few critical carnivores are left "disappointed" by the experience – and especially by the bill – but supporters are always ready to "prepare their appetites" for this splurge.

McNasby's [S] – | – | – | I

723 Second St. (Bay Shore Ave.), Eastport, 410-295-9022

This revered Eastport oysterman's waterside market, which has reopened under the management of nearby Davis' Pub, serves Bay fare like crab cakes and a rich fried rockfish sandwich; you place your order in a cinderblock bunker, and if weather permits, pass up its plastic-appointed interior for the picnic tables on the dock by the Naval Academy and dine watching the boat traffic.

Northwoods [S] 24 | 21 | 24 | $39

609 Melvin Ave. (Ridgely Ave.), 410-268-2609

■ "Especially nice for special occasions", this "cozy", "romantic" Annapolis "hideaway" has "stayed the same

Annapolis | F | D | S | C |

for years" and that's why loyalists "love it"; the "excellent" Continental menu is as "dependable" as ever, as is the "professional" service, while the "prix fixe is a bargain."

O'Learys Seafood S | 25 | 21 | 23 | $40 |
310 Third St. (Severn Ave.), Eastport, 410-263-0884
☑ "Skip the touristy" places in Eastport and "head to this gem" instead advise those in-the-know about this "great seafood-without-a-view" spot that lets you "custom mix-and-match" your finny fare and cooking preparation to have it "your way" (don't miss "one of the best crab cakes ever"); sure, it's a bit "noisy" and it "needs a bigger bar", as "there's no place to wait" for a table, but you'll leave "satisfied."

Paul's Homewood Cafe | – | – | – | M |
919 West St. (Taylor Ave.), 410-267-7891
West of Downtown Annapolis, Anna Marriott and Chris Nicholas' dad's 1949 lunch counter draws midday regulars for soft-crab sandwiches, souvlaki and burgers, and now evening specials like halibut with crabmeat and tarragon sauce as well; later, the pre–Maryland Hall dinner crowd turns over the art-filled dining room to couples and families, who linger till closing over big, homey, housemade desserts.

Phillips S | 15 | 15 | 14 | $28 |
12 Dock St. (Randall St.), 410-990-9888
See review in Baltimore Directory.

Piccola Roma Ristorante S | 23 | 19 | 22 | $38 |
200 Main St. (Church Circle), 410-268-7898
■ "Superb" Italian cooking that "rises above the ordinary" sets apart this "upscale" Annapolis ristorante blessed with a "prime location" where patrons like to "sit by the window" and "watch the passing Main Street parade" while dining on "stellar" pastas; the food is "not fussy, just great", and it's delivered in "inviting" environs by a team that pays "attention to the details."

Red Hot & Blue BBQ S | 19 | 14 | 16 | $20 |
200 Old Mill Bottom Rd. S. (Rte. 50, exit 28), 410-626-7427
See review in Washington, DC Directory.

Reynolds Tavern S | – | – | – | M |
7 Church Circle (West St.), 410-295-9555
Jill and Andrew Petit have reopened a grand old 1747 Georgian brick tavern and brought period antiques from their native England to do it up in style; a refined, salad-centric lunch and afternoon tea are served in the parlors, while the stone cellar has a pre-Revolutionary public house vibe (pub fare, flowing beer and live music); in good weather, a stately bricked-in patio serves midshipmen with parents in tow, refugees from the tourist zone and officials from the adjacent Statehouse.

Annapolis | F | D | S | C |

RUTH'S CHRIS STEAK HOUSE S | 24 | 23 | 23 | $49 |
301 Severn Ave. (3rd St.), Eastport, 410-990-0033
See review in Washington, DC Directory.

Sam's Waterfront Cafe S | 22 | 23 | 21 | $34 |
2020 Chesapeake Harbour Dr. E. (Edgewood Rd.), 410-263-3600
■ "A good port in a storm" is "worth finding", so you should make it your business to get to know this "local secret" "hidden" "out of the way" at the Annapolis harbor; it's an "elegant yet relaxing" place where the "picturesque" setting ("love watching the yachts come and go") only enhances the "excellent" New American seafood dishes; "don't miss" this "best bet."

Sputnik Café | – | – | – | M |
1397 Generals Hwy. (Crownsville Rd.), Crownsville, 410-923-3775
Anticipate a "food adventure" at "Crownsville's best-kept secret" whose Cold War decor (envision faux corrugated Quonset hut walls, plastic designer chairs and space-age chandeliers) provides an offbeat backdrop for the kitchen's International dishes (like its signature wasabi-and-sesame-crusted salmon with a vegetarian sushi roll); N.B. there's live entertainment on Thursdays and Saturdays.

Treaty of Paris S | 20 | 23 | 20 | $39 |
Maryland Inn, 16 Church Circle (Main St.), 410-216-6340
◪ At this "history lesson" of an inn that's as old as this country, bask in the "charming" "colonial" atmosphere; the Continental-American menu is "above average", "if not excellent", but critics lament it's a "shame" that the "unremarkable" food can't live up to "one of Annapolis' most historic settings."

Tsunami S | 24 | 17 | 21 | $29 |
51 West St. (Church Circle), 410-990-9868
■ On West Street's emerging restaurant scene, this "cool hangout" is the "'in' place to be", attracting a "young, hip crowd" that descends nightly for the "singles" action at the bar; don't be fooled, though, into thinking that the food is an afterthought, because the sushi is "outstanding" and the "styling" Pacific Rim "fusion" cuisine "original" and "terrific", making for "exotic fun" that's a "refreshing" change of pace for "brass-and-fern Annapolis."

Wild Orchid Cafe S | 23 | 19 | 22 | $32 |
909 Bay Ridge Ave. (Chesapeake Ave.), Eastport, 410-268-8009
■ "Delightful and intimate", this "converted" house tucked away in an "out-of-the-way location" in Eastport presents a daily changing New American menu that "always" features "interesting choices" based on a "complex mix of

ingredients that works"; the "beautifully arranged" dishes, "deep in flavor", are brought to table by "cheerful" folks in "charming" quarters, which explains why admirers "love" this "hidden treasure."

Yellowfin [S] – – – E

2840 MD Rte. 2 (at South River), Edgewater, 410-573-1371

South Beach comes to the South River with dance-club style replete with burly doormen, flashy yellow and steel decor and pulsing music; sure, it tries hard to be hip, but even gray-haired boat owners feel tuned in to dishes (and wines) that are mostly Traditional American, like 'The Wedge' of iceberg lettuce and big steaks; some fin fare, such as mahi mahi and 'Caribbean lobster tail', keeps the theme coastal, as does the fine sunset view over the water.

Yin Yankee Café [S] 23 19 21 $28

105 Main St. (Green St.), 410-268-8703

■ Amid the hustle and bustle of Annapolis' City Dock, this "hip sushi bar" offers a "different" option thanks to its "expansive selection" of "surprisingly" "excellent" Asian fusion dishes; add on "cool", "comfortable" digs, "personal" service and "not too expensive" tabs and the result is a "fun find", leading habitués to exclaim "we never tire of the innovative food or funky atmosphere."

Eastern Shore

	F	D	S	C

Alice's Café ⌀   ▽ 27 | 20 | 23 | $13
22 N. Harrison St. (bet. Dover & Goldsborough Sts.), Easton, 410-819-8590
■ Already cherished as a "favorite" in Easton, this teeny "diner cares about ingredients", and it's amply evident after one bite of its "wonderful roast beef"; while "fabulous", "creative" Eclectic sandwiches and "custom-baked cookies" rule at lunch, its "comforting" breakfast plates lure in many an early-riser in the AM; closes at 3 PM.

Bistro St. Michaels S   26 | 22 | 23 | $38
403 S. Talbot St. (Watkins Ln.), St. Michaels, 410-745-9111
◪ Fashion plates like to "get dressed before they drive out to St. Michaels" to sup at this "jewel" (it's also a favorite among "dressed-down boaters"), which pleases with "innovative", "dependably excellent" French bistro dishes ("don't miss" the "best-ever mussels") served by a "doting", "accommodating" staff; it can get "crowded and noisy" inside the "tastefully" decorated room, but the "lovely back porch" provides a "perfect" escape.

Blue Heron Cafe   ▽ 22 | 19 | 21 | $34
236 Cannon St. (Cross St.), Chestertown, 410-778-0188
◪ Enthusiasts "drive out of their way" to this "charming little" house set on a leafy residential street in colonial Chestertown for its "imaginative" menu of updated Eastern Shore fare; "steadily" turning out "good food in an everyday environment", it's a "local favorite", but critics lament that it "doesn't live up to its rave reviews."

Columbia   ▽ 27 | 26 | 26 | $46
28 S. Washington St. (Glenwood Ave.), Easton, 410-770-5172
■ Upstairs at this "understatedly elegant" "townhouse" in Easton is "superb" chef-owner Stephen Mangasarian's private residence, while downstairs is his "very special" labor of love, a "warm and charming" haven for a "quiet, romantic" meal; his "creative" New American menu changes every three weeks, but highlights always include a rack of lamb that's worth "dreaming about"; there are only nine tables in the "cozy" parlor and drawing room, so you can expect "personal, sincere" service.

Crab Claw S⌀   20 | 16 | 17 | $28
156 Mill St. (Talbot St.), St. Michaels, 410-745-2900
◪ After "a day of sightseeing", "sit by the water and crack crabs" at this seafood "shack" next to the Maritime

Eastern Shore   F | D | S | C

Museum in St. Michaels; it's a "fun outing" where you dig into a pile of steamed crustaceans dumped on picnic tables covered with "paper tablecloths" (for those who "don't want to get their fingers dirty", there's a proper dining room upstairs); of course, "it's packed" on summer weekends with "out-of-towners", so service can be "spotty."

Fisherman's Inn/Crab Deck S   20 | 19 | 19 | $28
3032 Main St. (Rte. 50), Grasonville, 410-827-8807

☑ Providing "a lovely respite" "on the way to the shore", this rambling Kent Narrows hub has dual personalities – the Fisherman's Inn is an "old established restaurant" (circa 1930) with an "old-fashioned" seafood menu and a "nautical" motif replete with an antique oyster plate collection, while the Crab Deck (as we go to press, being rebuilt after a fire) is an alfresco alternative with "wooden benches" and live music; if you "don't get too complicated" with your order, they're "good places to meet friends."

Harris Crab House S   21 | 16 | 18 | $28
433 Kent Narrows Way N. (Rte. 50, exit 42), Grasonville, 410-827-9500

■ "On your way to the Eastern Shore", this "classic crab house" "overlooking the Kent Narrows channel" (the "top deck" affords a "gorgeous" "view" of the "boats coming and going") is a "must stop"; it's all "about crabs and beer" (and homemade "nutty buddy" ice cream cones for dessert) here, so expect a highly "casual" atmosphere.

Holly's S   16 | 10 | 16 | $15
108 Jackson Creek Rd. (Rte. 50), Grasonville, 410-827-8711

☑ A handy "stopping point" for beach travelers "after clearing the Bay Bridge" in Kent Narrows, this "diner of yesteryear" housed in a motel is the "real deal" for "down-home" Eastern Shore eats that are "plain, like they should be"; "you won't go away hungry" after tucking into "maybe the best fried chicken in Maryland", "scrumptious chicken salad" and other "SOS comfort food", washed down by "real milkshakes", but critics caution only "in a pinch."

Imperial Hotel S   ▽ 24 | 24 | 23 | $43
208 High St. (Queen St.), Chestertown, 410-778-5000

■ "Off the beaten path" near colonial Chestertown's central square, this intimate "gem" set in a "lovely" restored hotel exemplifies the "elegance of days gone by" and makes a "great getaway for a romantic night" in "high style"; many feel the New American menu – "fine but never too fancy" – actually "exceeds its reputation."

Inn at Easton S   ▽ 25 | 25 | 24 | $44
28 S. Harrison St. (South Ln.), Easton, 410-822-4910

■ "Civilized dining" in a grand Federal-style mansion is the draw at this Easton inn restored by Liz and Andrew Evans,

Eastern Shore F | D | S | C

a "quiet, elegant" showcase for his "simply superb" Eclectic treatments of local ingredients, paired with a "limited albeit very good wine list" and served by an "exceptional" staff; it's a "real treasure that hasn't yet been fully discovered", so if you're seeking to find "excellence in everything", this is the place.

INN AT PERRY CABIN S — | — | — | E
308 Watkins Ln. (Talbot St.), St. Michaels, 410-745-2200
Taking better advantage of its "magnificent" "waterside setting" in St. Michaels, this "class act" "retreat" (operated by Orient-Express Hotels) has a redesigned dining room, expanded to be closer to the bay, and is appointed with big windows and a nautical theme that gives it an airy look; still manning the stove, though, is Mark Salter, who has introduced an à la carte Continental menu that features Chesapeake Bay seafood specialties.

Kennedyville Inn S ▽ 25 | 22 | 23 | $36
11986 Rte. 213 (5 mi. north of Chestertown), Kennedyville, 410-348-2400
■ "Hard to find, harder to forget" swoon the smitten about this "hidden gem" in the countryside of Kennedyville; "everything is wonderful" here – from chef-owner Kevin McKinney's "quirky" yet "fancy" Chesapeake Bay fare (his signature "oyster fritters and crab steak alone are worth the trip") and BBQ to the "cute" decor to the "excellent" service, adding up to a "treat" that "should not be missed."

Latitude 38° S ▽ 24 | 22 | 24 | $30
26342 Oxford Rd. (Bonfield Ave.), Oxford, 410-226-5303
■ "Catch up on area gossip" at this "pride of Oxford", a "local favorite" among tradespeople, landowners and sailors; "bravo to chef" Douglas Kirby for his "delicious", frequently changing New American bistro menu based on local ingredients (the "bar dinners are an outstanding bargain") and to the "friendly" crew; "what a find!"

Mason's ▽ 26 | 22 | 22 | $39
22 S. Harrison St. (South Ln.), Easton, 410-822-3204
■ Mary and Matthew Mason's grand old family house on what's becoming Easton's restaurant row is home to an "eclectic" mix of "outstanding" New American dishes distinguished by "great depth of flavor"; though the "main dining room" is "wonderfully comfortable", the "enjoyable" garden is a veritable "oasis", but wherever your table, you'll be tended to by an "outgoing" staff.

Michael Rork's Town Dock S 20 | 18 | 19 | $33
125 Mulberry St. (Talbot St.), St. Michaels, 410-745-5577
◪ "Nifty chef-owner" Michael Rork gives his undivided attention to this "casual" American seafood house "superbly located" on a site in St. Michaels with scenic

vote at zagat.com

Eastern Shore F | D | S | C

views of the harbor and the river (naturally, the best tables are out on the "relaxing" "dockside" deck); dissenters, though, crab "disappointing after all the hype."

Narrows S 25 | 21 | 22 | $33
3023 Kent Narrows Way S. (Rte. 50, exit 41), Grasonville, 410-827-8113
■ "A perfect way to start a vacation" in Kent Narrows is to spend a "lovely summer day overlooking the water" at this genteel Chesapeake Bay fare dining room, long a "local favorite" for the "best crab cakes on the Shore" and an "equally great cream of crab soup"; "everything is right" again at dusk, when a meal is accompanied by a "gorgeous view of the sunset"; "we wouldn't miss it on the way to or from the beach."

Out of the Fire ▽ 21 | 22 | 23 | $34
22 Goldsborough St. (Washington St.), Easton, 410-770-4777
■ "Attractively" decorated with a "revolving art display", this "neat" hangout in the historic district of Easton centers around a stone hearth in the open Mediterranean/Eclectic kitchen, from which emerge "delicious wood-fired" breads and pizzas and "super" roasted entrees; locals "love this place" and dine at the chef's counter or the wine bar in the back.

Robert Morris Inn S 21 | 23 | 22 | $39
314 N. Morris St. (Tred Avon Rd.), Oxford, 410-226-5111
■ Near the Oxford ferry dock, this "quaint", "comfy" inn dating back to 1710 hasn't changed its Chesapeake Bay seafood menu in three decades, which is just fine with longtime followers who gladly "make the trip" for the "still divine" crab cakes ("James Michener was right – they really are some of the best on the Eastern Shore"); even some stalwarts, though, concede that "everything else here is irrelevant", while foes find it all too "bland and basic" ("time to update the kitchen").

208 Talbot S 27 | 23 | 26 | $48
208 N. Talbot St. (North St.), St. Michaels, 410-745-3838
■ "Quite a surprise" for the "little sailing town" of St. Michaels, this "sophisticated" "all-time favorite" is "superb in every way", from chef-owner Paul Milne's (a "magician with sauces") "superior" Continental seafood dishes (the "Saturday prix fixe menu is fabulous") to the "romantic" surroundings to the "outstanding" service; "overall, it's a real winner", "worth a drive from anywhere" for "truly fine dining" that makes a meal a "special occasion."

Baltimore, Annapolis and the Eastern Shore Indexes

CUISINES
LOCATIONS
SPECIAL FEATURES

Indexes list the best of many within each category.

All restaurants are in the Baltimore area unless otherwise noted (A=Annapolis and E=Eastern Shore).

vote at zagat.com

Baltimore – Cuisine Index

CUISINES

Afghan
Helmand

American (New)
Abacrombie
Acacia
AIDA Bistro
Antrim 1844
Aqua Terra/A
Atlantic
b
Baldwin's Station
Carrol's Creek/A
Center City
Chameleon Café
Charleston
Cibo
City Cafe
Columbia/E
Corks
4 West
Hampton's
Healing Heart Blues
Helen's Garden
Henninger's Tavern
Henry's
Imperial Hotel/E
Ironbridge Wine
JJ's Everyday
Joy America
Kings Contrivance
Latitude 38°/E
Linwood's
Louisiana
Mason's/E
Michael Rork's/E
Paul's Homewood/A
Sam's Waterfront/A
Sascha's 527
Spike & Charlie's
Stone Manor
Strawberry's Bistro
Tasting Room
Treaty of Paris/A
Viccino Bistro
Wild Orchid Cafe/A
Windows

American (Traditional)
Baugher's
Blue Moon
Brass Elephant
Cafe Hon
Cheesecake Factory
Clyde's
Dutch's Daughter
4 West
Friendly Farm
Hard Times Cafe
Harryman Hse.
Jennings Cafe
Manor Tavern
Milton Inn
Oregon Grille
Peppermill
Reynolds Tavern/A
SoBo Cafe
Union Hotel
Woman's Ind. Ex.
Woodfire
Yellowfin/A

Asian Fusion
Eurasian Harbor
Ixia
Purple Orchid
Red Maple
Roy's
Soigné
Tsunami/A
Yin Yankee Café/A

Barbecue
Kennedyville Inn/E
Red Hot & Blue/A

Cajun/Creole
Ethel & Ramone's
Louisiana

Californian
Paolo's

Chesapeake Regional
Blue Heron/E
Brighton's
Captain Harvey's
Faidley's Seafood
G&M
Gertrude's
Harry Browne's/A
Inn at Perry Cabin/E
Kelly's
Kennedyville Inn/E

Baltimore – Cuisine Index

McNasby's/A
Michael Rork's/E
Narrows/E
O'Learys Seafood/A
Pierpoint
Robert Morris Inn/E
Timbuktu

Chinese
Asean Bistro
Cafe Zen
P.F. Chang's
Szechuan
Szechuan Best
Szechuan House

Coffeehouses/Dessert
b
Cafe Hon
City Cafe
Crêpe du Jour
Paul's Homewood/A
Ze Mean Bean

Coffee Shops/Diners
Chick & Ruth's/A
Holly's/E
Jimmy's
Papermoon Diner

Continental
Brass Elephant
Harry Browne's/A
Inn at Perry Cabin/E
Josef's Country Inn
Marconi's
Northwoods/A
Rudys' 2900
Treaty of Paris/A
208 Talbot/E

Crab Houses
Barn
Bill's Terrace Inn
Cantler's Riverside/A
Captain Harvey's
Costas Crab
Crab Claw/E
Faidley's Seafood
Fisherman's Inn/Crab/E
Harris Crab/E
Kelly's
L.P. Steamers
Obrycki's Crab
River Watch

Delis/Sandwich Shops
Alice's Café/E
Attman's Deli

Eastern European
Ze Mean Bean

Eclectic/International
Alice's Café/E
b
Bicycle
Combalou Cafe
Elkridge Furnace
Ethel & Ramone's
Inn at Easton/E
Martick's
Out of the Fire/E
Peter's Inn
Sputnik Café/A
Tasting Room
Zodiac

French
Elkridge Furnace
Jeannier's
Martick's
Purple Orchid
Tersiguel's

French (Bistro)
Bistro St. Michaels/E
Cafe de Paris
Cafe Normandie/A
Crêpe du Jour
La Madeleine Bakery
Les Folies/A
Petit Louis Bistro

German
Josef's Country Inn

Greek
Ikaros
Kali's Court
Paul's Homewood/A
Samos
Zorba's

Hamburgers
Jennings Cafe
Linwood's
McCabe's

Indian
Ambassador Din. Rm.
Banjara

Baltimore – Cuisine Index

Irish
Galway Bay/A

Italian
(N=Northern; S=Southern)
Aldo's (S)
Amicci's
Angelina's
Boccaccio (N)
Café Troia (N)
Cangialosi's
Cibo
Da Mimmo
Della Notte
Due (N)
La Mona Lisa/A
La Scala
Liberatore's
Paolo's
Pazza Luna
Piccola Roma/A
Sabatino's
Sotto Sopra
That's Amore (S)
Tiburzi's (S)
Trattoria Alberto (N)
Vespa

Japanese
Edo Sushi
Fuji
Joss Café/Sushi/A
Matsuri
Sushi Hana
Suzie's Soba
Tsunami/A
Yin Yankee Café/A

Lebanese
Carlyle Club
Lebanese Taverna/A

Mediterranean
Black Olive
Kali's Court
Tapas Teatro

Mexican/Tex-Mex
Austin Grill
Blue Agave
Holy Frijoles
Jalapeño/A

Middle Eastern
Lebanese Taverna/A
Orchard Market

Noodle Shops
Suzie's Soba

Nuevo Latino
Babalu Grill

Pan-Asian
Asean Bistro
Purple Orchid
Red Coral
Red Maple
Suzie's Soba

Persian
Orchard Market

Pizza
b
Cibo
Out of the Fire/E
Viccino Bistro

Pub Food
Bertha's
Brewer's Alley
Davis' Pub/A
Galway Bay/A
Henninger's Tavern
Kelly's
McCabe's

Seafood
Atlantic
Black Olive
Captain Harvey's
Carrol's Creek/A
City Crab
Costas Crab
Crab Claw/E
Dutch's Daughter
Faidley's Seafood
Fisherman's Inn/Crab/E
Gertrude's
Inn at Perry Cabin/E
John Steven
Legal Sea Foods
L.P. Steamers
McCormick/Schmick's
McNasby's/A
Michael Rork's/E
Narrows/E
O'Learys Seafood/A
Phillips
Pierpoint
Pisces

Baltimore – Cuisine Index

River Watch
Robert Morris Inn/E
Sam's Waterfront/A
Timbuktu
208 Talbot/E
Yellowfin/A

South American
Fernando's Salsa

Spanish
Jalapeño/A
Tio Pepe

Steakhouses
Fleming's
Jordan's Steakhse.
Lewnes' Steakhse./A
Morton's
Oregon Grille
Prime Rib
Ruth's Chris
Shula's Steak

Tapas
Jalapeño/A
Out of the Fire/E
Red Coral
Red Maple
Tapas Teatro

Thai
San Sushi
Thai
Thai Arroy
Thai Landing

Vegetarian
Cafe Zen
Zodiac

Vietnamese
Saigon Remembered

LOCATIONS

BALTIMORE

Business District/ Downtown/Convention Center/Camden Yards/ Inner Harbor
Babalu Grill
Brighton's
Cangialosi's
Cheesecake Factory
Eurasian Harbor
Faidley's Seafood
Hampton's
Joy America
Legal Sea Foods
Marconi's
Martick's
McCormick/Schmick's
Morton's
Paolo's
Phillips
Pisces
Purple Orchid
Red Coral
Ruth's Chris
Shula's Steak
Tio Pepe
Windows

Canton
Atlantic
Austin Grill
Helen's Garden
Tiburzi's

Downtown North/ Charles St./Mt. Vernon
Abacrombie
b
Brass Elephant
Center City
City Cafe
Combalou Cafe
Helmand
Ixia
Prime Rib
Red Maple
Sascha's 527
Sotto Sopra
Spike & Charlie's
Tapas Teatro
Thai Landing
Viccino Bistro
Woman's Ind. Ex.
Zodiac

East Baltimore
Attman's Deli
Kelly's
Obrycki's Crab

Federal Hill/ South Baltimore
Banjara
Bicycle
Blue Agave
Corks
L.P. Steamers
Matsuri
Pazza Luna
SoBo Cafe
Soigné
Szechuan
Thai Arroy
Vespa

Fells Point
Bertha's
Black Olive
Blue Moon
Henninger's Tavern
Jimmy's
John Steven
Kali's Court
Louisiana
Peter's Inn
Pierpoint
Ze Mean Bean

Hampden/Roland Park/ Homewood/ Charles Village
Ambassador Din. Rm.
Cafe Hon
Carlyle Club
4 West
Gertrude's
Holy Frijoles
Jeannier's
McCabe's
Papermoon Diner

Baltimore – Location Index

Petit Louis Bistro
Suzie's Soba

Highlandtown/Greektown
Ikaros
Samos
Zorba's

Inner Harbor East/
Little Italy
Aldo's
Amicci's
Boccaccio
Charleston
Da Mimmo

Della Notte
Fleming's
La Scala
Roy's
Sabatino's

Mt. Washington
Crêpe du Jour
Ethel & Ramone's

North Baltimore/
York Road Corridor
Cafe Zen
Saigon Remembered
Thai

OUTER BALTIMORE/CENTRAL MARYLAND

Bowie
Strawberry's Bistro

Brooklandville
City Crab

BWI/Linthicum/Elkridge
Elkridge Furnace
G&M
Timbuktu

Columbia
AIDA Bistro
Asean Bistro
Cafe de Paris
Clyde's
Hard Times Cafe
Ironbridge Wine
Kings Contrivance
La Madeleine Bakery
P.F. Chang's
That's Amore

Ellicott City/Catonsville
Fernando's Salsa
Fuji
Jennings Cafe
Jordan's Steakhse.
Tersiguel's

Essex/Dundalk
Bill's Terrace Inn
Costas Crab
River Watch

Frederick
Acacia
Brewer's Alley

Dutch's Daughter
Stone Manor
Tasting Room

Glen Burnie/Severna Park/
Pasadena
Trattoria Alberto
Woodfire

Hunt Valley/
North Baltimore Co.
Friendly Farm
Henry's
Manor Tavern
Milton Inn
Oregon Grille

Lutherville/Timonium/
Cockeysville
Edo Sushi
JJ's Everyday
Liberatore's
Peppermill
San Sushi
Szechuan House

Northeast Baltimore/
Parkville/Perry Hall
Angelina's
Barn
Chameleon Café

Owings Mills/
Reisterstown/
Pikesville
Captain Harvey's
Cibo

Baltimore – Location Index

Due
Edo Sushi
Harryman Hse.
Liberatore's
Linwood's
Rudys' 2900
Ruth's Chris

Randallstown/Eldersburg/Sykesville
Baldwin's Station
Healing Heart Blues
Liberatore's
Szechuan Best

Towson
Café Troia
Orchard Market
Paolo's
San Sushi
Sushi Hana

Westminster/Taneytown
Antrim 1844
Baugher's
Liberatore's

White Marsh/Bel Air/Harford County
Josef's Country Inn
Union Hotel

ANNAPOLIS

Annapolis
Aqua Terra
Cafe Normandie
Cantler's Riverside
Chick & Ruth's
Galway Bay
Harry Browne's
Jalapeño
Joss Café/Sushi
La Mona Lisa
Lebanese Taverna
Les Folies
Northwoods
Paul's Homewood
Phillips
Piccola Roma
Red Hot & Blue
Reynolds Tavern
Sam's Waterfront
Sputnik Café
Treaty of Paris
Tsunami
Yellowfin
Yin Yankee Café

Eastport
Carrol's Creek
Davis' Pub
Lewnes' Steakhse.
McNasby's
O'Learys Seafood
Ruth's Chris
Wild Orchid Cafe

EASTERN SHORE

Alice's Café
Bistro St. Michaels
Blue Heron
Columbia
Crab Claw
Fisherman's Inn/Crab
Harris Crab
Holly's
Imperial Hotel
Inn at Easton
Inn at Perry Cabin
Kennedyville Inn
Latitude 38°
Mason's
Michael Rork's
Narrows
Out of the Fire
Robert Morris Inn
208 Talbot

Baltimore – Special Feature Index

SPECIAL FEATURES

(Restaurants followed by a † may not offer that feature at every location.)

Additions
Abacrombie
Acacia
AIDA Bistro
b
Cangialosi's
Carlyle Club
Center City
Cibo
City Crab
Fernando's Salsa
4 West
Healing Heart Blues
Ironbridge Wine
La Mona Lisa/A
McNasby's/A
Paul's Homewood/A
Red Coral
Reynolds Tavern/A
Saigon Remembered
Strawberry's Bistro
Thai Arroy
Tiburzi's
Yellowfin/A

Breakfast
(See also Hotel Dining)
Alice's Café/E
Baugher's
Blue Moon
Brighton's
Cafe Hon
Chick & Ruth's/A
City Cafe
Holly's/E
Jimmy's

Brunch
Ambassador Din. Rm.
Blue Moon
City Cafe
Helen's Garden
Pisces
Reynolds Tavern/A
Windows
Ze Mean Bean

Buffet Served
(Check availability)
Ambassador Din. Rm.
Banjara
Pisces
Szechuan Best
Windows

Business Dining
Aldo's
Blue Heron/E
Boccaccio
Brass Elephant
Brighton's
Cafe de Paris
Charleston
Cibo
Dutch's Daughter
Fleming's
4 West
Hampton's
Harry Browne's/A
Lewnes' Steakhse./A
Linwood's
Morton's
Peppermill
Prime Rib
Roy's
Rudys' 2900
Ruth's Chris
Trattoria Alberto
Viccino Bistro
Windows

BYO
Cafe Zen
Edo Sushi
Fernando's Salsa
JJ's Everyday
Orchard Market
Samos
Thai Arroy

Catering
Alice's Café/E
Attman's Deli
Brass Elephant
Cafe Hon

vote at zagat.com 213

Baltimore – Special Feature Index

Paul's Homewood/A
Samos
Sascha's 527
Wild Orchid Cafe/A

Child-Friendly
(Besides the normal fast-food places; * children's menu available)
Baugher's*
Cafe Hon*
Chick & Ruth's/A
Friendly Farm*
Holly's/E

Delivery/Takeout
(D=delivery, T=takeout)
Alice's Café/E (T)
Attman's Deli (D,T)
Cafe de Paris (T)
Faidley's Seafood (T)
Holly's/E (T)
Samos (D,T)
Szechuan House (D,T)

Dessert
Alice's Café/E
b
Baugher's
Blue Moon
Cafe Hon
Eurasian Harbor
Holly's/E
Paul's Homewood/A
Tapas Teatro

Entertainment
(Call for days and times of performances)
AIDA Bistro (jazz)
Asean Bistro (guitar/piano)
Atlantic (jazz/Latin)
Babalu Grill (DJ/Latin)
Baldwin's Station (folk)
Bertha's (blues/jazz)
Brighton's (jazz/piano)
Carlyle Club (jazz)
City Crab (guitar)
Clyde's (varies)
Da Mimmo (piano/vocals)
Della Notte (piano)
4 West (jazz)
Gertrude's (jazz)
Healing Heart Blues (blues/jazz)
Les Folies/A (varies)
Oregon Grille (bass/piano)
Out of the Fire/E (guitar)
Pisces (jazz)
Prime Rib (bass/piano)
Red Coral (DJ)
Red Maple (DJ)
Reynolds Tavern/A (varies)
River Watch (bands)
Sputnik Café/A (varies)
Strawberry's Bistro (jazz)
Treaty of Paris/A (jazz)
Windows (jazz)
Woodfire (varies)
Ze Mean Bean (folk/jazz)

Fireplaces
Antrim 1844
Elkridge Furnace
Harry Browne's/A
Harryman Hse.
Manor Tavern
Milton Inn
Petit Louis Bistro
Robert Morris Inn/E
Rudys' 2900
Treaty of Paris/A
Union Hotel
Ze Mean Bean

Historic Places
(Year opened; *building)
1740 Milton Inn*
1744 Elkridge Furnace*
1747 Reynolds Tavern/A
1772 Treaty of Paris/A*
1790s Bertha's*
1791 Harryman Hse.*
1850 Brass Elephant*
1850 Martick's*
1860 Woman's Ind. Ex.*
1880 Manor Tavern*
1883 Baldwin's Station*
1890 Tersiguel's*
1890s Petit Louis Bistro*
1902 Imperial Hotel/E*
1920 Marconi's

Hotel Dining
Antrim 1844
   Antrim 1844
Badger Inn
   Abacrombie

Baltimore – Special Feature Index

Harbor Court
  Brighton's
  Hampton's
Hyatt Regency
  Pisces
Imperial Hotel
  Imperial Hotel/E
Inn at Easton
  Inn at Easton/E
Inn at Perry Cabin
  Inn at Perry Cabin/E
Inn at the Colonnade
  4 West
Maryland Inn
  Treaty of Paris/A
Pier 5 Hotel
  Eurasian Harbor
  McCormick/Schmick's
Renaissance Harborplace
  Windows
Robert Morris Inn
  Robert Morris Inn/E
Sheraton Inner Harbor
  Morton's
Stone Manor
  Stone Manor
Union Hotel
  Union Hotel
Wyndham Baltimore
  Shula's Steak

Late Dining
(Weekday closing hour)
Sabatino's (3 AM)
Zorba's (2 AM)

Meet for a Drink
(Most top hotels and the following standouts)
AIDA Bistro
Bertha's
Blue Agave
Brass Elephant
Cafe de Paris
Center City
City Crab
4 West
Healing Heart Blues
Henry's
Ironbridge Wine
John Steven
Kelly's
Manor Tavern
Soigné

Tasting Room
Tiburzi's

Offbeat
Alice's Café/E
b
Bertha's
Cafe Hon
Center City
Chick & Ruth's/A
City Cafe
Ethel & Ramone's
Faidley's Seafood
Fernando's Salsa
Healing Heart Blues
Helen's Garden
Jimmy's
John Steven
Kelly's
Martick's
McNasby's/A
Papermoon Diner
Peter's Inn
River Watch
SoBo Cafe
Sputnik Café/A
Tapas Teatro
Zodiac

Outdoor Dining
(G=garden; P=patio/porch;
S=sidewalk; T=terrace;
W=waterside)
Ambassador Din. Rm. (G)
Antrim 1844 (T)
Babalu Grill (S)
Baldwin's Station (T)
Bicycle (G,P)
Bistro St. Michaels/E (P)
Blue Heron/E (P)
Café Troia (S)
Cantler's Riverside/A (T,W)
Carrol's Creek/A (T,W)
Cheesecake Factory (P,W)
City Cafe (S)
City Crab (P)
Clyde's (P,W)
Crab Claw/E (P,W)
Crêpe du Jour (T)
Davis' Pub/A (P)
Ethel & Ramone's (P)
Eurasian Harbor (P)
Fernando's Salsa (S)

Baltimore – Special Feature Index

Fisherman's Inn/Crab/E (P,W)
Gertrude's (G)
Harris Crab/E (P,W)
Harry Browne's/A (P)
Harryman Hse. (P)
Helen's Garden (T)
Imperial Hotel/E (G)
Inn at Easton/E (P)
Inn at Perry Cabin/E (T)
Josef's Country Inn (G,P)
Joy America (T)
Kali's Court (P)
Linwood's (P)
L.P. Steamers (T)
Manor Tavern (P)
Mason's/E (G)
McCormick/Schmick's (P,W)
Michael Rork's/E (T,W)
Northwoods/A (P)
Oregon Grille (P)
Phillips (P,W)
Reynolds Tavern/A (P)
River Watch (P,W)
Sam's Waterfront/A (P,W)
Stone Manor (P)
Tapas Teatro (S)
Vespa (S)
Wild Orchid Cafe/A (P)
Yin Yankee Café/A (S)
Ze Mean Bean (S)

Parking

(V=valet, *=validated)
Aldo's (V)
Ambassador Din. Rm. (V)
Black Olive (V)
Boccaccio (V)
Brighton's (V)
Charleston (V)
Da Mimmo (V)
Eurasian Harbor (V)
Fleming's (V)
Hampton's (V)
Ixia (V)
Kali's Court (V)
Louisiana (V)
Marconi's (V)
McCormick/Schmick's*
Morton's (V)
Pisces (V)
Prime Rib (V)
Purple Orchid (V)
Roy's (V)
Ruth's Chris (V)
Shula's Steak*
Sotto Sopra (V)
Treaty of Paris/A (V)
Viccino Bistro (V)
Windows*

People-Watching

Barn
Baugher's
Bill's Terrace Inn
City Cafe
Faidley's Seafood
4 West
Harry Browne's/A
Jimmy's
La Mona Lisa/A
Papermoon Diner
Red Maple
River Watch
Sabatino's
Tiburzi's
Yellowfin/A
Zodiac

Power Scenes

Boccaccio
Charleston
4 West
Hampton's
Harry Browne's/A
Lewnes' Steakhse./A
Oregon Grille
Prime Rib
Windows

Private Rooms

(Call for capacity)
Abacrombie
Aldo's
Black Olive
Boccaccio
Brass Elephant
Cafe de Paris
Cafe Hon
Café Troia
Charleston
Dutch's Daughter
Eurasian Harbor
Fleming's
Harry Browne's/A
Ikaros
Jordan's Steakhse.
Lewnes' Steakhse./A

Baltimore – Special Feature Index

Manor Tavern
McCormick/Schmick's
Milton Inn
Morton's
Oregon Grille
Pisces
Red Coral
Reynolds Tavern/A
Roy's
Sabatino's
Stone Manor
Tersiguel's

Prix Fixe Menus
(Call for prices and times)
Antrim 1844
Asean Bistro
Café Troia
Corks
Hampton's
Inn at Easton/E
Kings Contrivance
Milton Inn
Northwoods/A
Stone Manor
Tersiguel's
Treaty of Paris/A
208 Talbot/E
Viccino Bistro

Quiet Conversation
Abacrombie
Acacia
Ambassador Din. Rm.
Cafe de Paris
Carlyle Club
Columbia/E
Ironbridge Wine
Jordan's Steakhse.
Paul's Homewood/A
Strawberry's Bistro
Thai Arroy
208 Talbot/E
Ze Mean Bean

Reserve Ahead
Aldo's
Ambassador Din. Rm.
Antrim 1844
Bicycle
Bistro St. Michaels/E
Black Olive
Boccaccio
Brighton's

Café Troia
Captain Harvey's
Chameleon Café
Charleston
Columbia/E
Costas Crab
Da Mimmo
Hampton's
Harry Browne's/A
Harryman Hse.
Healing Heart Blues
Helen's Garden
Helmand
Inn at Easton/E
Inn at Perry Cabin/E
Jalapeño/A
Josef's Country Inn
Kelly's
La Mona Lisa/A
Les Folies/A
Lewnes' Steakhse./A
Liberatore's
Linwood's
Louisiana
Milton Inn
O'Learys Seafood/A
Oregon Grille
Paul's Homewood/A
Pierpoint
Pisces
Prime Rib
Red Coral
Red Maple
Reynolds Tavern/A
Sotto Sopra
Stone Manor
Tersiguel's
Trattoria Alberto
208 Talbot/E
Wild Orchid Cafe/A
Windows

Romantic Places
Ambassador Din. Rm.
b
Cafe de Paris
Charleston
Columbia/E
Hampton's
Healing Heart Blues
Helen's Garden
Ironbridge Wine
Jordan's Steakhse.
La Mona Lisa/A

Baltimore – Special Feature Index

Milton Inn
Thai Arroy
208 Talbot/E
Woman's Ind. Ex.
Ze Mean Bean

Senior Appeal
Bistro St. Michaels/E
Cafe de Paris
Cafe Normandie/A
Crêpe du Jour
La Madeleine Bakery
Les Folies/A
Petit Louis Bistro

Singles Scenes
Henry's
Red Maple
Tasting Room

Sleepers
(Good to excellent food, but little known)
City Cafe
Fuji
Peppermill

Tea Service
Bertha's
Brighton's
Inn at Perry Cabin/E
Reynolds Tavern/A
Stone Manor
Wild Orchid Cafe/A

Views
Baldwin's Station
Brighton's
Cantler's Riverside/A
Fisherman's Inn/Crab/E
Friendly Farm
Gertrude's
Hampton's
Harris Crab/E
Inn at Perry Cabin/E
Ironbridge Wine
Joy America
L.P. Steamers
McNasby's/A
Michael Rork's/E
Phillips†
Pisces
River Watch
Windows
Yellowfin/A

Visitors on Expense Account
Acacia
Black Olive
Boccaccio
Brighton's
Charleston
4 West
Hampton's
Harry Browne's/A
Inn at Easton/E
Inn at Perry Cabin/E
La Mona Lisa/A
Lewnes' Steakhse./A
Morton's
Oregon Grille
Prime Rib
Ruth's Chris
Shula's Steak
Soigné
Tersiguel's
Trattoria Alberto
208 Talbot/E

Winning Wine Lists
AIDA Bistro
b
Cafe de Paris
Charleston
Corks
Fleming's
4 West
Helen's Garden
Ironbridge Wine
Oregon Grille
Petit Louis Bistro
Tasting Room
Tersiguel's

Worth a Trip
Annapolis
    Cantler's Riverside/A
    Joss Café/Sushi/A
    McNasby's/A
BWI/Linthicum
    Timbuktu
Columbia
    Cafe de Paris
Easton
    Alice's Café/E
    Columbia/E
    Inn at Easton/E
Essex
    Bill's Terrace Inn

Baltimore – Special Feature Index

Grasonville
  Harris Crab/E
  Narrows/E
Kennedyville
  Kennedyville Inn/E
Middletown
  Stone Manor
Parkville
  Barn

St. Michaels
  208 Talbot/E
Taneytown
  Antrim 1844
Upperco
  Friendly Farm
Westminster
  Baugher's

Wine Vintage Chart

This chart is designed to help you select wine to go with your meal. It is based on the same 0 to 30 scale used throughout this *Survey*. The ratings (prepared by our friend **Howard Stravitz**, a professor at the University of South Carolina) reflect both the quality of the vintage and the wine's readiness for present consumption. Thus, if a wine is not fully mature or is over the hill, its rating has been reduced. We do not include 1987, 1991–1993 vintages because they are not especially recommended for most areas.

	'85	'86	'88	'89	'90	'94	'95	'96	'97	'98	'99	'00	'01
WHITES													
French:													
Alsace	24	18	22	28	28	26	25	23	23	25	23	25	26
Burgundy	26	25	17	25	24	15	29	28	25	24	25	22	20
Loire Valley	–	–	–	–	25	23	24	26	24	23	24	25	23
Champagne	28	25	24	26	29	–	26	27	24	24	25	25	–
Sauternes	21	28	29	25	27	–	20	23	27	22	22	22	28
California (Napa, Sonoma, Mendocino):													
Chardonnay	–	–	–	–	–	22	27	23	27	25	25	23	26
Sauvignon Blanc/Semillon	–	–	–	–	–	–	–	–	24	24	25	22	26
REDS													
French:													
Bordeaux	25	26	24	27	29	22	26	25	23	24	23	25	23
Burgundy	23	–	21	25	28	–	26	27	25	22	27	22	20
Rhône	25	19	27	29	29	24	25	23	25	28	26	27	24
Beaujolais	–	–	–	–	–	–	–	–	23	22	25	25	18
California (Napa, Sonoma, Mendocino):													
Cab./Merlot	26	26	–	21	28	29	27	25	28	23	26	23	26
Pinot Noir	–	–	–	–	27	24	24	26	25	26	25	27	
Zinfandel	–	–	–	–	–	25	22	23	21	22	24	19	24
Italian:													
Tuscany	26	–	24	–	26	22	25	20	28	24	27	26	25
Piedmont	26	–	26	28	29	–	23	28	26	25	24	22	

Look before you watch.

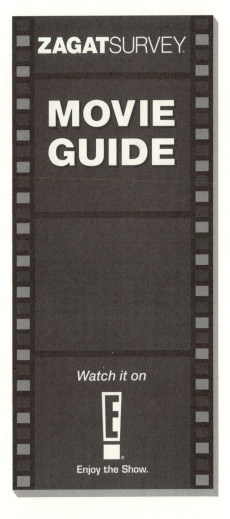

After 24+ years of helping choose the right restaurant, Zagat Survey is now helping you with the rest of the evening's entertainment by introducing the Zagat Survey Movie Guide, covering the top 1,000 films of all time. Ratings and reviews are by avid moviegoers, i.e. people like you.

Available wherever books are sold, at zagat.com
or by calling 888-371-5440.